Can't Regulate This

An insider's true story of how greed and self-realized financial gain in public and private companies are affecting EVERYONE'S financial future

D. J. Burgundy

Published by Waldorf Publishing
2140 Hall Johnson Road
#102-345
Grapevine, Texas 76051
www.WaldorfPublishing.com

Can't Regulate This

ISBN: 9781645708773
Library of Congress Control Number: 2019945183

Copyright © 2019

All rights reserved. No part of this book may be reproduced or transmitted in any form or by any means whatsoever without express written permission from the author, except in the case of brief quotations embodied in critical articles and reviews. Please refer all pertinent questions to the publisher. All rights reserved. No part of this book may be reproduced or transmitted in any form or by any means, electronic or mechanical, including photocopying, recording, or by an information storage and retrieval system except by a reviewer who may quote brief passages in a review to be printed in a magazine or newspaper without permission in writing from the publisher.

Table of Contents

Preface 1
Protecting the Naïve 13
"Of the Cloth" 16
Circumstances That are Ripe
for Fraud – Caveat Emptor: 21
Desperate People Do Desperate Things 27
You Can Run, but
the Problems Will Not Hide................... 34

The Collins & Aikman Experience............ 46
The 110 Plan 60
C&A, Y2K and 110M - 70
An Unwelcome Surprise........................ 84
Tick-tock, Tick-tock............................... 92
The Magic Carpet Ride 93
Denied! 136
Lots of Boxes, Titles and Names- 184
Old habits die hard................................ 199

The BestRideAuto Experience.................. 206

The PUFFiltrationExperience 236
Ferdalez Wisdom................................... 274

From the Author.................................... 279

Epilogue - Meet Mr. Patrick Sulyeam 286
Steel Company Drowns in the Downstream . 351

Author Bio 356

Preface

This book of factual historical record contains actual excerpts and exhibits ("materials") that are not ordinarily found in the public domain. Given the subject matter of the materials and the context of the matters at hand, I needed to secure these materials as a matter of personal protection in the event that I was personally harmed, fired, discharged, etc. as the direct result of causing the named companies to disclose the truth about their financial position and results of operations. These excerpts and exhibits, including a transcript of auditory recordings, would come to my aid as evidence of the facts had I been adversely affected as a result of and in the effort of doing the right thing.

This factual historical record also contains references to the individual perpetrator's ethnicity, land of origin, race and religion for the purpose of demonstrating that the act of fraud is nondiscriminatory, is all-inclusive and resistant to stereotyping or profiling. Contrary to popular belief, in this book there are many individuals named of various sizes, shapes and colors in addition to the stereotypical White Male Inhabitants of Wall Street at the southern tip of Manhattan.

The story will demonstrate that you cannot effectively regulate people telling the truth when large personal financial gain with deceit and mediocre financial compensation for doing the right thing are the alternatives; the administration and regulators actually do not know what they are dealing with. They also do not appreciate the nonproductive excessively onerous cost related to greater and greater regulation, with no productive outcome as the result.

While this book describes actual circumstances, experiences, events and outcomes that the author has endured, the names of individuals who have not been named in related court and SEC documents have been changed, including that of the author.

There are priorities, motivations and subjective areas entering into some of our life choices:

Love
Judgment
Money
Black and White
Grey Area
Good Judgment
Ego
Bad Judgment
Power
Ethics / Morals
Sex

It's late on a Saturday night, nine days after I resigned from my last chief financial officer post of a portfolio company owned by a private equity firm, and I am tired. Tired of persuasion, persuasion coming from CEOs and most recently chairmen and private equity owner principals attempting to convince and persuade me that it is not only acceptable but also justified to break the rules—yes, break the rules. What does this mean? When we were kids, it was relatively simple. Breaking the rules meant that you took a piece of bread from the dinner table that was eloquently prepared for guests by your mother, and for that, you received a "time-out" or a short scolding. Youth, sheer naivety and the need for social coaching, all were clear reasons as to why the rules were broken. Soon, after the deed had been done, a satiated appetite along with a sincere apology returned you to good standing with Mother and we redeemed our youthful innocence, that is until the next offense which may have come on the following Sunday when family and friends amass once again for one of Mother's fantastically prepared feasts. God rest her soul. A Cherokee Indian, Scottish and English woman from Missouri, she cooked Lebanese food better than the whole of my father's family who emigrated from Lebanon in 1913. Delicacies that you were tempted to pinch off and wish that you could take with you into your next life experience.

As adults and accomplished businessmen and women, we go about our daily tasks, some rudimentary, some requiring decision making and unadulterated judgment. We attempt to be mindful of the risks, advantages, pros and cons, internal and external consequences of these decisions involving judgment, and try to come up with the best position for all stakeholders involved. Broadly, stakeholders can be defined as, but not limited to, shareholders, customers, employees, financing institutions (banks), private investors and debt holders (including mezzanine / high-risk lender financing), the community, suppliers, the environment, and local and federal governments. All of these stakeholders can be and often are affected by decisions that are made in an intimate office setting, often with the sole motivation being personal financial gain; placed ahead of the fairness and duty owed to the aforementioned stakeholders. Personal gain that is supposed to be derived from true value creation so that all individuals can enjoy either the fruits of their labor (the ultimate satisfying reward), returns from smart investing, or both. Not financial gamesmanship that is the result of sequestered decision making in a boardroom, with the decision makers working to bring profit unto themselves and no one else.

I have been at this game for nearly three decades in senior operational and financial management capacity. I can tell you that I have exercised judgment in the grey areas, that have helped a company and its management achieve its financial performance objectives and investors achieve and exceed their required return on investment, and doing so while playing the game of business inside of the white lines and in accordance with the rules and regulations set forth by the authorities and agencies providing these rulings. These rulings have been developed and implemented through regulation and, so as to level the playing field among all investors and creditors (in the broadest sense, all stakeholders) to help them decide where to put their money, time and resources. This decision process involves the assessment of the informational inputs, such as the financial statements, market conditions, growth prospects, macroeconomic factors, along with the associated risks. Investors, generally, do not give second thoughts as to whether the (audited) financial statements are accurate, or fraudulently altered to achieve a desired result of management. Since they are audited, the prospective investors, lenders and other stakeholders believe that the financial statements are the written truth.

I also can tell you that I have found myself in situations when doing the "right thing" in reporting the financial results of operations in accordance with Generally Accepted Accounting Principles ("GAAP"), or International Financial Reporting Standards ("IFRS"), is a secondary thought of those in executive positions, whose compensation and recognition are based on the financial results of operations (CEOs, CFOs, presidents, COOs, chairmen, private equity and non-private equity owners of businesses). I have been in "persuasive" discussions, which I will share with you the written form transcripts of auditory media that were meant to justify the illicit portrayal of financial results and convince me that breaking the rules was appropriate. These discussions that wedged me, the CFO, between the truth and the lie that otherwise would have been told were conveyed by people whom you would otherwise regard as intelligent. These discussions, held in one-on-one settings, literally turned my insides out via their naked disregard for the regulatory rules by which this reporting is governed. What was worse was their blatant neglect for and lack of responsibility of individuals on the other end of their dirty deed who would be adversely affected in one form or another. We're talking about pensioners who are counting on proceeds from pension funds that have invested in the stock of companies whose financial statements were relied on but later, the companies have turned insolvent due to the lies and misleading information contained in those financial statements. We're talking about employees who regularly rely on a weekly paycheck from their employer whose leadership issued financial statements containing lies when filed with their lenders as they bled the company of borrowed funds rendering the company insolvent and unable to meet the weekly payrolls.

I have debated over whether or not to write this book and the utility of such a chronology. In making this decision, I have considered the following:

- Putting this knowledge and these experiences in

the hands of individuals who are considering a similar career path certainly can help them build the necessary character which, when combined with their necessary education, will allow them to make the right choices while demonstrating that they are not in unchartered water;

- The potential effects, negative or positive, that such a book would have on my career;
- Increasing regulation in the financial industry as the solution to the greed-based illicit behavior of influential business people who are "on the take," and conversely, the handcuffing and overburdening of fair and honest decision makers who would suffer as a result of such increased regulation;
- The level of hard work, study and dedication required to perfect my art of reflecting results of operations in accordance with the appropriate regulations while optimizing those same operation's financial results. I call this playing the game inside of the "white lines";
- The fact that during my hiring and onboarding experiences, after disclosing some of my unsavory experiences with these "persuasive influential decision makers," the promises that came from hiring company managers (which effectively were the hiring company's guarantee that "that will never happen here") only to have them renege on these convenient and circumstantial words when conditions warranted to advantage themselves in some way.

To the President of the United States, previously Barack Obama, to the U.S. Congress and to the regulators: You can make the rules and tighten them as much as you care to. I am here to tell you that you "CAN'T REGULATE THIS!" behavior away. History has shown this as well as the experiences that I am about to reveal.

The stripes on a zebra are hard-coded and do not change. The brains of the greedy are hardwired. They will find ways around the rules. The good and honest business people will continue fighting the good fight and play the game between the white lines... There are many of them, I wish to say: the strong majority. Further, regulation will only choke the honest ones further and make it far more costly to run their businesses. Regulation was fine "pre-Obama." It was enforcement and awareness that was lacking.

Disclaimer: This book is written in such a manner to protect the ignorant. Notice that I did not use the word "innocent." These are actual experiences; however, the names of the people and some of the companies are fiction.

I could have been much farther ahead, both in my career and financially, than I am today if I had chosen to succumb to the illicit behavior that I was compelled by others to implement or I could have found myself in jail and sued civilly. I have my strong character to thank, which my mother helped to foster and cultivate. This book is dedicated to her and to my family.

I have some thank you's to dole out:

Thank you, Trudy, my loving and dedicated wife, for putting up with me in my quest for a meaningful and productive career within a tough profession. Most of all, thank you for your undying and unconditional love and for holding our shared values so near and dear.

Thank you, Trina, Lance, Trace and Stacy, our fabulous children, for living with and through my staunch beliefs and vocal opinions about what is right, for listening to my advice and counsel about doing the right thing and for not throwing your dinner plate across the table at me!

Thank you, Bill Waldon, for coming to my aid in a time of dire need to help me find a safe solution to a very difficult professional situation that resulted in the preservation of my integrity. If not for you in that very difficult time, I'm not sure what the result would have been (either way, the company's numbers would have been the right ones, damn it!). Thank you for your legal counsel and advice, which were invaluable, as is your continuing friendship.

Thank you, Richard Margosian, Tim Abrhams and Bill Carson, for the culture you put forth at Masco that was no "BS" (matter of fact!) and passionately oriented at creating value with the utmost ethics while holding your human capital as the most important investment in your business. I was fortunate to spend ten years with you and I reflect fondly on that time often.

Business and Profits: The Root of all Good and the lifestyle we enjoy in the United States of Capitalism are captured in advents like this:

> Electricity
> The Motor Car
> The Home You Live In
> Vacations and Hospitality
> Facebook
> Financial Transaction Automation
> Solar Panels for Efficient Energy Generation
> WiFi Connectivity
> Financial Services Preserving/Creating your Wealth
> Google
> Microsoft
> Cloud Computing

Tesla and the Electric Car
Apple iPad
Samuel Adams Craft Beer
Apple iPhone 10X
Aerial Drones

"Who Built That?!" Not government!

People, by design, are interested in doing good things and bringing these things to market. This enriches their lives, the lives of those who consume their goods and services and the greater world at large. To receive a fair value for the goods and services that good people create, as established by a willing and able inventor / maker / manufacturer / service provider / seller and as paid for by a willing and able consumer, is capitalism's true essence and dates back prior to the advent of money as the medium of exchange. At one time or another in history, three fox pelts, the product of a hunter, were bartered for five steel pails produced by a blacksmith; the basis for what we call American capitalism.

In 1397 A.D., the Italians invented the first modern bank (Medici, Rome), creating a place of safekeeping for a store of value. Once this was established, the metering of the value for goods, services and property was possible in an indexing manner and the concept of monetary relativity began. Also, the measure of wealth was transformed from how many horses one possessed, to the compilation of the monetary value of one's cash and possessions. Simply, the system worked with little government intervention and regulation, other than to ensure that the transactions were conducted with valid currency. Certainly, the government had and continues to have laws governing what is legal to sell and what is not. This writing is less about the development and transformation of the regulatory environment in the United States, but the mention is certainly to highlight it, as there are certain things that cannot and will not be regulated. Having more rules is not the answer.

It is unfortunate that during the 2009-2016 presidency of Barack Obama, the administration's perspective was such that everyone is entitled to some pelts, medical treatment and a cell phone even if one didn't go to the trouble of developing a skill that enables them to create something of fair value in exchange. Under the Democratic administration of Bill Clinton, his drive to increase home ownership and the government policies that followed were a significant contributor and the precipitating factors to the mortgage crisis and the Great Recession that the country, its economy, you and I endured. And out of this mess, the great hate for business and the banks responsible for our current facilitation of exchange has emanated, been inspired and incited by Obama and his administration. The socialists who are trying to transform the basis of American's economic existence and the taint and disdain upon businesses who are responsible for our progress thus far is a deep disservice to those who have fostered their wonderful contributions to our society and lifestyle. This false narrative must stop.

The regulation that existed prior to President Obama was largely adequate. As the pendulum has swung, Trump may be going too far in over-correcting for the Obama actions. Proper enforcement of the pre-Obama rules was and continues to be the answer—in lieu of more regulation—because there is deceit that will continue to go undetected and unregulated even in the era of layer upon layer of mega-regulation. The same deceit that Obama had tried to vilify will morph itself into another form of deceit in gaming the system in a different way. This is the nature of the deceitful individuals. "You cannot regulate this!" to eliminate such behavior.

Protecting the Naïve

I was good with arithmetic, so at a very young age, I had decided to model my brother's career path: accounting. My brother was my role model and mentor. Having a sickly and elderly father caused me to look for leadership elsewhere. So, I was nine years old and thought that modeling my brother would be a good idea.

As I had progressed through my secondary school education, I began to take accounting courses and entered the strange debit and credit world of the double entry bookkeeping system. The best way I can describe the double entry bookkeeping system is there are two entries related to each and any transaction; one being the source (or perhaps source of funds) and the second being their application. This is but one way to think of it; there are many others, I am sure.

The only way the teacher explained the science and methodology to this weird stuff was to advise the class that debits are on the window side of the room and credits are on the hallway wall side of the room. I thought to myself, "How in God's creation will this have any relevance to my honing a skill with which to earn a living, much less what relevance could this have in the real world?" I was quite confused; however, I decided to stick with it because this was going to be "my ticket," or so I thought.

I soon learned that these debits and credits are the means and by which are the foundation of governance for financial accounting. They would be applied to the way in which a company portrayed itself to the population of third parties who would have a stake, or some risk, relative to the company's ability to generate earnings and economic value. These include, but are not limited to owners, shareholders, commercial banks, investors, debt financiers, employees, customers, vendors, suppliers, the government and surrounding communities. At that early age, I had no clue that we all are connected to each other in those certain monetary ways. Let the Enron and Tyco catastrophes be examples of how connected we are and how improperly applying these debits and credits devastated innocent individuals by destroying the value of their pensions (pension advisors directed pensioners' investments to these companies). These acts of greed and impropriety ruined lives and the future wherewithal of individuals to economically survive.

Bear in mind, there were rules already in place at the time of the Enron improprieties which, if adhered to, would have guarded against the resulting insolvency and personal hurt that so many individuals suffered. It wasn't the "lacking" regulation; it was the greed of the senior management, collectively.

It is unfortunate that these events needed to occur to apprise the general public of the importance of properly accounting for the events and activities of a company. Prior to these events, the average person did not understand the implication chain whereby the improper and fraudulent application of the double entry bookkeeping system could manifest itself in the personal financial ruin of so many unknowing and innocent individuals.

You will read about the most major event of mine that predated the Enron and Tyco frauds where I, as CFO of a $1.8 billion enterprise, was caused to cut ties with my senior management in order for the company to report the proper numbers in its year 2000 financial statements. As uncomfortable as it was made for me to do this, I found the drive to overcome their influences to commit fraud as I caused the company to file correct and accurate financial statements with the SEC before it was popular and in vogue to do the right thing after the Enron debacle. After I left the company, the leadership's deviant ways returned and lies and fraudulent financials were reported. This behavior continued as did their large paychecks until the company's ultimate insolvency, bankruptcy and dissolution. It was only at this time that their leadership of lies ended.

"Of the Cloth"

I have often used the term "of the cloth" to describe the (inferred) oath which fellow brethren (and sisters) take in putting themselves forth as "accountants." We, as accountants, possess the knowledge that the naïve, innocent and unknowing do not. The training is lengthy and extensive. For those of us who are CPAs, the in-depth and specific training is long on what a material misstatement of financial information looks like, fraud detection and the appropriate response should fraud be detected. This training also imparts to us the deep duty owed to the ultimate stakeholders of a business by senior managers, officers and directors, including the CFO. This is the highest duty known to law and is known as the fiduciary duty. The essence of fiduciary duty is such that the business professional places the individual(s) to whom the fiduciary duty is owed in a position of protection, in fact, a position of care that is higher than they give to themselves. As an analogy, imagine a doctor who smokes cigarettes and the advice contrary to cigarette smoking that they give their patients. In matters of money, the care is such that the professional decides on matters pertaining to the protection of assets and optimization of wealth with the best interests of the person owed the duty (e.g.: ownership, creditors in the case of a bankruptcy) always at heart. That is what the professional is paid to do, even where these decisions and their resulting outcome may advantage the professional in some way. Therefore where a strong conflict of interests exists, the professional must disclose this conflict to the appropriate parties, and in some cases either subordinate their interest, or substitute themselves with a person or a firm who will not have the same conflict. It is explicit within this duty that the professional abides by the laws and regulations pertaining to the profession. If not for that, decisions may be made that would violate the regulations and standards to advantage ownership and management and, therefore, place the very individuals to whom the fiduciary duty is owed at greater risk and directly in harm's way.

Because of this duty, and the compulsion to do the right thing on behalf of all of the stakeholders—most notably to those who are owed the fiduciary duty—I coined the phrase "of the cloth," likening this duty to the virtues of the priesthood. No matter the personal gain that may be had by twisting the truths, we must do the right thing and put others ahead of ourselves.

I must say that throughout my career, and I believe that I can speak for the majority of professionals in this field, I have found it a privilege to be entrusted to protect the assets of ownership, optimize the earnings potential of businesses and, thereby, the wealth of the ownership, and do so with a command of the rules and regulations such that "real value" was created and protected "within the white lines" and on a level playing field. Implicit in this is the portrayal of financial information to third parties who would know no better if the financials were purposely misleading: those who are blind to the intended deceit that some senior managers bake into their published results. We, as the general public, believe that just because a company and its results of operations and statements of financial position and cash flows have been audited, and the auditor / independent accountant decides on providing an unqualified (clean) opinion that the financial statements present the numbers fairly and in accordance with generally accepted accounting principles, that they are in fact the right numbers. I am here to tell you in this book that often times they are not. I am providing you real life examples such that the quality of information purveyed is dependent upon the character of the senior management, including the chief financial officer, whether or not readers of financial statements are actually getting the truth. If not for me in some of these real life cases, lies would have been served up and the readers and users of the financial statements would have developed different conclusions other than the truth about the company and acted in ways that may have put themselves at greater risk, lest they had known the truth. With the right information, decisions on investment, lending, supplying, procuring activities can be evaluated accurately to serve their own best interests and the interests of their companies. With the wrong information, these parties will make decisions and act in such a manner that may present peril to themselves and their companies.

Anybody can cheat and take the easy way out. True professionals take the higher road and deal with the intrinsic elements to manage the company and produce results; they don't cosmetically change the numbers to falsely portray that they have met their objectives.

Causing a company to be compliant with rules, regulations and accepted principles of accounting and financial reporting is but one aspect of the job of the chief financial officer. The CFO doesn't actually perform the bookkeeping activity. Generally, there is a "company controller" who is responsible for recording the transactions and required financial recognition of the affairs of the company. It is the company controller and his team who perform these duties; however, it is incumbent on the CFO to be fully aware of the company's financial position and policies for accounting treatment as the ultimate compliance responsibility lies with him or her.

The CFO must also serve in the capacities of business leader, sometimes chief negotiator, strategist, performance monitor, colleague, growth enabler, cost reducer, CEO confidante, profit enhancer, ethical gatekeeper and motivator. It is these other elements of the job that may confuse CEOs, chairmen, presidents and owners about the balance of "playing by the rules, inside the white lines," and furthering their interests of generating maximum profits and cash. In my experience, the motivations that drive illicit behavior in financial reporting are when executives are positioning the enterprise for an event such as a sale or merger, or there are significant bonuses to be paid upon the successful achievement of milestone financial performance. We soon shall explore the career experiences that I have had, where my superiors were conflicted about the full scope of my job requirements as CFO and had chosen to influence me toward the "dark side." In their mind, "This (these distortions of the company financial performance) is just between us," and "No one will find out," and "This is right and just that the customer is overpaying us because they should be paying more for our products," so "Keep the revenue in the books, they'll never come after us."

I have had a long career spanning forty-plus years, twenty-eight of which were in a senior financial management capacity. At this point of time, nine employers had employed me (including the two exampled in the book's epilogue), two with notable entrepreneurial inspiration and impeccable ethics. I drove a culture, along with the CEO and chairman—separate individuals holding those posts—in this direction. Two others I would rank as good in those categories, but not notable. That leaves the remaining four which you are about to read of the experiences that poked and prodded my character, tested my person and caused me to really get to know myself. These experiences drove me to be stronger and more upstanding than I ever thought I could be.

As you read this book, I ask you to ponder the circumstances: the potential outcomes, both positive and negative. Put yourself in my shoes. For those of you whose job is within a financial discipline, or one that holds a fiduciary duty, I hope to convey this in the fashion that you are experiencing this "in the first person" so you too can experience the telling signs that were there, as I did, and so you can identify with them on a forward basis to predict what may be coming at you down the line, should you encounter such unfortunate circumstances.

It can be a confusing thing. It was for me. On one hand, I was in a position of influence that, with my authorization, the company would have been fictitiously overvalued by nearly a $100 million. Stock would have been transacted and people made wealthy or wealthier, including myself. On the other hand, I was in a position of influence that, with the stroke of my pen, the company would have been properly valued, and I could sit across the kitchen table from my loving wife and children and advise them to "do the right thing," and those words would not be words only, empty in truth and content like the skeleton of evil and untruths that this world can be full of. The words would be truthful, meaningful and more valid because they came from truth, not lies.

Simply, do the right thing!

Circumstances That are Ripe for Fraud – Caveat Emptor:
Short-term gain with relatively no pain.

There have been numerous debates, both on congressional and regulatory/SEC record, about the alignment of short-term increases in earnings to an executive's (and an executive's team) compensation and the need to "regulate" this element in disconnecting the short-term gains to executive compensation. The thought is such that removing the element of compensation that benefits the executive for increasing quarterly or annual earnings, this will change the overall behavior of the executive such that the impetus to generate and create a fraud that ostensibly increases earnings per share will diminish to the point of nil. Well, I ask you, in this day and age of creative finance and back room negotiation in the form of side-letters to your employment contract, etc., is this really possible? Certainly short-term, quarterly earnings targeted increases, especially in "earnings per share – driven" SEC companies are suspect.

After analyzing SEC companies' reporting, does anyone wonder why earnings per share either hit or marginally exceeded analysts' expectations? Is this really possible? The data spills the truth. Forgetting about Sarbanes-Oxley [1] for the moment (a valiant effort at onerous regulation), of S&P 500 member companies, the following data shows that, of SEC-regulated reporting companies. "Quarterly earnings have exceeded estimates for roughly 70% of the S&P 500 member companies that have reported results." This for the fourth quarter of 2014. (information per MFS, Boston, MA):

Can these companies really be hitting / exceeding the

numbers that the analysts put forth so frequently? Certainly, the analysts are intelligent individuals, but perhaps they are not fully experts on the company nor the industry in the majority of the time. But time after time, quarter after quarter, the results are meeting with analysts' expectations or exceeding them. Rarely is there a blow. Are the analysts that in tune with the business, or because the stock price is the indication of the present value of future cash flow, is it the desire of senior management to hit or exceed analysts' estimates so as to increase the stock price to meet the analysts' expectations, who are often investment bankers and sellers of the companies' stock?

The grey areas of accounting are wide; that is why they call accounting an "art" and not a science. Accounting is subject to (broad) interpretation, often interpretation that is not consistent with the desire to "get it right,". Often, playing within the grey area to achieve the short-term financial goals of management and ownership is what it turns into.

So, that may be a discussion that permeates the world of SEC reporting companies; however, that discussion certainly transgresses into the private equity / private company world. Return on investment is a term that is near and dear to the heart of private company ownership as well as shareholders and senior management of publicly traded enterprises.

Private equity normally establishes a fund to purchase businesses to which the enterprise value can be enhanced through increased financial performance. These funds are comprised of contributions by independent investors (silent partners [2], most likely), which may include insurance companies and pension funds of public and private companies, as well as municipalities. Certainly, the private equity firm principals also may contribute their personal capital toward the effort of making a return on their personal investment. Generally, this is the case, along with the portfolio company's (companies in which private equity invests) management. This is the hook. When financial interests become aligned, then it becomes possible for everyone to win as the result of the collective hard work by all, or the misdeeds of a few.

It is normal and customary for a private equity fund to be established with a limited duration, meaning the point in which investment in a portfolio company occurs and the divestiture and subsequent return of capital and profit (capital gain on carried interest) is returned to the individual investor. Often this limited (fund) duration is approximately three years; in other words, from the first dollar in to the last dollar out and returned to investors, a period of three years is allowed by contract. Should an adequate return not be earned in comparison to expectations set forth by the managers of the private equity fund, depending upon the magnitude of the investment in proportion to the fund and the experience of the private equity firm principals, all hell could break loose with the partners because of the spoiled situation. Of course, everyone involved wants to be a winner and that is why they invested in the fund and entrusted their wealth to the Private Equity (active) Partners and Directors in the first place.

So, let us contemplate the conditions under which the misdeed—falsification of financial statements—can be, would be and has been committed, which constitutes fraud, no matter the size and magnitude of the lie, act of omission, or commission may be. These situations are nearly all the result of underperformance of the business to expectations and consequently, either mismanagement of the business or setting of investor expectations that are too optimistic, for whatever reason.

The setting of lofty, far too stretched "stretch" goals, and their advertisement to third parties (lenders, investors and creditors—press and public) in terms of earnings per share, trailing twelve months of EBITDA (Earnings before Interest, Taxes, Depreciation and Amortization) is where the senior executive, whose riches are set on the achievement of these "made public" objectives, falters. This in effect is the first act of fraud, overselling the capabilities of the business to these third party stakeholders who I referred to earlier as the "naïve and innocent," those who do not have the inside knowledge nor, in many cases, the financial moxie to call out the executive on this bogus leading statement which is the hook set to entice these naïve and innocent third parties to participate.

Footnote Explanations

(1) Sarbanes–Oxley ("SOX") was a 2002 regulatory law, named after sponsors U.S. Senator Paul Sarbanes (D-MD) and US Representative Michael G. Oxley (R-OH). SOX requires chief executive officers, chief financial officers and potentially other senior management to individually certify the accuracy of financial information. By comparison to prior to when this law was enacted, penalties for fraudulent financial activity are punitively severe to a much higher degree. Also, SOX increased the oversight role of boards of directors, required a proportion of "outside the company" directors and necessitated the independence of the outside auditors who review the accuracy of corporate financial statements.

The bill is made up of eleven sections and was enacted as a reaction to a number of major corporate and accounting scandals, including those affecting companies and resultantly shareholders of Enron, Tyco International, Adelphia, Peregrine Systems, and WorldCom. These scandals cost investors billions of dollars when the share prices of affected companies collapsed and shook public confidence in the US securities markets. Varying views of the law are had, both by the proponents of more regulation and those not in favor. One view being that this law adds too much complexity and cost burden to companies subject to it. Other views are such that the effects of this law are likely worth it. It is largely debatable as to whether the true effectiveness of the law is as intended, or if the same would have been accomplished through better enforcement of the existing laws and regulations prior to its enactment.

(2) Silent Partners are silent "owners" of a business who merely contribute money as investment to a business and exercise no management control or influence.

Desperate People Do Desperate Things

So how does one become desperate? Can people be born with desperation in their DNA? Is desperation a choice that we make? A conditioned response? Can there be predispositions? Certainly there are some predispositions that are nongenetic; is it possible that a predisposition may be genetic? It seems that a combination of insecurity and greed will breed desperation. Overselling one's capabilities to turn a business into a gold mine is ripe for desperation. Clearly, when those expected "gold mine results" don't hit, one looks for alternatives that can lead to desperate and fraudulent acts of commission and omission. I have witnessed this too many times in my career and you are about to experience them from my CFO chair.

Consider a young, Muslim, Eastern Indian who lived with ten families, one of which was his own, in an open floor plan on just one floor of an apartment building with a communal bathroom in India. This person desires for a better life, so he becomes well-educated in his specialty field, electrical engineering. At a relatively early age, he then finds himself a way to get to the States. In the States, he continues his education as General Electric recruits him. At GE, he is responsible for program management in the building and sale of large electrical generators, under contract with the US Department of Defense. He is young, bright and successful in his job and is integrated into the "GE Way."[3] He takes very well to this environment. While he was accomplished in his job, he was not identified as a "key-high potential" employee; nonetheless, he operated and performed well for GE.

Continuing to be highly smart and self-motivated,

he is interested in advancement and comes across a position with Motors Engine, a Fortune 500, publicly-traded company specializing in the manufacture of engines used in heavy duty applications. He enters the Light Duty Filtration business segment (a noncore business for Motors Engine) as product quality manager, then moves into an overall plant management role and from there on and into general management within the Light Duty Filtration business segment. He is tapped to lead the sale process of the business segment to a private equity ("PE") firm. This low-middle market business produces approximately 20% EBITDA returns on a pro forma (prospective) basis, as was displayed in the winning PE firm's prospective financials for the business as a stand-alone entity.

This smart young man proceeds down a path with one PE firm whose intent is to layer on senior management positions and burden this successful business with exorbitant management fees. For some reason, after Motors' experience with this PE firm on a prior divestiture, the potential deal goes south and now comes the successful suitor; a big city based, non-diverse PE firm with some relatively inexperienced leaders at the top of the firm, along with an older, relatively used-up ex-consultant (A. T. Kearney and KPMG) as the operating partner and lead-man / chairman of this new portfolio company. This PE firm acquired the business and named the person in charge of selling the business, on behalf of Motors Engine, as the company's chief executive officer.

The PE firm paid an amount greater than 5X EBITDA (1X Sales Value) to take control of the company, utilizing a blended equity structure consisting of 2/3 debt, the balance being the equity investment out of one of their funds, along with management participation. There were so many protections for Motors on clawback (recourse litigation) which were built into the sale documents. Given that, the improper diligence conducted by the PE firm on certain items about the assumptions for revenue realization and other key success factors that Motors was responsible for, as a part of the deal, to make this investment a success required more than hope and hard work. Poor diligence items on the part of the PE firm also revealed, in my tenure, the need to double capitalize the Shanghai, China business as well as poor business set-up by the PE firm (this required draws on the North American bank line of credit to recapitalize this business; the PE firm was NOT going back to the fund to admit their errors and request additional funding to right their errors). Another large miss was failure to identify a failing business segment within the Light Duty Filtration business, due to a major trend in offshoring much of the supply to satisfy customers' demand for this business' core product....

Fast-forward four months and the company is borderline in violation of its credit agreements and soon to be in breach of its bank covenants. Does he break the rules AND influence others to put themselves in the crosshairs, or does he have the moral fiber to call it like it is AND cause the firm to take a step back?

Consider the Eastern European, older, relatively used-up ex-consultant (A.T. Kearney and KPMG, big consulting houses) who, as the operating partner and lead-man / chairman of this new portfolio company, was joyously advertising to all with regularity, prematurely beating the drum with sounds of what a successful investment this is. The largest investment of the PE firm to date, his purpose was to entice the weak by touting how we all will win big on the later and ultimate sale of the business with the cashing-in of our stock grants and options; this all the while, the more intelligent ones in his audience, myself included after becoming acclimated with the situation and business prospects, being of the mind that the PE firm overpaid for such a business and knowing that the options may not be worth the paper that they were written on. Is this guy too far gone to even contemplate what his intentions are? Does he even realize what he is saying?

Consider the Anglo-Saxon CEO of a Blackstone / Wasserstein Perella 87% owned portfolio company who will cash in big if he can turn the financial performance of this business sufficiently so that Blackstone and Wasserstein Perella can get out from under this underperforming, debt-saddled business. Incentive: big payday, if successful.

Consider a middle-aged, dominant Iranian who is a technically savvy engineering type and who is placed in charge of a noncore business (US subsidiary) owned by a Euro multinational German-based privately owned company who wishes to spin-off this noncore business into a 50-50 merger of global equals and do so while optimizing enterprise value, the business as the contributory consideration to the joint venture. This individual has strong short-term and long-term financial incentives to accomplish this mission, whatever it takes. He really wants to make a name for himself among the Euro hierarchy and run the combined business in North America. There are elements of control, greed and narcissism here that could not be described here and are a better subject to be addressed in a writing in the field of psychology.

These individuals have no exclusive right to succeed in business, with their families, at work, in life and (more pointedly) financially, yet they believe they do. Their motivations are common among Muslims, Middle Easterners, Americans, Europeans, Africans, and those who have and those who have not: to lead a life of happiness, fulfillment and financial security. We all have these desires and motivations. The difference is that their formula for success, given the certain collection of circumstances, includes the realm of anything and everything creatively and illicitly that will cause them to succeed at their mission of the premium payday.

Can you or a credible government regulate this societal condition that stems from the individual? In all of my experiences, the answer to this question is, without a doubt, NO. Certainly, regulation is required and wanted in its proper and effective doses. Just as children, in the process of growing, appreciate establishment boundaries, the consequences of crossing them and the effective enforcement of the rules, so does business (of course not likening business to immaturity). Regulation, which does not strangle the life out of the entrepreneurial spirit and the willingness of business people to take a risk, is generally welcomed in our capitalistic society as we have historically known it. But just because it seemingly is in vogue to come down hard on business as a response to the perceived causes of the "Great Recession," in another "Bush-bash," it flat out does not make sense to kill the spirit with more and more (in some cases useless, overly burdensome and way-costly) regulation. The types of things that go on, as you will find out in this book, happen behind closed doors, in a confidential setting, are whispered with the "wink-wink" treatment and in most cases will not be caught proactively through more regulation. These things will go on, continue to go on, with whatever level of regulation is law. These things will likely pass a Generally Accepted Accounting Principles or International Financial Reporting Standards audit, because the alignment of management in conducting this fraud is tight. Remember, "We will all win together and realize the payday if we succeed with the mission."

My experiences in this realm both predate and postdate Enron, Tyco International, Adelphia, Peregrine Systems, WorldCom, and the other highly publicized frauds and, resultingly, the failure and ultimate dissolution of the notable "Big 4" independent accounting and auditing firm, Arthur Andersen. These named frauds did occur while regulation was in place (absent Sarbanes-Oxley), and were caught only years beyond the acts of commission and omission. It is unfortunate that only individuals of sound judgment and character with a strong enough backbone, who cannot be tempted with this big payday syndrome, are the only catchall, save-all to these unfortunate circumstances. The buck stops with this person; if not for that, lies will be told, financial statements will be signed off, frauds will be committed and people (re: the naive) will be hurt through resulting financial losses due to these breaches of fiduciary duty. It is most likely to be some years later that these lies and fraud will be detected and diagnosed, just as in the prior factual examples. It is then too late.

Footnote Explanations

(3) Those of us in industry who have worked with or developed relationships with ex-GE employees have learned that General Electric grooms high-potential employees by sending them to an internal GE school of management training called Crotonville Management Training Center. Crotonville, a parcel of leafy land about an hour north of New York City is where GE grooms its future management executives in tactics, values and culture. Former CEO Jack Welch wrote in his 2000 letter to GE shareholders that, forced to choose between: 1) a manager who shares GE values but isn't quite making his/her numbers; or 2) a manager who delivers the numbers but doesn't fit the corporate culture, he'd give a few more chances to the former but immediately fire the latter. Those who don't share the company's values "have the power, by themselves, to destroy the open, informal, trust-based culture we need to win today and tomorrow," wrote Welch.

You Can Run, but the Problems Will Not Hide

Consider the white Anglo-Saxon CEO of a Blackstone/Wasserstein Perella 87% owned portfolio company who will cash in big if he can turn the financial performance of this business sufficiently so that Blackstone and Wasserstein Perella can get out from under this underperforming, debt-laden business.

Unfortunately for these investors, or financial engineers, on May 17, 2005, the Automotive News published an article, "Collins & Aikman Files Chapter 11 Bankruptcy."

The article describes that the bankruptcy was actually no surprise and how just five days prior, David Stockman, then fifty-seven years old, quit as the chairman and CEO, off-putting these responsibilities on one of his soldiers, the principal of an acquiree that Collins & Aikman picked up in the midst of its own hysterical mess. A member of a bankruptcy and turn-around/ "work-out" firm ("financial advisor," as they prefer to be called) of New York was then appointed "chief restructuring officer," of which there were a few during this period of unwinding the behemoth. The article further goes on to say that, "The beleaguered auto interior and trim supplier had fully used its credit line" (previously acquired through false financial reporting) "and was relying on 'accommodation' payments from customers to fund its operation."

"Accommodation payments" are those that usually OEM customers, such as Ford, General Motors, Toyota, BMW, etc., will provide to financially distressed supplier(s), far beyond just the purchase price of the automotive components for which they are under contract. If not for these accommodations, the customer—car makers—would go without their parts and their cars would not be made. These payments, often in the several millions of dollars, shore-up the net negative cash flows, or "cash-burn," of these financially distressed businesses.

Outsiders would believe that this was the beginning of the end of this company, but I, D. J. Burgundy, the CFO of the majority share of the company, knew the end began when, after I left the company in 2001, the lies began to be told about the company's true financial condition. You will see what was really happening, on the inside, through my eyes.

On August 12, 2005, Crain's Detroit, a go-to for business news in Detroit, reported "Car Parts Supplier Receives a U.S. Grand Jury Subpoena." "DETROIT, Aug. 12 – Collins & Aikman, the auto parts supplier that filed for bankruptcy protection in May, said Friday that it had received a federal grand jury subpoena for financial records going back more than five years. A company spokesman, David Olman, said the grand jury subpoena was in addition to a request from the Securities and Exchange Commission for similar financial records. Mr. Olman said the S.E.C. had asked for the documents earlier this summer. As Collins & Aikman neared bankruptcy, it disclosed that it was conducting an internal investigation into how it had accounted for approximately $88 million in rebates from vendors from 2002 to 2004. The company later said it might have to reduce its earnings from that period by $10 million to $12 million."

This article goes on to say, "The financial problems at Collins & Aikman have drawn an added degree of interest from Wall Street and the media because of the company's former chairman and chief executive, David A. Stockman. Mr. Stockman, who served as budget director to President Ronald Reagan, resigned from the company under pressure days before its bankruptcy filing. Another executive, the vice president and treasurer, John Galante, left the company last month."

It was late July of 1999 when a mutual friend introduced me to Mr. Gene Wyler, the President of the North American Interior Systems super-group of Collins and Aikman Corporation. When spending the prior 21 years under the hood and in the wheel wells of the automobile, I thought it was time to enjoy a little bit of sexiness of the automotive industry; that being said, I began contemplating joining a firm specializing in the manufacture and sale of the touchy-feely areas of the automobile: the interior. Fabrics, carpet, acoustics, instrument panels, air conditioning vents, door interiors, arm rests, consoles, glove boxes and floor mats were way more sexy than the differential gears and pinions, piston pins, steering linkage, constant velocity joints, idler arms, axles shafts, sun gears, ball joints or connecting rods (although the last two may sound sexy, depending upon the company and the company in which you find yourself, but not really!). The President of the North American Interior Systems group was a real great guy and we hit it off immediately. He was intense about his business; clearly, he was all about managing the (the large sector—75% of the total Collins & Aikman) company based on data driven decisions and mutual respect among all colleagues in the spirit of supplying good quality product to his customers, on time and at the proper value proposition. I was attentive, respectful and assertive while I emphasized my twenty-plus year career accomplishments and how I could help him with his goals and objectives for the company.

While they were conducting diligence about me with regard to my potential hire into the important position of vice president of finance / chief financial officer, I was off doing a bit of diligence on my own, pertaining to the company's competitive position, customer base, customer standing and financial condition of the business. My investigation found that in 1999, the Collins and Aikman Corporation was the largest manufacturer and supplier of automotive carpet and acoustics (underlay) to the automotive original equipment manufacturers (OEMs). Albemarle, North Carolina, was the mother ship for this product segment; manufacturing tufted carpet rolls in standard sizes and a multitude of colors specified by the OEM. With a similar operation, near in size and related production located in Farnum, Quebec, Canada; together, these locations were feeder operations for the downstream product manufacture that occurred in Old Fort, North Carolina; Parker, South Carolina; and Lacolle, Quebec, Canada.

The technology in this company was second to none for this product segment. Of course, a lot of this information came from knowledge obtained from sites seen after my joining on, but the subsequent knowledge confirmed my diligence about the operations and corroborated much of the facts learned of the company. I marveled at the operation; seeing the automated thread placement into tufting machines that weaved the miles long of carpet rolls. Operationally, the Albemarle and Farnum facilities were technically advanced and well-engineered. I particularly remember, as one would never forget, a dye range in the Albemarle, NC, operation. The dye range color treated the carpeting to the customer specifications; color shades and hues as set forth by the customers. This "range" was approximately 15 – 18 feet in width, with an approximate length of a football field.

At the front end of the dye range, where the dye coloring is introduced, a person mans the set-up and color change station. With the flip of a switch / turn of a dial, the color immediately changes to the color selection desired; however, drastic changes in color (black to sky blue) would result in a spoilage that would be several feet in length due to overlapping colors; the phase-in of the new color and the phase-out of the color it was changing from. When considering the speed that the carpeting would travel in the dye range as the rolls are unwound in a de-coiling type of process at the front end of the dye range, a significant blurring/combining of the colors would last until the old color was completely phased out and the new color was completely phased in. For this reason, there would be a progression of colors that would be scheduled. So long as the company was aware of the customer color requirements scheduled for that day, the company could optimize the output (decrease the amount of color scrap) by scheduling which colors followed each other with each change involving a slight color change (e.g.: black to brown to charcoal grey to navy blue to light blue to light beige, etc.). Having access to the factory due to tours in observing either capital equipment implementations, efficiency improvements, new work cell configurations, etc., I would always take a special moment to observe this phenomenon of technology and engineering. This was a true testament to the company's market leadership position that I learned about during my pre-employment diligence.

Another technology at which I marveled was the

molding and cutting of the underlay and carpet to the shape of the automobile's interior floor. This technology was located in the "downstream" operating plants of Parker, SC, and Lacolle, Quebec, Canada . Large rectangles of paired underlay and carpet would be set into the lower mold of the mold-press at which point the upper and lower molds would close and heat would be applied. Once the carpet and underlay, now integrated, permanently took the shape of the automobile's interior floor, the molds opened and an automated robotic arm holding a water gun (a high-pressure water spray device that resembled a gun) would prepare to perform surgery. At the point when the water gun was in position, it blasted water out of the gun at a bazillion pounds per square inch and the robotic arm proceeded to trace the outer edge of the specific automobile's floor until the outline was free of the excess rectangle. This was all computer program controlled. AMAZING stuff in manufacturing!

Once again, the company was full of great technology and had highly capable senior operating management—emphasis on "operating" management. In addition to Wyler, a legacy Collins & Aikman employee, through the good times and the transitional ones, was Mr. Lynard Strong, a long-time career military guy who performed every action, including the drinking of his coffee, by "the book." Standardization and standardized processes, the hallmark of the US military, had become the vehicle for success in the automotive supplier businesses. While Wyler headed the North American Automotive Interior Systems, Strong reported to Wyler as his head of "US Carpet and Acoustics." While being respectfully obsessive, Strong commanded the allegiance and attention of his direct reports.

The structure of the US Carpet and Acoustics group was historically traditional for a successful large-scale industrial business with alignment to the head of operations of all of the functional areas of the business. A business of such girth and market share is only successful based on the technical product engineering, industrial engineering, operational management, customer focused program management, and customer driven sales and marketing operations - Collins & Aikman had it all. Their direct customer base spanned continents and included Toyota, Honda, Nissan, General Motors, Chrysler, Ford and Daimler, among others. You cannot have such class-A customer retention without excellent / superior product quality and customer service being driven by superior technology, engineering and operating management in the 21st century. You may have gotten away with consistently mediocre performance in the later segments of the prior half-century, but that hasn't worked since the late 1990s and will not and cannot return.

The balance of Collins and Aikman North American Automotive Interior Systems (NAAIS) was fairly in-line with this structural business concept, both in the products that it offered, customer focus and the operating construct of its business; Canada Carpet and Acoustics, Floor Mats and Accessories and Fabrics with the exception of its plastics business which was in disarray, until such time as we integrated it with the remainder of the business' operating philosophy. A relatively new acquisition, "Manchester Plastics," under prior ownership, was a noteworthy business; however, it was stuck in operational mediocrity. When combining this mediocrity with the cannibalized commodity pricing, as the OEMs were famous for taking any product segment supplied by a third party and commoditizing it, from the perspective of forcing price-downs to the point of severe pain and later insolvency—as we have learned and experienced—this business was victimized and was in need of leadership so that it could regain dignity as a valid and viable automotive supplier. This was our mission for this (newly) acquired product segment.

While the level of monetary investment supporting such a business is rather large, notice that in this segment, I have not raised the topic of money. We will eventually get there, but let us first talk about "value" and the "value proposition." We all make our purchasing decisions based on equilibrium. This equilibrium is rooted in consideration. The consideration that I receive must be equivalent (or greater, in the case of a real deal) than the consideration that I give up to acquire such article; no matter if it is a sweater, an iPhone, a house or, in this case, an automobile. So when you walk through the door of the automobile dealership, you have a genuine thought about some value that you are willing to pay (paid consideration) for the service, reliability, luxury, look and transportation of an automobile (consideration received). The amount that you actually pay to the dealership is broken down among the profit / fee kept by the dealership, profit or (loss) derived by the original equipment manufacturer, the cost of the OEM's inside resource operations and the value paid to automotive parts suppliers, which is further broken down into profit or (loss) derived by the supplier, the cost of internal resource operations of the supplier and amounts paid to raw material or purchased component sources that go into making the product… and so on.

As demonstrated earlier, Collins and Aikman was a

solid operational company. The company, chock-full of engineering, technical and operational talent, knew its costs of operation, including the cost of its raw materials and purchased components, and the market price of its products, the force of which was operating profit. Sure, the company weathered the storm of OEM price downs, which were year on year repeating and demanded often and regularly, but the basis of the company—as with all companies—was one of profitability. The company was executing on all fronts, but was not executing in a critical area highlighted below:

Part of my diligence was the review of the financial condition of the business. I was provided the most recent annual report for the company, which was dated December 31, 1998. The following were my noted take-aways:

Shareholder Equity: - $79,771,000 (negative)

Shareholder Equity consisted of –
Paid-in Capital of: $524,322,000
Retained Earnings /
    (Deficit) of: - $604,093,000 (negative)

Debt Financing
Consisting of –
Long-term Debt: $846,107,000
Other, including
Post Retirement
Benefit Obligation: $271,869,000
Short-term Liabilities
(mostly Trade and
Accrued Liabilities): $344,006,000

Total Debt $1,461,982,000

With effectively no shareholder equity (actually largely negative equity) partially due to egregious interest expense of $212,832,000, the magnitude of the debt level was paramount on this business. While Collins and Aikman was operationally fine, with a debt to equity ratio (the amount of money owed to third parties as compared to the owner's / shareholders' net worth of the company) of -18.33 to 1 (the negative indicates negative equity), the business—by any stretch of the imagination—was financially distressed due to the financial engineering aspect on the company's and the private equity ownership's (Blackstone and Wasserstein-Perella) approach to financing structure. The interest expense in the year that I was reviewing in my diligence activity was in excess of $82,000,000. Assuming a business produces an operating margin of 20%, this would mean that the business would be required to produce revenues of $400,000,000 just to meet the interest obligation on the debt, not to mention payment of any principal amounts due.

So approximately one-quarter of the revenues and all of the activities required to produce those revenues—including capital expenditures required, staffing and resourcing, material procurement and distribution, all manufacturing activity, sales and administration for a $400,000,000 business—were expended solely for the purpose of paying interest, while not a red cent went to profit or shareholder value creation, the reason for a (for profit) business' execution and existence. Known as a "leveraged buyout," this type of financing was popular beginning in the early 1980s with the advent of what we now call private equity. Today, incurring significant debt is the norm for most private equity acquisition activity, albeit not of this magnitude.

How is it possible that such a sound operational company can enter these financially troubled waters? From my experience, it begins with the notion that (some) private equity groups and others involved in senior corporate management believe that they can take a risk with others' money. The hope becomes such that when employing this financing as capital at risk, then levering the company up with two-thirds debt or greater in proportion to total financing, with a roll of the dice and a little luck, the company (will be) awarded major incremental revenue contracts. Or, alternatively, rationalize operations to be more efficient and therefore more profitable, manage the supply chain to consolidate buys, pressure suppliers for price reductions and finance their inventories through more generous terms; these are the levers of profit generation that may be employed. When private equity is purchasing an enterprise, another avenue of wealth creation results from striking such deals with less cognizant or knowledgeable sellers about the earnings potential of the business. These deals can be (perceived) bargains on relative enterprise value such that the portfolio company will generate such great cash flow/cash flow earnings (EBITDA) as is indicated in that wonderful financial model that some late twenties / early thirties MBA-bound financial mogul wannabe has generated in a chic high-rise office in the middle of Chicago or Manhattan. (Often months or years down the line, the private equity firm is asking, "Where are those profits?")

That being said, given the fact that the company was operationally sound, had great talent and given that I liked and respected Gene Wyler, the North American

Automotive Interior Systems President with whom I would be working intimately, I decided to join on and meet the challenge. I also believed that I possessed the bill of goods that could help move this business to further operational success. Via the implication chain, this would lead ultimately to financial success and deleveraging of the balance sheet (increasing the proportion of equity to debt financing) through superior earnings, just as I had done at my most significant career achievements at the prior company. I was up to this, for sure, as this is what feeds my industrial soul and spirit.

The

Ca Collins & Aikman

Experience

It was a mid-Sunday morning in the late August, early September timeframe of 1999. My wife, at the time, and I were in upper Michigan at a family vacation home and having a good old time of it. Shortly, I was to start my position as vice president of finance / chief financial officer for the North American Automotive Interiors Systems group (NAAIS) of Collins & Aikman Corporation. The total revenues for this business segment were approximately $1.4 billion of the total company's $1.8 billion revenue base (78% of the company). As was explained by my boss, Gene Wyler, my mission and key deliverable was to integrate five independent separate operating divisions into one super-interiors group that would go to market as the "total interiors solution" to the OEMs, with common financial policies, procedures, metrics, working capital management, quoting practices, and return on investment and profitability / productivity measures.

In addition to this, I was to provide key leadership and participation in moving the needle on earnings such that the company would get the required attention from "the Street" so that the stock price could reach a level that would be acceptable for The Blackstone Group and Wasserstein-Perella to get out from under their onerous and lagging investment in the company (they owned 87% of the company at that time). At this time, Collins and Aikman was an SEC registrant and traded on the New York Stock Exchange. Being owned by private equity in such a significant amount, the company operated in a mutated fashion: having all of the rules and regulations that pertain to a publicly owned company, including financial reporting, yet having the drive of cash earnings of the normal PE environment, it was also driven by earnings per share ("EPS"). EPS was the conduit to the stock trading at a higher value.

Not knowing it at the time, nor was senior management remotely cognizant of the fact that a significant upgrading of the finance function in NAAIS was required. The accounting and finance group had absolutely no esteem or credibility with the senior operations staff. This was in part because they commanded no respect and gave no respect for the rules governing financial reporting, a.k.a., Generally Accepted Accounting Principles ("GAAP"). The five separate independent and autonomous divisions had "divisional controllers." When the operational migration from the five separate and autonomous divisions to the super group (North American Automotive Interior Systems) occurred, these individuals reported to me. Carla Quick was controller of the plastics division, a business previously known as Manchester Plastics and acquired by Collins and Aikman approximately three years prior to my signing on; Charlie Danville was controller of the Floormats and Accessories Division, a legacy C&A business; Pierre St. Joulliet, controller of the Canada Carpet and Acoustics Division; John Kyte, controller of the US Carpet and Acoustics Division; and much later in this endeavor, Paul William was aligned to me after the "Fabrics Division" was rolled under my leadership. Prior to my joining the company, and shortly after in my cultural indoctrination, the operating executives would have a large say in the accounting treatment of certain business-related conditions and transactions so much so that they would suggest that certain journal entries be recorded with desired financial reporting effects. I did not want to consider this a case to be made for earnings management at that time, but I was certain that a cultural transformation was needed. I was either going to be the person to drive this culture change, or I was not going to succeed in my professional career. After all, I was a CPA who was bred and raised in a school that was known for providing an excellent education in how to become a professional accountant. My typical day, while I was developing my education, was eight to twelve hours of work as I studied in night school at Walsh College of Accountancy and Business Administration, followed or preceded by six to eight hours of study, or combined study and classes, the balance of the twenty-four was sleep, most often two to four hours and sometimes none. I had to master this profession, without question, and was driven to do so by knowing US GAAP and the United States Tax Code. After ten years with a major corporation, in leadership senior finance positions, eight of which I was CFO for, one who was not "of the cloth" would be mistaken if they thought they were going to even so much as suggest to me how to account for a business.

The people who reported to me were of varying levels of education and experience, but for the most part were hard working and like everyone, I gave them a chance to prove themselves in their function. I was to learn, in time, that one of them for sure was a keeper, three would require some action and the last one required a serious change in mindset about responsibility for and ownership of the financial records of a business, otherwise he would put my critical mission in jeopardy; technically, he was excellent but he suffered from the disease of operating-bosspleasiology, a disease that affects a lot of good (not great) financial professionals.

This Sunday morning in northern Michigan was a

special one, though. Dinesh Shaw, CFO of the holding company and one of my two bosses, was introducing me via conference call to Pierre, Carla, John and Charlie as their new functional leadership to discuss who I was and what my prior accomplishments were in a get-to-know session. I also was curious, at first blush, about the certain business challenges confronting the individual divisions of this newly formed super group. After my introduction and relatively short synopsis of my earlier career, the call quickly migrated into the individual division's challenges. Not so surprising, since C&A dominated the market in certain product categories, the word "growth" did not show in the challenge discussion. Two words did, though, and resoundingly: "MORE PROFIT"!

These folks sounded as desperate as they did bewildered. This wasn't a good sign.

The strong push to get C&A out of the Blackstone portfolio was seemingly pale in comparison to the drive to move David Stockman, the ex-federal budget director of the Ronald Reagan administration out of Blackstone, as I learned somewhat later in reading the biography of Steven Schwarzman, co-founder and managing partner of The Blackstone Group, "King of Capital." The early resigner from the Reagan administration, being from western Michigan, had a relatively strong affinity toward the automotive industry and believed that there was significant opportunity for financial gain in investing in this industry and segment at that time. About six months prior, he had established "Heartland Industrial Partners" and targeted rust-belt automotive businesses, acquiring MascoTech, Inc. and Simpson Industries, his first targets, and rolling them into what was then labeled "Metaldyne." This was Stockman's first foray into this segment on his own. Having learned through reading the book and actually experiencing some of its manifestation at C&A, there was a love-hate relationship between Schwarzman and Stockman that lasted during Stockman's tenure at Blackstone.

The following 6 paragraphs are excerpts from the book "King of Capital" which pertain to the Collins & Aikman experience and Mr. Stockman.

Stockman had cracked the Wickes nut, or so he thought. He plotted to break up the company, whittling it down to a single business: Collins & Aikman, a maker of textiles, carpeting, and wallpaper. Blackstone and Wasserstein-Perella each sank $122 million into the buyout that closed the same month as Transtar – the largest investment by Blackstone for the next seven years.

Things went awry almost from the start, in early 1989, when the US economy started to soften. An early sign of trouble came that spring, when Wickes put Builders Emporium, then the largest home-improvement retail chain in California, up for sale. Blackstone expected it to fetch as much as $250 million, one former employee says. "But we ended up having to sell it over time for like $50 million." Slowing auto sales also dug into the auto fabrics side of the business.

The buyers also soon discovered that Wickes's former CEO Sandy Sigoloff – a corporate turnaround artist and notorious cost slasher nicknamed Ming the Merciless – had hacked away rather too exuberantly at Wickes's management ranks. "What we had found was that Sigoloff was used to getting rid of whole layers of management for companies that were in trouble. But this company wasn't in trouble," says Schwarzman. "He fired a lot of people anyhow, so there was nobody around to do the work." Nearly from the start, then, the company was a problem."

The Edgcomb acquisition was the brainchild of Steven Winograd, a thirty-one-year-old M&A prodigy Blackstone lured away from Drexel. At Drexel, Winograd had played a role in a $150 million, management-led LBO of Edgcomb in 1986 and later that year helped take the steel fabricator public making a rich man of Edgcomb's CEO, Michael Scharf, and huge profits for Texas's Bass family and other backers of the buyout.

From the moment Winograd settled in at 345 Park Avenue, he pressed the idea of a second buyout of Edgcomb, whose stock had languished after it went public. Schwarzman quickly said yes. In May, Blackstone negotiated a $330 million deal to take Edcomb private for eight dollars a share, two dollars above the IPO price of 1986. Like Transtar, the Edgcomb buyout was leveraged to the rafters, with Blackstone contributing just $23 million for a 65 percent equity stake. The buyout closed in June.

David Stockman opposed the deal. Since his arrival at Blackstone a year earlier, Stockman had carved out a role for himself as a devil's advocate and doomsayer, and he argued fervently against the Edgcomb buyout. Stockman's input didn't win him any fans at headquarters. "He had a habit of criticizing other people's deals, particularly in the early years," says one former partner. "Right or wrong, David was never in doubt," says David Batten, another ex-partner. Stockman's Casandra act soon wore thin not only because it put him at loggerheads with his partners, but because he often was just wrong.

Understanding all of these "plays" many years later gave reason to the bizarre experiences which I was both cursed and blessed with at the pinnacle of my midlife career. It is not that I wasn't aware of the financial implications and motivations related to the outcomes that would translate to the various interested parties; these were obvious to me. What I am curious of is the human element, as I always am: the attraction and, conversely, the repelling nature of certain personalities that can make life highly pleasurable or extremely difficult. Having read the book several years after my experience, it was somewhat of a surprise that this was the case at Blackstone as it was completely out of our knowledge at the level of company operations (although we had kind of known that Stockman had to get the heck out of Blackstone, we weren't expecting C&A to be his parting gift). This does explain some of the urgency that was conveyed to me along the process of readying this behemoth of a company for the event of a transaction that would involve the sale of a majority of the company's shares.

What I learned early in my first few days at C&A was why such a level of desperation and bewilderment existed among the business unit controllers, along with the (abnormally) strong push for profit. The reason: with the approximate revenue level of $1.8 billion, the company was expecting debt service in the form of interest payments approximating $100,000,000. Yes, one hundred million dollars. Operating income, from which interest expense is deducted, in the year prior was $98,478,000, which meant that with all else being equal, the company couldn't cover its required interest payments. It is typical that when more operational profit is needed in a large-scale business, the senior leadership (C-level suites) of the company will lean on and pressure the strongest, most profitable business units to produce even more profit. In the early stages of the process of stroking the performing business units to produce more profit, Tom Nivens, C&A's holding company CEO, would often use the forum of humorous "needling" with the leaders over the strong business units, and with a chuckle. Within the fun of it, how can one resist?? After all, we're buddies and having a good time at it, aren't we?

As time moves on and the week progresses with status meetings on various issues, all of this "fun" turns to serious discussion and the assignment of profit task (a designated number of additional profit that will be earned) often occurs in a personal meeting between the business unit head, his/her VP of finance/CFO, the holding company CEO and CFO. The interesting thing is that it is initially not a bottoms-up approach to developing how much profit improvement can be had, but a mere "assignment" of additional net income that the business unit will give to the corporation. One person will make that decision, and that's the CEO (probably in counsel/ with consent of his/her CFO). At that point, the "scramble" starts! "Where does (s)he think we're going to come up with that amount of money?" are often the first words uttered from the business unit executives.

Part of the scramble process includes the operating company CFO / VP of finance, controllers and operating executives coming together to brainstorm ideas as to where the improvements will come from, naming the projects and quantifying a range of values that may be counted, individually and in the aggregate. This process produces a list of these initiatives, along with their individual value assignments. The list is disseminated to the lower operating levels of the business unit for further validation of both the initiatives and the values. Once the lower levels are through with their part of the process, the business unit controller will compile the results and report back to the operating company CFO/VP of finance of the aggregating business group—in this case, the North American Automotive Interior Systems group.

At every point in the process, when these improvement numbers are conveyed to the next highest level, often there is a negotiation that takes place between the purveyor of information and the person to whom the numbers are reported, including the assignment of probability and a weighted average sum of improvement that can be somewhat relied upon (somewhat, because one sneeze and the plan for improvement can take an adverse turn placing the overall profit improvement in jeopardy). That being said, even with deep thought and hard work, the business units often do not meet the CEO's profitability task assignment. When this happens, "unidentified task" is often the label that is given to the shortfall. This is so that the total task "assignment" stays intact and perhaps is incorporated into the next profit plan (even though a gap exists and no identifiable actions which would fill that gap are named at that point).

Often with the desire to satisfy, on the part of the business unit operating head, s/he will likely only ever-so-softly "qualify" the total improvement plan and related dollars by advising the CEO that, "We have some work to do to get there." The consequences of this can be great. On one hand, incentive compensation is likely linked to the amount of stretch contained in the financial plan (in other words, there is personal money to be made by achieving the task). On the other hand, not wanting to dissatisfy, for the obvious reasons, this sets up a condition that presents itself as the need to hit the assigned numbers, no matter how we hit them and no matter the consequences of how we hit them.

The human nature of "willing to please," the desire for "financial gain" and the culture of the company can set a tone for a disaster in the making. The culture of C&A NAAIS was one that operated under the guise of "mutual respect," as President Gene Wyler conveyed to me regularly since my first meeting with him. In all respects, Gene is a true gentleman and friend. I hold a great deal of respect for Gene, his business acumen and his drive for excellence in business. He had spent the better of two decades (plus) with Collins & Aikman, beginning as a quality technician, moving into supervision, sales, sales and marketing management, then general management and president of some of the divisions which reported into he and I, as the heads of the NAAIS, the new super-group of C&A.

Given that Gene had been with C&A for such tenure, with his good nature and manner, he had built several long-lasting relationships within the company and with individuals who now reported to him. A byproduct of the relationships that Gene had built over his long career with C&A was loyalty. Many people in this circle to which I am referring would do most anything for Gene. I believe this loyalty paid off in a lot of ways and that payoff likely went both ways.

Such loyalty and dedication can be beneficial to a company, its management and its employees, so long as the loyalty is kept within certain boundaries, meaning the things one does to remain loyal do not cross a certain line. Although this was not Gene's intention, I had some early signs that this loyalty penetrated and permeated all areas of the business, including areas of finance that could fog good decision making about what the numbers need to represent, hence the desperation and bewilderment of my direct reports; desperate for good results and the confusion of choosing not to report the right numbers while erring in the direction of not wanting to disappoint.

Little did I know, my work was cut out for me to change the culture, bring discipline to the function and cause the right numbers to be reported.

Collins & Aikman Moves Headquarters from Charlotte, North Carolina, to Troy, Michigan

During the late 1990s, supplier consolidation and "systems" supply was a megatrend in the automotive industry. This generally meant that the shaping of an automotive supplier had to be such that you, as a supplier, were at or approaching one billion dollars in automotive supply revenues and provided an "aggregate system," or specific "module" of the vehicle, to the Original Equipment Manufacturers ("OEMs"), or their tier one suppliers, depending upon where you, as supplier, fit into the supply chain.

As an automotive supplier, (greater) Detroit was seen as the place to have your headquarters. Just as well, having the company's sales, marketing and administrative groups here was deemed most advantageous due to the fact that most of Ford's, General Motors' and Chrysler's sourcing groups, which consisted of purchasing and engineering, were located in Detroit (Ford, General Motors and Chrysler were then known as the "Big-Three").

With modular supply in the offing at C&A and the company's move to Troy, Michigan, the last thing was the public relations aspect. Imagine this major business being tucked in the south, truly where most of the textile companies were born and operated. C&A was one of these in its earlier years, producing wall coverings and floor coverings with some automotive business. Being that automotive was by now the lion's share of the company, it had to act, live and breathe like the rest of automotive suppliers serving the North American market. The major transformations of the company, its girth and the move to Detroit had to be largely publicized in order for the company to get the attention required for it to gain traction on Wall Street so that the stock price would positively move and facilitate the brokering of C&A to new majority ownership.

Well, Blackstone got just the guy! Mr. Thomas Nivens, a veteran to the auto scene, most recently responsible for a transformation (good or bad, jury's still out) of Tenneco Automotive, an exhaust system manufacturer. Tom was our CEO and my God; you knew when Tom was on your floor, much less in the building. His persona was larger than his stout 5' 7" or 8" stature, and so was his volume.

Tom had the ability to tell you that elephants can fly. After he told you that, your perception of how high elephants can fly was only influenced by how much direct influence Tom had on your future (as for me, I didn't believe Tom's lines because I had a job to do and by all means, I was going to do it!).

During Tom's quest for "Wall Street traction," he was in the local paper, "The Detroit Free Press," and the local business publication, "Crain's Detroit Business," nearly every week, if not twice within a week. Tom was great at telling (what he thought to be) the world about everything that was right with C&A, what great accomplishments were ongoing and why C&A was the premier automotive supplier to be riding, either in the car or as an investment. It didn't matter if Tom was addressing the public or talking to colleagues and associates inside of the company. The message was the same. It never stopped. It could have been about any topic and you would wind up in the same spot. He was so "on," one could not come away with any other impression but that it was all just "too thick." The same shit he was telling you was too damn thick to believe, and boy did he know how to layer it on. You could just sense that his words were beyond reality, most of the time.

This is the guy we reported to, ultimately, the guy who approved our incentive compensation.

With Tom's influence, this whole situation was dangerous.

The 110 Plan

The time when I joined with C&A is commonly known as "budget/forecast season" in the automotive industry, which launches in mid- to late-July with estimates of vehicle builds, by platform (primary vehicle construction, drivetrain and suspension upon which variants are derived) and individual models. This information historically has been supplied by J. D. Powers, the firm that surveys the public and develops quality ratings for many industries; but now, a company named "IHS" has taken over the automotive forecast business, with their acquisition of a company known as "CSM" who specialized in make, model and volume estimates for the automakers. This is the brain trust that most all of the suppliers use to develop their volume forecasts, as they apply their portfolio of products to these estimates (one per vehicle, two per vehicle, just as there are four tires on each automobile, etc.). This allows the automotive suppliers to understand how many of their products they should plan to produce in the following year and develop the beloved sales revenue forecast.

The primary reason an independent source is utilized by the supply base in establishing the amount of units to be produced is because the OEMs will provide inflated numbers, many times with the intent of pushing up to the supplier's "tooled capacity"[4]. The reason that the OEMs typically will provide inflated numbers is because they wish for the suppliers to be ready to facilitate maximum production of the vehicle in the case the vehicle is a real hit with consumers. Another semi-related reason is that the OEM, upon a request for quotation for a new or revised part/product, will pump the volume to the tooled capacity (in the request for quotation) so as to obtain the lowest / optimized price possible. The OEM purchasing personnel believe that the more volume that is assumed to be produced, the lesser the price will be obtained from the supplier. Often, these pumped volumes are mostly never achieved, leaving the supplier with more fixed costs [5] hitting their P&L than they had planned, thus creating either less profits than planned or losses. As time marched on, suppliers became cognizant of such OEM ploys and, therefore, reduce reliance on OEM supplied information for volume estimates. The element of trust between suppliers and OEMs could be described as nearly non-existent. If trust exists, it's only a façade.

As we all gathered in Wyler's (the President's) office, there was a certain high degree of uneasiness among the sales and marketing staff who were assembled to review, validate and compile the sales plan on a customer-by-customer, product-by-product basis. It began as a disorganized effort as folks were unsure as to how to view their respective business units other than by gross volumes and prices. Hence, I could tell that not much intelligence was built into prior plans

I was well equipped with an item out of my tool box that allowed the group to fertilize the raw data with some intelligence that would allow them, and us as senior management, to develop and understand what is changing in the customer, market and product that leads to the ultimately compiled sales plan. I saw how this was going, so I provided the group with a structure to organize and present their information. We walked through a few scenarios, and this helped focus the group. The group had begun to catch on and was somewhat calmed with this approach, but this did not clear the fog of uneasiness in the room.

Little did I know at the time that Wyler leaked the CEO's profit directive of $110 million to some of his close confidantes in the sales staff, who leaked it to their close confidantes, who leaked it to their close confidantes, and so on. These guys were like nervous cats on a hot tin roof. My sense was that in the many years of seniority that many of these individuals had with the company, the level of seriousness that was now required and the need to perform had never existed at these levels. It was clear to me that the newly acquired level of business seriousness was only surpassed by the fear they possessed should they reveal information in the plan that would be inconsistent with the production of the $110 million; much less, not to perform to such plan. Wyler most certainly had the dedication, alignment and loyalty from his sales lieutenants, but please remember that loyalty goes both ways. Early indications, from what I could tell and have experienced being in the game for some time now, is that the certain loyalty that existed was also covering some incompetence in a few of the individuals. Ultimately, I was too early in my tenure to judge, but time would tell.

The next step in the process, once sales were finalized and approved, was to hang expense off of these numbers: cost of raw material, purchased components, direct and indirect labor, supplies, electricity, salaries, general and administrative expenses, etc. But first, sales were the call of the moment; therefore, I dedicated the remainder of my week to counseling and advising the sales group on the compilation of their individual plans which would be amalgamated into the total sales plan for the North American Automotive Interior Systems of C&A.

I received an invitation from the holding company CFO for another Sunday morning conference call. I was sure that this call was to take on a different character than the prior conference call. The call, which started at 10 a.m., which I decided to take on our backyard deck, was intensely focused on improvements in profitability for both the current year and the next. Attendees on the call were Dinesh Singh, C&A Holding Company CFO; Ron Angelotti, corporate controller; Thursten Beyers, corporate treasurer; and my controller direct reports for support.

Dinesh feverishly launched off into the Parker, SC, plant's level of inside truck (forklift) drivers and in his estimation, there were too many by a magnitude of 2X. As a source of increased profits, Dinesh was advocating that we layoff 50% of the inside truck drivers. Although I had not yet been to the Parker manufacturing facility, I understood that this was a sprawling facility which had been modified and adapted to the required molded automotive floor manufacturing. In a previous life, this facility was a distribution warehouse where semi-truck and trailers would port, pick-up and deliver wholesale and retail goods. You can begin to imagine a disjointed facility, even after adapting it to manufacturing. The product flow was quite bad, thereby necessitating more inside truck drivers than you would normally encounter in a simpler factory.

I always opted on the side of the operating executives when it came to staffing resources since they hold the ultimate responsibility of quality, delivery and customer service. This was one of Lynard Strong's operations. Lynard and his right-hand Parker operations guy, Cal Peoples, were principled business people and would fight the good fight and ultimately win this mandate with a strong argument. As I recall, the mandate was given and people were laid off, only to realize the plant could not operate with this level of staff in the inside trucking department; therefore, requiring a recall and reversal of that poor decision made by a bean counter in some Taj-Mahal style office. I recall at that time, I couldn't believe what an idiot this guy was. After my pre-employment diligence an article surfaced about how Mr. Singh unlawfully liquidated an employee pension fund at another company to meet his prior company's financial performance targets.

The discussion migrated through material cost to salaried staffing and indirect labor, plant-by-plant. Dinesh's favorite saying was "all costs walk on two feet." I was mostly listening because I was keenly aware that after years of meeting mandatory customer price-downs through material cost reductions and efficiency drives while keeping company profitability intact, most of the low hanging fruit had been plucked. With several bean-counters on a call on Sunday morning (no manufacturing or commercial representatives from the company), the best one could expect is to come up with easily identified opportunities for profit improvement, hence the term "low hanging fruit."

My single contribution to the profit push came with a suggestion on a technical accounting issue. Most often, a large entity with many manufacturing operations does not do a good job of costing their product inventory. Typically, a standard (estimated) cost is used, in a scientific and procedural approach. This "standard cost" approach to valuing the company's product inventory typically is not accurate and, given the level of sophistication and intelligence within the finance community upon my arrival, I was guessing that this area of the accounting ledger may have been deficient of attention.

Generally accepted accounting on inventory valuation is the "lower of actual cost or market"; therefore, should the estimated (standard) cost be less than the actual cost of manufacture and price, there is an opportunity to bring some of the cost which previously had a negative impact on the income statement within the current quarter onto the balance sheet into the value of inventories as a declaration of value, thereby crediting (increasing) income in the period.

The call concluded at 3 p.m. and resulted in a compiled listing of opportunities to be followed-up on. Another valiant effort turned fire drill that was a precursor to what was to come in 2000. I reviewed the plan with the operating managers. They viewed the plan developed without their involvement and opinion to be absurd. Clearly, they were at odds with the operating items and especially some of the suggestions affecting them that would compromise the efficacy of their business (the Parker forklift inside truck driver initiative being one).

Among many priorities, the months of September and October were comprised of traveling to many of the major company factories to review budgets and operating results, sharing my views on how the business must be structured, and reviewing and analyzing results in a sensible format which yielded a way of cutting through a lot of the fuss and muss to determine cause and effect in a simplistic manner. As the end of the year approached, monthly results of one operation would be $400,000 favorable to the prior forecast (given one month earlier), only to be met with another operation that would be $500,000 unfavorable. This was somewhat typical during that period of the industry, especially in companies where financial and operational expertise were not properly melding to develop realistic projections. This needed significant correction on a forward basis, and it was on my watch and leadership to fix this problem.

We ended the year not too far off of the 1999 4th quarter macro estimate for NAAIS that I developed and Wyler approved. This was somewhat comforting as understanding and credibility for the business was under development; however, this result still left significant gaps yet to accomplish in achieving the following year's $110,000,000 top down assignment.

Once I had compiled the prospective results for the year 2000—after successive reviews and modifications as suggested by Wyler and fully vetted and negotiated with his operating lieutenants—I reviewed the consolidated numbers with Wyler and, while we were short of the $110 million, we labeled the gap as "unidentified operating task," which hopefully would be narrowed and closed with initiatives that were to be brought forth and materialized during the following year of operations. Even stretched as we were (with a gap of approximately seven million dollars), upon submission of our plan to Nivens and Singh, we had expected them to ask us for a roadmap on how we would actually deliver the year 2000 prospective results.

Instead, what we received in final approved budget format was a number that was greater than $110 million. Their assumption was that if we were shooting for numbers higher than the actual goal, we most certainly would reach the acceptable number. Even though we already stretched to a point that may take seven days per week of dedication from everyone to execute, monitor, readjust, execute and monitor—in addition to acquiring some luck to help us find the unidentified elements to fill the gap and execute upon them—we received more unidentified task that pumped the number close to $120 million for our target. Oddly enough, even though the number was trumped up, I along with some others of the senior staff were assured that even though our target had matured to be bigger than life, the number that we would be judged on for incentive compensation would be the $110 million (which was a real reach anyway!).

This made for an interesting dynamic at the 1999 C&A Christmas party that was held at the Birmingham (Michigan) Country Club. Greeting everyone in a jubilant and upbeat manner was Mr. Tom Nivens along with his Florida-based wife. Tom lived in Waukegan, IL, a high society area in Greater Chicago land. Tom rode the company jet on Monday mornings to the Oakland-Pontiac Michigan Airport just in time to pick up his green BMW 5 Series to drive to the newly established Troy headquarters into which the corporate staff moved over the course of the Christmas break and early January 2000 and parked his BMW on Friday afternoon in order to be airlifted, on the company's dime, across Lake Michigan to his weekend social circles.

The new corporate headquarters structure was an immaculate, half-crescent, two-story building and was notable, both aesthetically pleasing and modern from the outside as well as state of the art, work facilitating for all. The company's executives enjoyed top-end office accommodations. My perimeter office had angled walls to fit the contour of the building's exterior while molding a cove for our (the president's and my) shared administrative assistant nicely placed between the entrance of Wyler's and my office. My office had an entrance-way swatch of square footage ahead of the actual work area that was adorned with a remarkably modern and facilitative desk and credenza unit—cherry wood I am guessing—with overhead shelves and a matching conference table efficiently placed eight feet from my desk. My guess is that my office was one-quarter of the size of the small Birmingham ranch home that I tore down and replaced with a modest two story prior to joining on to C&A.

While my office was characteristic of the size and accompaniment of most of the individuals' offices who reported to Gene, Wyler's office was 1.5X that. While you may expect that individuals with tenure and industry experience such as ours would be provided such digs to conduct their business, you wouldn't expect this type of treatment to be bestowed by a company with such poor financial condition. I justified it in my mind to be the result of a company with a $1.8 billion top line, the need for such a showplace for customer enticement and the fact that operationally, the company was sound while awaiting a turn in financial fortune.

This Christmas party was a corporate dynamic that I had never experienced at a company Christmas party; Tom's jubilant greetings and buoyancy relating to his pumped-you-up outlook for this business and himself; the business had not yet carved a spot of financial permanence and due to this, industry sustenance, yet large dollars were flowing for the corporate lifestyle of a thriving business. This air of the party was tempered by the

NAAIS staff who were realistic yet hopeful about the company and our performance. These individuals attended the party in the spirit of the holiday and being together but appeared to "carry the weight of the world on their shoulders." I knew this by the solemn look of their brows which were anchored by a warm smile upon greeting. Cordial exchanges between colleagues and spouses were accompanied by a toast for a good holiday, and then the discussion focused on the business and the height of the mountain that we were expected to climb in the following year (2000). Year 2000 would be ever telling about (1) the makeup of the senior leadership, (2) the ultimate tactics and resulting destiny of the company, and (3) who I really was as a human being.

This experience really revealed to me that our lives are comprised of a series of tests: tests of love, tests of mental and physical aptitude, tests of care and charity and tests of moral character and ethics. The sum of results of these tests ultimately determine our future, the circle of our friends, our social status, our long-term financial standing and on what side of truth and fairness we stand and fight for. Here I was, in the middle of establishing the foundation of a long, rewarding career (hopefully both in subject matter and personal finances) and about to embark upon the most challenging and self-defining event of my professional career and life, one that would test who I was and what I really cared about—professionally and personally—by trying my moral and ethical character.

C&A, Y2K and 110M - A Challenging Combination:

The new year, 2000, came with a bang of celebration and a high degree of uncertainty in most peoples' lives about whether or not their computer systems would continue to function. The design of many (dated) systems incorporated only two digits for the year, therefore, coming from 99, 00 would revert to the year 1900 because the architects of these old systems did not have the foresight to design a four digit year so that the progression of time could bring integrity to data systems beyond the year (19)99. Fortunately, Kraig Hester, NAAIS I/T director assured Wyler and I that our systems were year 2000+ compliant and that the change of the century would pose no significant issues to our business. He was correct; however, there were a few minor glitches, so minor that I cannot recall the insignificant consequences posed, but nonetheless, an early morning January 1 call from Kraig advised that all was well, aside from these slight hiccups.

While the team jelled well and rallied around the need to produce superior numbers, the business was not producing numbers consistent with the lofty goals for year 2000. By and large, consistently upon reporting monthly results, we were coming in to numbers that ranged 75-90% of the time-phased $110 million (annualized $82.5 - $99.0 million). Clearly, this was not going to get it done for us and the time of desperation hit early in the year. We had traveled monthly around the U.S. and Canada for our regular "operations review" meetings which would include one to one and one-half days of meetings and tours of the operations to validate improvements which were discussed. The operations review meeting would touch all areas of the business, not only the financials: a summary by the president (Wyler), product engineering, manufacturing operations, sales and marketing, human resources and safety, purchasing / supply chain, finance and any other pertinent topics that were impacting the business. A substantial part of our profit improvement was coming from the purchasing / supply chain area whereby the Purchasing / Supply Chain management group would competitively shop raw materials and purchased components (versus manufactured) for price and terms to compare against the related information of the incumbent supplier. This would bear the threat of re-sourcing the items procured from the incumbent, should better prices and terms be found, leaving the incumbent with substantially less business that would have adverse effects on the incumbent supplying company.

After taking part in a few of the operations review meetings, it became quite apparent that Tom Nivens was intent on imparting some cultural change at C&A, especially at the NAAIS group. As I had mentioned Wyler's significant tenure with C&A, the number of long-time relationships that he had and that ostensible reciprocal loyalty that had matured throughout the years. To an outsider—which Tom Nivens was, having been with the company somewhat less than one year—these relationships have seemingly manifested themselves into a fair amount of complacency which, in his mind, explained why the profit needle had not significantly moved since he had joined on.

The first operations meeting of 2000 was not a pleasant one. With effectively coming close to / nearly making our sales forecast for the period, and in some cases exceeding it, the profit numbers were not coming through at the levels of the 110 Plan, not to mention the "Stretch Plan" arbitrarily assigned by Tom and Dinesh. As I had mentioned, there was about a 30% gap, with a significant share of the gap falling in the area of the task assigned to the Purchasing / Supply Chain group. Bill O'Shaunessy, a great and respected friend of Gene's, headed up this area. Originally coming from the sales and marketing side of C&A, Bill, in my early estimation, was a competent and sensible individual. Having been groomed in the C&A way, Bill knew the product and supply base rather well and was clearly a professional.

Well, it was clear that this opinion was not shared with Nivens as he began to treat Bill O'Shaunessy as a punching bag in these meetings. Nivens belittled O'Shaunessy in a manner that made the remainder of us cringe. O'Shaunessy did his best to answer for the shortfalls, doing so in his usual gentlemanly manner. This was painful for all, except for Nivens, all the while enjoying his bully style approach at senior management. We all knew O'Shaunessy was a great guy whose head and heart were in the right spot. You could see the empathy on the faces of O'Shaunessy's colleagues.

One of the initiatives which we undertook to help address the unassigned task number was an attempt to convince General Motors that C&A NAAIS was harmed by supply contract pricing, where cross border Canada supply of the product occurred while the price was set in US dollars. It was a major effort and condition of doing business with General Motors that the acquisition transactions for products sourced for their US Market vehicle sales were denominated in US dollars. The purpose for this would be to eliminate or limit GM's risk of foreign currency fluctuation when purchasing parts. Being as all purchase orders from the OEMs come with a set of terms and conditions (T's & C's), I knew that this was going to be a huge uphill battle. In understanding the assertion of loss, I was to compile all sales to GM that were made from our Canada facilities, then take the differential in the currencies, which happened from the point of awarding the business to C&A, and quantify the level of economic loss that had occurred since the business was awarded. This loss was the result of the strengthening US dollar over time when compared to the Canadian dollar when compared to the relationship of the respective dollars at the time that the business was awarded much earlier in time (3-8 years ago). As C&A was paid in US dollars with having its costs to manufacture the products in Canadian dollars, as the US dollar strengthened against the Canadian dollar, it took more Canadian dollars, proportionately. Since C&A was paid in US dollars, it would have taken more US dollars being paid to C&A via a price increase, to make up for the increased cost in Canadian dollars, as the Canadian dollar was worth less in US dollars than when the business was awarded. This was the claim to be asserted. I had worked at the direction of and in conjunction with Wyler. The first time through with the numbers, as compiled, yielded a wild number such as $14-$15 million, due to the strengthening of the US dollar in comparison to the Canadian dollar. A meeting was set with the lead GM purchasing vice president for petroleum-based products, Mr. Bill Simmons.

 I guess the thought, after submitting this plea summary to Bill Simmons and his staff, was as if we would just walk into the meeting, pick up a $15 million check and all of our profit problems would disappear. **"Ya right!"** GM had profitability issues of its own that would complicate any significant pricing recovery. After arriving at the GM Engineering Center—its sprawling Warren, MI, campus that doubled as the extension of its downtown Detroit headquarters—we were led to a conference room where Bill and his team surrounded a large table. Our attendees included Wyler, Bill O'Shaunessy, VP of Purchasing Bob Smiley, VP of sales and marketing and myself, VP and CFO.

As Simmons and staff were prewarned of the subject matter and had familiarized themselves with it, the commencement of the meeting was both cordial and somber: cordial because of the intimate nature of the C&A supplied products to the overall GM automobile offering, and somber because any supplier doesn't just lob a $15 million claim at GM, or any OEM automotive manufacturer, and expect a warm and fuzzy reaction. We were viewed by the GM team to be ridiculous, desperate, unconscionable, bizarre, beyond reality—perhaps insane. As a matter of fact, I believe that word was actually used in the meeting. While the GM stance was clear from the beginning of the meeting that the contracts were awarded in US dollar denomination, with no foreign currency protection provision, they were kind enough to view our slides, acting as if they understood their content, careful to not acknowledge any level of implicit monetary harm that came to C&A via the fluctuation in the relative currency valuation, nor acknowledge any obligation of GM to make C&A whole on this item. The meeting concluded with a promise to get back with us on their decision. This, little did we know, would take a number of weeks that eventually turned into months.

Not too long after the Simmons meeting, we received a meeting request from one of GM's go-to people who is in the business of assessing and fixing distressed suppliers: BBK, Ltd. BBK was well known for protecting GM's interest where supply of parts/products may be placed in jeopardy due to either operational or financial distress. This was less of a meeting request and more of a notice that a meeting would take place in approximately one week. While we were shocked by this ("How can the customer be concerned about C&A's financial or operational viability, a company with our resources and backing?" and, "This is only a temporary issue that we are experiencing so that the business can effectively be sold."), we were quite confident that this individual, as expert as they may be, didn't know the business and the current situation as well as we did, and that we could easily demonstrate that this business was a healthy business. The truth of the matter is that anyone who could read a financial statement could tell that we had significant challenges, and the meeting with Bill Simmons didn't help matters as we did demonstrate a level of desperation with the mere presentation and request that we put forth.

The February operations review meeting was one of similar candor to January's. With the frustration building after successively missing financial goals in a similar magnitude, you had begun to get a sense that the fervor in these meetings was akin to sharks circling around someone with a large and raw wound swimming in the ocean. Nivens was vicious during the review. He was almost to the point of boiling for the entire meeting. Red-faced and sweating, he attacked most of the presenters in the meeting, even throwing barbs at the non-business / non-commercial function leads within the business. It had become so that nothing was off limits, even the areas where Tom had no functional technical knowledge such as engineering and product research and development.

And then came the Purchasing/Supply Chain functional review, a bloody mess. That is about the best description that I could come up with. Nivens laid into O'Shaunessy like I have never seen in an open forum; I might say that O'Shaunessy, after some time of understanding that he was a marked man, had begun to respectfully stand up for himself and the things that he and his team were doing. While I might add that this is an area where we may have been doing better for the business, it certainly did not warrant this level of disdain and embarrassment in the front of all of us; perhaps some things are best left for behind closed doors. Upon O'Shaunessy's businesslike persuasion and retort, Nivens lambasted him and O'Shaunessy had nothing left for himself but to stand there in front of the crowd, as if here was a six-year-old receiving a strong discipline from his father and had no place to hide.

Tom, a 50+ year-old with long company tenure, was summarily dismissed from his position the next day upon return to our Troy, Michigan, headquarters. The whole senior staff grieved this as Tom was a good man and colleague and, if handled in the right way, he could have been successful in achieving the company objectives…. Maybe, that is depending upon what those company objectives were. As vice president of purchasing / supply chain, Bill O'Shaunessy was replaced by a guy named Joe Furtuck, a Nivens yes-man who suffers from the appeasing "Bobble-Head Syndrome"[6]. Furtuck was "everybody's man," seeming to think of himself as if he walked on water and could solve everyone's problems every time. This I could tell was going to be a problem for (me and) good accounting from the start.

Well, from the start, the operational cadence, since Furtuck commenced with his activities, went something like this:

1. Tom Nivens and Dinesh Singh would summon Furtuck to their office suite,

2. Nivens would try out some cockamamie scheme with which to approach certain suppliers with on Furtuck. Furtuck bites,

3. Furtuck goes to the major supplier, puts forth his wild pitch, strikes up a negotiated deal (most often remuneration to keep their existing business into the future),

4. Furtuck returns to C&A Troy HQ,

5. Furtuck meets with Nivens and Singh and advises of a rebate based on keeping future business,

6. Nivens and Singh celebrate a six or seven digit win to ostensibly drive earnings in a positive direction,

7. Furtuck comes and visits with me,

8. Furtuck discloses the details of the deal which he has struck with said supplier,

9. I congratulate Furtuck on his accomplishment and advise Furtuck that this will have no immediate favorable P&L impact but must be recognized over the future purchases on a pro-rata basis because it pertains to future business.

10. Furtuck, disappointed, leaves my office and reports to Nivens and Singh that the one-time purported immediate earnings gain is said to be fiction by Burgundy (me) and the amount negotiated must be amortized over future purchases.

11. This accounting would stick.

After a second Furtuck attempt with similar results

(what is the definition of insanity?), Joe Furtuck adjusted his approach to the following:

1. Tom Nivens and Dinesh Singh would summon Furtuck to their office suite,

2. Nivens would try out some cockamamie scheme with to approach certain suppliers with on Furtuck. Furtuck bites,

3. Furtuck would check with me on the strategy,

4. I would review and either approve such that these are immediate earnings gains, or counsel and advise Furtuck on what is appropriate for immediate recognition, based on the concepts discussed,

5. Furtuck would (most likely) adjust the supplier proposed deal,

6. Furtuck goes to the major supplier, puts forth his wild pitch, strikes up a negotiated deal,

7. Furtuck returns to C&A Troy HQ,

8. Furtuck meets with Nivens and Singh and advises of a rebate based on keeping future business,

9. Nivens and Singh celebrate a six or seven digit win to ostensibly drive earnings in a positive direction,

10. Furtuck comes and visits with me, in confirmation of contemplated deal,

11. Furtuck discloses the details of the deal which he has struck with said supplier,

12. I congratulate Furtuck on his accomplishment.

13. This appropriate deal and proper accounting would stick in accordance with GAAP.

As I had mentioned, I had to get Furtuck's attention more than one time. As things progressed, he would bring me other ultra-creative deals that were coached/ influenced by Nivens and Singh, post negotiation and communication. All of these items were slanted in a manner to game the financials with supplier cooperation but gain no real economic value. This went on both with the sales and purchasing sides of the game.

Nivens needed me to accompany him to one of our operations for a review of sorts while Singh and Wyler were unavailable. I had other business to attend to also while there, so we shared the company plane to one of the southern plants. As I had mentioned, Nivens was hell-bent on breaking the cultural loyalty within Wyler's staff. About a month prior to the trip, Nivens pressured Wyler to fire Bob Smiley—our vice president of sales and marketing and longtime industry professional who knew C&A's product, markets and customers cold—otherwise Nivens was going to do it himself (this is the story that I learned from Wyler).

Wyler was distraught. As you can well imagine, these guys had been through a lot together, major business awards / wins and disappointments, struggles over pricing, acquisitions leading to broader businesses to manage, customer collaboration, births, marriages, deaths, etc. Steve Steiner, who had less of a broad business knowledge and involved in a smaller segment of the business, was appointed Bob's successor. Steve also suffered from the "Bobble-Head syndrome"[6], acquiescing to anyone who signs his paycheck. Steve accompanied Nivens and I on the plane and as usual the stipends of coffee, bagels, pastries, orange juice and other morning accouterments were provided as the idle pilot catered to us. Steve was along for a knowledge-gaining experience since he clearly was over his head when entering NAAIS due to the mass, product complexity and range of high-profile customers. From the sales and marketing side, Steve managed a business that was one-tenth of the size of NAAIS. He clearly had a lot to catch up on and in a hurry.

We got through most of the flight and the conversation turned to improving profit with the engagement of the sales and marketing team and the cooperation of our customer base. This was convenient because Nivens had the both the head of finance and the newly appointed head of sales, the responsible parties to (1) negotiate a deal with a customer and (2) account for the deal.

Nivens' theory was vitally, substantively and morally flawed. It was laid out by Nivens as follows:

1. In the current year (the year with a targeted $110M operating income), approach the customer with a price increase request.

2. The price increase would be sizable, probably about $4-7 Million when applied to the volumes.

3. Ask the customer to pay C&A this value in the current year.

4. Promise the customer that you would give that value back to them in the following year, plus interest, or the cost of money for the period that we held their money prior to repayment.

5. Account for this price increase as increased sales revenue and profit in the current year (helping to facilitate earnings enough to get the stock price high so Blackstone could get out and Nivens and Singh could collect their large success bonuses).

Upon having to give the money back, who the hell knows what the fraudulent accounting would be, I sure as hell had no clue... A rebate? ... What? ... One thing I did know for sure, I wasn't going to direct the accounting related to any such sham!

Needing to have the appearance that I was a team

player (all for one, one for all), I asked Tom Nivens for a deal to be brought to me and at a later time I would review it under the proper GAAP treatment and accounting.

The reality of this, whether or not Tom was smart enough to know this, is that this type of arrangement constitutes a loan, or financing, NOT A PRICE INCREASE FOR VALUE THAT THE COMPANY COULD KEEP AND BOOK TO SALES REVENUE. Tom was smart enough to think that he could influence someone who he had a great deal of influence over to do the wrong thing; he threw out a line, but I wasn't biting.

I think Tom knew better.

So Tom drove to my Birmingham, MI, home the morning of the trip, and we took my car which at the time was a new Lincoln LS, the small high-end car that was designed by the BMW designer who was responsible for the 3 and 5 series. NAAIS had significant content on this car, so it was a good drive to Oakland-Pontiac Airport. Upon return from our destination, Tom and I jumped in my car and headed to my home where his car was parked. I asked if he would like to come in for a glass of wine before he left, and he accepted. As we sat in my dining room sipping away, Tom told me of the (hidden behind a retractable wall) car museum that he has in his living room and what a "good time" we could have if I flew across Lake Michigan with him to his home and spent a weekend. Bait thrown. If I bit, I'd be obligated to help him achieve his personal objectives. I knew better. We weren't friends who came together over common ideals and blood, sweat and tears; we were guys collectively trying to make a buck. One of us was trying to manipulate the other into a fraud. The better of us was trying to do a great job, earn a fair buck and be on with life.

While I love cars, museums and having fun, I love truth, liberty and freedom more.

Do the right thing.

Footnote Explanations

(4) The amount of production that is possible by one machine and related tooling, given that all conditions are perfect.

(5) Fixed costs are costs such as building maintenance or property taxes that do not change with unit volume.

(6) The "Bobble-Head Syndrome" is a term developed by the author which describes the spineless approach that many loyal executives take toward their boss whereby the boss is always correct and the head of the bobble shakes up and down, no matter what is said, no matter what is asked and no matter the ethics that may be breached along the way.

An Unwelcome Surprise

One morning in mid-March 2000, I received a call from Stuart Blumenthal, our GM account executive in charge of sales to General Motors. He requested a meeting with me to include two of his "program managers" assigned to the GM Cadillac DeVille (DTS) interior door project. It was not every day I received such a call; the sales and marketing side of the business pretty much runs their own show, so I immediately accepted and asked them to come down to my office.

Upon their arrival, they knocked at my door and I reciprocated with a warm greeting. These guys were hard working and dedicated individuals with the want of company and personal success, something to be respected and fostered. As they made their way into my office, as we had begun to sit around my conference table, they suggested, "David, we think we may have a problem."

As encouraging as I possibly could be, I offered, "There is no problem that we cannot collectively solve."

They continued, "You know of the Cadillac DeVille (DTS) rear door interior program we launched in the current model year?"

"Sure," I acknowledged.

"Well, we make two versions of the door: one with a sunshade and one without a sunshade."

"OK, got it so far."

"Pricing for the sunshade version is $225.00 each, and for the non-sunshade version, pricing is $175.00 each."

Thinking that this was a pricing and profitability issue, I volleyed back, "OK, and are we making money on both versions?"

"Well, we believe we are, but the story goes deeper. We received purchase orders from GM with a mistake made on the non-sunshade version. Instead of $175, they mistakenly applied the sunshade price to the purchase order; therefore, we are overbilling them and collecting too much cash for the non-sun shade version."

In disbelief, I asked, "Are you sure?"

"Absolutely we are. We even checked with billing and verified that volume on all of the doors are going out as $225.00."

I asked, "Do we have a sense of the number of doors that this mistake applies to and the amount of the money owed back to GM?" They produced a schedule of shipments and billings, along with the purchase orders and an example of the invoices and sure enough, there was in excess of a $2 million liability owed to GM.

I immediately thanked them for bringing this to my attention and in the name of doing the right thing. I assured that the right thing would be done on our watch. Feeling quite bad for a mistake that wasn't theirs, they asked if there was something more that they may need to do to help with the problem. I assured them that "at this stage there wasn't and that I would take it from there."

So much for the 110 Plan, as this pricing error was incorporated into all of our forecast projections, in addition to the inclusion in year to date (and prior year) results. As Wyler was out at customers earlier that morning, and bad news spreads much slower than good, I had the honor of greeting him later that morning with the news. He, just like I, was astounded. Of course the diligence questions came, "Did you verify this information?"

I advised, "I did prior to your arrival back here, all the way through cash collections." Gene immediately phoned both Nivens and Singh and they came down to his office while I remained.

Tom Nivens and Dinesh Singh made themselves comfortable around Wyler's conference table and we disclosed the news, with the appropriate evidence. Lots of deep breaths from Nivens and Singh, an Eastern Indian by descent, turned two shades lighter upon the news. After the news settled in, a strange, almost commercially legalistic argument arose from Nivens.

Nivens was actually justifying keeping the money and continuing to recognize the revenue in our financial statement and associated performance. Nivens, in his justification, cited GM owing C&A money for "currency devaluation, material price increase recovery that GM has not agreed to pay" and a myriad of other (un)justified irrationalities. I advised Mr. Nivens that we must view these items individually, as they must be, because each individual item he identified had a distinct economic reality and result that is unrelated to the other. I advised him that the door overpayment and excess revenue recognition "is a real liability" and we should recognize it in the financials. I further advised that I didn't care what he and the company did with the cash, however, it would make great business sense to advertise to our customer GM by walking into the GM purchasing head's office and dropping a bag of $3 Million on his desk and proclaim "look what we found." "This is GM's money and is the result of some sort of internal error that led to a purchase order pricing error," I told them. Then in the same breath, remind the GM purchasing head that you are in the running for the new Epsilon interior program and ask his consideration for being awarded that package.

Nivens would have no part of that! He was in the middle of a stock deal, doing anything he could (legal and otherwise) to increase earnings, and he would pulverize any deterrent he met along the way in pursuit of his big pay day and the actions that would lead to that. They left Wyler's office and we sat there deflated, me as CFO much more than Wyler as I well knew the ramifications of not recognizing the liability anytime, but especially during a major stock sale. In short, the word is "fraud," for (1) willfully taking customer's money unjustifiably while concealing it, and (2) knowing of such a condition that falsely increased the value of the company upon which a pending sale would occur. Such a condition, if properly handled, would lead anyone to value the company relatively lower than it otherwise would be valued with results that included the fraud. I vowed to myself that in time we would recognize the liability because it was the right thing to do and for now and a short time beyond, I guess we would smile, play it their way and hope for a windfall that would allow us to keep our current forecast while recognizing this abnormally large amount owed to GM.

The money owed back to GM (the hidden liability) was growing with each Cadillac DTS (Deville Touring Sedan) that hit the road. It was nearing late summer and in the operations review, I highlighted the NAAIS risks and opportunities with the GM door issue on the top of the list with an estimated $3 million of risk. The financial portion of the presentation revealed that the business was hitting 70-80% of the 110 Plan including the fraudulent inclusion of the erroneous increased door pricing, on a time-phased basis. I was increasingly concerned that profit increases would not come from added sales volume. Being as we were past the traditional high volume parts of the year (1st and 2nd quarters), we could not rely on proportionately higher profits from higher sales volume as the large production quarters now left in our rearview mirror. Instead, we continually and repeatedly lent on commercial recoveries from both our customer and supply base to shore-up the numbers. The largest opportunity was the claim we set forth to GM on foreign currency issues ($15 million). Joe Furtuck and his purchasing shenanigans produced marginal improvements that when properly accounted for, didn't give much to the bottom line in current quarters.

GM reported back to us on our currency conversion claim request. Of the $15 million that Wyler believed to be justified, GM graced us with approximately $2 million. GM, after their advisor's review, had begun to know the serious financial condition that C&A was in and as a result, was benevolent enough to gift the company some help. On the stand alone merits of the claim, there was nothing there and GM had no obligation, but the goodwill between the companies, the market share that C&A commanded along with GM's need for continued supply of product all led to a good business decision by Simmons and his team to justify and provide some working capital to the company. Wyler was significantly disappointed and underwhelmed with GM's response. Also, given the "settlement" on the currency issue and no following action, we received a letter on behalf of GM, which was the result of the BBK review. The result was such that C&A would be monitored on a go forward basis, to ensure GM supply of product so that they could continue to manufacture automobiles, until such time as the financial viability of the company was corrected and improved.

By now, Nivens' patience was beginning to wane. Results on a year-to-year basis were essentially flat. It was an obsessively competitive environment in automotive. All suppliers were vying to maintain their market share, while attempting to take conquest business from their competition. The OEMs were nearly successful in turning any and all products from technologically rich into simply a commoditized business, thereby eroding the prices paid to the suppliers.

Just as in the first decade of the 21st century, through the Great Recession of 2008, financial distress was becoming commonplace among the suppliers and it was during this time that there was a business created just to deal with troubled suppliers. The OEMs fragmented their purchasing staffs with troubled supplier specialists, just to monitor their financial and operational risk and when the shoe fell, to engage these turnaround firms either to fix the businesses in trouble or put them to sleep in a work-out, pseudo bankruptcy process. For those too far gone, bankruptcy was not an option but an enforced imperative.

The company results were not changing favorably whatsoever; in fact, they were stagnant to negative. This was getting in the way of Nivens' attempts to sell the business at a value that would be acceptable to Blackstone. Nivens, however, was making regular trips to Greenwich, Connecticut, to meet with Stockman to help engineer the acquisition of C&A by Heartland Industrial Partners. Upon returning from Greenwich, later one afternoon I received a call from Nivens with Singh in his office. Clearly upset with the wavering results, Nivens began to blame Wyler's leadership. Nivens cited his perceived downfall on Wyler's performance across all of the functional areas of the business and naming the specifics.

Then, the inevitable question came. What did I think of Wyler as the leader of this morphing organization? This clearly could have been a political question with a more politically charged response. As I thought through how I should respond, I paused long enough to gain the composure to develop a thoughtful and intelligent response. I decided to site Gene's strengths and weaknesses. To paraphrase: "From the product and customer perspective, Wyler was immersed. Having worked in the quality organization and having been in charge of sales and marketing, it was evident that this intelligence traveled with Gene throughout his career and he carries this with him in his capacity as president of NAAIS. From a leadership perspective, in my observance of Gene and the cultural protocol, I haven't actually seen Wyler challenge the ones who are loyal to him. It seems that if there is a challenging issue, one that should create some strong and fierce but respectful debate, we'll get a good ol' boy approach to it and most likely a "go-along to get-along" response. After observing this on a regular basis, it seems as if there is no exception to this approach."

I had a habit of working in the office until approximately 6:30 or 7:00 p.m. As I recall, Wyler was summoned to Nivens' office around 5:00. He was up on the second floor for quite a while. He returned after 6:00 and I learned that he had been fired. Gene's wife was out of town, back in North Carolina where their broader family resided. Gene and I had established a pretty good relationship, professionally and personally, from time to time, doing social things as friends and couples from time to time.

I felt awful. I knew that my words about Gene were not a large contributing factor to the decision. Although, as CFO of the organization, I was required to respond objectively and, in my mind, heart and soul, I remained apolitical, factual and emphasized both his strengths and weaknesses. Any investor would expect such a response. We met later that evening at one of Gene's favorite haunts. My role changed from chief financial officer to chief friend and consoler. Gene is a great guy. Like I said, we all have strengths and weaknesses.

Nivens was on a terror to change the culture and throw out that which was not optimizing value; at the same time, he was throwing out what also was good about C&A, ruining a previously great operating company and driving it to bankruptcy. In the end, Tom got more than just the culture change that he was after.

Tick-tock, Tick-tock

This was not only the sound of the clock, but also a bomb. Actually two bombs. One was inside Nivens' head (upon bad news, his face could turn redder than a Gulf of Mexico sunset, and I was sure an aneurism was soon to come) and the second was the bomb to go off when all of this news hit the financials, which I was certainly intending to execute on my watch.

Things were becoming intense during the third quarter of our 110 Plan Year. Results, for the most part, were consistent with approximately 80% of the plan—slightly behind in some months, slightly ahead in others—this of course not considering the hidden liability. While the liability was growing, I didn't deem it material enough in relation to the company's earnings in the first and second quarter reports (10Q's). In my mind, the materiality would have grown throughout the year, and in the fourth quarter the company would have to fess-up to the truth. I wasn't quite sure how I was going to accomplish this and keep my job. All of 40 years young, this certainly was something that I never experienced in my career.

Hence, I was becoming a bit nervous because I knew well that this thing, contrary to Nivens' and Singh's opinions, was not going to correct itself and go away. With 20 years' experience in businesses of various size and scale, nothing like this had ever happened where financial information was concealed from the public to favorably affect the stock price.

The Magic Carpet Ride

One day in early September, I received a solicitation call from Mr. Tony Fiore. You will learn later that I viewed Tony as a Godsend. Tony was the business development leader for a "trade-credit" organization known as ViaMedia. Tony explained to me that he brokers excess and obsolete goods and services for other excess goods and services and this whole value chain winds up being monetized in media advertising. While I could buy into the concept, I couldn't very well understand it. This would take careful study and likely involve a flowchart, something I didn't have time for. The interesting thing about the process was that 50% of the excess and obsolete goods brokered from you could be remunerated in cash.

While on the call, I immediately pulled a query of our inventory accounts and confirmed what I had thought: the carpet and acoustics segment of our business had a reserve for obsolescence in the amount of $10,000,000 (that's $10 million!). This was becoming more interesting by the minute. This meant that there were $10 million of goods that we still had physical possession of but were written-off in our P&L (expensed and declared valueless). If I could somehow turn some or a portion of these items into value through a transaction, I could bring their value back on books and upon the sale transaction, declare the income.

Being relatively new to the company, I hadn't had the luxury of touring all company-owned sites, so I asked Tony Fiore to hold so that I could check with Charlie Danville, the site controller in verification of the physical possession and location of the goods. Sure enough, the goods were there in our Zanesville, Ohio, warehouse and Charlie's physical headquarters was Canton, OH, about one hour away. I returned to the call with Tony Fiore and advised him that there was likely a good chance that we could help each other. I asked Tony for next steps and he advised that within two weeks, he and his valuation expert would fly down to Zanesville from New York City. I told Tony that me and my director of financial planning would meet him in Zanesville, OH.

Before we fully committed to this program, I wanted some hard verification that this would go well and we would be able to financially recognize the gain. At the time our independent accountant (auditor) was Arthur Andersen [7]. I had conferred with the lead audit manager who advised that we could recognize the gain, to the extent that we received cash, or value (not just trade credits) for the obsolete items. It took me a while to work through this because if we received the trade credits, which were redeemable, wasn't this value? Carmella, the audit manager, successfully persuaded me that the redemption must not be in an essentially valueless piece of paper ("valueless" because of the contingency of whether the true value would ever be realized with a subsequent transaction), but in actually receiving cash or the equivalent tangible value in the form of goods and services. I agreed and acquiesced gratefully! This meant that I had a minimum earnings pick-up (gain) of $5,000,000 (yes, that's $5 million) and deferred revenue of an additional $5 million—that is, only if the valuation expert confirmed the value of the obsolete goods in Zanesville.

A sunny day two weeks after the Tony Fiore discussion, we met in lovely Zanesville, Ohio. The sprawling, dirty warehouse contained obsolete press machinery, spare parts and yes, obsolete product inventory. The rows of obsolete inventory stretched as far as the eye could see. There were carpet rolls large enough that only a massive forklift truck could lift. Lots of them. They all appeared to be in OK shape, meaning that they were not dirty or damaged; they may have had a thick layer of dust on them, but the value appeared to be there.

There were thick cushion-type mats. A lot of them. Rows of stacks and stacks, the type that would go behind a bar, to cushion a bartender's feet and relieve back stress, or in the front of a stove for a restaurant cook. Go figure! God dropped a gift upon me (not actually *me*, but the company) that was helping me facilitate doing the right thing. The reason I say this is because I wouldn't have the need to erode my forecast by the value of the GM door liability. I had probably a $5 million goodie in my right pocket, and probably a $5 million bad-guy in my left pocket that wash to a nice zero impact on my forecast. Nivens would be happy. Singh would be happy. I would be happy.

In continued pursuit of "the deal" and his subsequent supreme payday, Nivens was making his frequent trips to Greenwich. Tom Nivens, by no means, was an even-tempered individual. "Cool as a cucumber" does not describe Tom. So, you can imagine that Nivens' mood ebbed and flowed with how the deal was developing. A month with relatively bad results would have everyone avoiding Tom, nearly at all costs.

Being as we produced monthly projections for the remainder of the year, at my direction, the same would apply to good forecasts and bad forecasts. Given that the prospective forecast would be finalized and released approximately three to four days after the actual results for the given month would be published, we were open for either whippings, congratulations, or some combination thereof, all to occur within five business days.

Time progressed with mixed results, as discussed earlier. We were encouraged by Singh to only recognize and give rise to the good news in our numbers, and for the most part, ignore the bad. We continued to operate without a president into the fourth quarter. Gene Wyler had taken his administrative assistant with him to his next job, so both of those integral spots remained vacant.

We received confirmation from Tony Fiore, Mr. Trade Credit, that the obsolete inventory was worth $10 million, gross value. Tony asked how we wanted it paid and I opted for the maximum in cash that was 50%, or $5 million, with the balance to be granted in trade credits that could be redeemed at our discretion. Tony sent over the contract and I sent it to our inside legal counsel. There were no issues with the contract, and I was advised and given that this obsolete inventory was gravy: there was little to no exposure on this deal. Three days later, now in October, Tony Fiore showed up with a check for $5,000,000. I swear I saw golden wings on his back and a halo above his head. My angel with the "get out of jail free ticket!"

In review of my NAAIS fourth quarter and full year forecast with Singh, I advised that we would be keeping our numbers from the prior month constant as business conditions and performance were consistent with the last submission. Singh asked, "Why doesn't your forecast for the fourth quarter and year increase by $5 million?" (Singh and Nivens had learned of my obsolete carpet and mat deal from Jeff Woodson, I suspect; a.k.a. the sea going snitch. Woodson had a history with Singh's corporate controller who you will soon learn about.) I advised with my pocket theory, approximately $5 million good ones in the right pocket and approximately $5 million bad ones in my left pocket, reminding him I had month after month in each operations review of the GM pricing mistake and resulting liability. Singh wasn't buying this. He was not only reluctant to agree, he furthermore instructed me to increase my quarter and full year forecast by $5 million, thus taking the gain and ignoring the liability. This was not only opportunistic; it was criminal and telling of what "the game" was all about to Singh: "gaming it to win the large pay-day."

Upon the directive, the forecast was increased to the level that Singh wished. I didn't have a clue as to how to combat this ill-contrived mind set. At this late date, there would be an interesting approach that I would find and utilize a bit later, but the time was not yet optimum for this one. I preferred to work with these guys to get the right result (emphasis on "right"); therefore, I utilized all friendly approaches, coaching and coddling as to what we collectively as a management team would and should realize as the right thing to do. If not for this approach, I would be dead in the water and ineffective as the VP of finance / CFO of NAAIS as I would not be viewed as a team player and be banished off of the island. I had to play ball with these guys because I needed "effect" on the business issues requiring my input and cooperation from all on the various items that confronted C&A. It was apparent that after nine months of this approach, all but one bullet was spent in my six-shot revolver. All I needed was an accurate aim and the gumption to pull the trigger.

As the end of the year was approaching, the activity related to the Stockman deal was heating up since year-end is a natural and convenient time to effect a change of ownership. With just a couple of days of notice, we were summoned to the Albemarle, NC, operation for a meeting with Stockman. We carried all of our materials—financial and otherwise—that would be pertinent to Stockman's Heartland Industrial Partners acquiring Collins and Aikman. I was the most senior person representing NAAIS. Lynard Strong, Cal Peoples, John Kyte, Mike Reagan (VP-GM of floormats and accessories), Steve Steiner (sales & marketing VP), Tom Nivens and Dinesh Singh were there awaiting the arrival of David Stockman, etc.

Recalling the images of Stockman from his budget director days at the US Office of Management and Budget, I recalled a relatively lean, well-groomed and well-heeled young man who had a command of numbers and facts that was large. I, like many others, paid a great respect to the work he did in the early years of the Reagan administration, for it was at this point that a great deal of "hard work" was required to get the US back on its feet while trying to heal itself of the plague of "Stagflation" that the years of Carter and others had bestowed upon our great country and its citizens. I expected maybe more years on him, but a bright, sharp and crisp demeanor accompanied by a quick wit and spirited man.

From the second-floor conference room window facing the driveway and parking lot, we viewed their arrival in two stretch limousines. Stockman exited the first limousine to arrive, accompanied by no less than ten twenty-somethings who must have just graduated business school and were carrying the traditional "accountant's briefcase" (leather bound with dimensions of 30 inches long, 24 inches wide and 12 inches deep). When they entered the conference room, I was amazed that Stockman was not even near the image that I would have estimated. In lieu of my description of the earlier Stockman, he appeared to be a recluse, somewhat balding and with long, un-groomed hair flowing beneath his shirt collar, almost down his back. While the cost of his apparel I am sure exceeded ours collectively as a group, David was sloppily dressed. It kind of appeared that he did not do a good job of cleaning his face that morning. *Kind of scary,* I thought to myself. *Seriously*?!

His team, along with David, undid their briefcases and piled numerous bound books of work materials and information supplied to them, onto the conference room table. They shared no information but proceeded to peruse through these books and, at various stopping points, ask rather pointed questions of us. I recall one was on the topic of scrap and labor cost content. Stockman and team were curious why the scrap rates were different among the various operations of NAAIS and why the percentage of labor cost in relation to sales revenue were also different, operation by operation. The simple answer was, "Processes are different between carpet and acoustic making versus producing and selling consoles or glove boxes." This in fact is what I replied with. Here is a guy (Stockman) who had been involved with this company for several years, minding this investment for Blackstone, claiming an affinity to the automotive industry, and he was unaware that the distinctly different processes and products of the various C&A locations had different rates of scrap and labor cost, and that the different locations produced different and distinct products with different manufacturing processes. They seemed to want to go deeper, but deeper meant reviewing standard cost routings for the levels of manning required to produce one product. John Kyte returned to his office to pull some of that information together.

One of the business models that Stockman used to extract value from manufacturing companies was to create a service company, let's say a utility, that would provide all the utility services to the manufacturing company and charge an amount that would be at the top end of acceptable in transfer price theory and logic. That being said, in many of our processes, scrap is a byproduct. This scrap byproduct can be reground and reintroduced into the manufacturing process, in limited quantity. Customer specifications would allow limited quantities of regrind to be blended with "virgin" materials and introduced into the production process.

Contemporary and lean manufacturing processes call for "one-piece" flow or manufacture. In this scenario, having the regrind processing as close to the productive machine—let's say a plastic mold press—was considered to be most efficient and lean. This keeps (the cost of) handling down and increases the throughput (rate of production), thereby further reducing product cost. When product production cost comes down, competitiveness increases and affords companies' growth by further customer awards of incremental business.

That being said, Mr. Stockman had something else in mind: a "central" regrind facility in the center of the US that would service all C&A locations. As Stockman volleyed that into the mix, the remainder of us who know anything about lean manufacturing and value creation in the contemporary world looked at each other around the table in wonderment of how you tell the guy who is selling the company to himself, in pseudo fashion, that this is a cockamamie idea? With an investment analysis, it would be revealed that there is no economic value creation from that idea. Knowing this, we all pushed back with logic, and as I recall, let his idea die a worthy death.

Stockman's claimed level of intelligence and expertise over most any business-related topic was further demonstrated in the process of acquiring the first portfolio company of Heartland Industrial Partners, the business that I left to join C&A. I recall my prior boss at MascoTech [8] sharing with me that when Stockman was in due diligence in the purchase process of that enterprise and questioning line item expense details, Bill Carson, the VP and controller of MascoTech, Inc., had demonstrated to Stockman and his lieutenants their methodology of accounting for workers' compensation insurance and claims. Predominantly, MascoTech was self-insured. Self-insurance was allowed in most states of the company's operation. As with any liability, the expense and liabilities are recorded when it is "probable" to occur and "estimable" in amount.

The process is such that an estimate is provided by subject matter experts, for the forthcoming year, and adjusted based upon the amount of valid claims that have the likelihood of adjudication, award and payment within a given period. These adjustments happen periodically and with the foresight of claims in process, the subject matter experts who provide such input, can make educated assessments of the values of award and payment and provide these amounts, claim by claim, in a time-phased approach so that the accountants can translate these values into the financial statements. These prospective views are generally provided quarterly, unless a catastrophic claim is raised, in such case an immediate communication and recognition would occur. In addition to the claims, there is a third-party administrator fixed fee that is incorporated into the expense and liability recognition and subsequent payments.

As Bill, gentlemanly as he is, conveyed this information in a businesslike response to Stockman and his crew during Stockman's due diligence process in acquiring MascoTech, Stockman, in utter disbelief (probably because he believed in the cash basis expense recognition, based on when payments are made, which would be more friendly to the periodic profit numbers), arrogantly blurted out, "Is this how all companies in the world account for workers' compensation?"

Bill's response, which was fueled by many of Stockman's unreasonable volleys of query, was, "David, I don't know if every company in this world accounts for workers' compensation expense this way, but I can assure you that every (good) company in the Universe does it this way."

The questions continued with Stockman firing them with the desperate taint of a man with confused and competing priorities; on one hand, Blackstone was leaning hard on the company to produce better financial performance, and on the other hand, a buyer was poking and prodding at the company's senior management as to how the future could be different to generate increased wealth for himself and his circle of business friends. The long conversation was somewhat limited to such candor, given that Mr. Stockman knew both the history and the present of the company since his tenure with Blackstone reached back into the Wickes acquisition days by the

New York private equity firm [9].

After a long day of this "diligence," we concluded as it neared 5:00 p.m., we were to head to a well-known country club in the area for refreshments and dinner. Lynard Strong, a self-conscious and nervous man, was ever more so. Being put on the firing line, for a good part of the session, he was in need of reinforcement. Nobody knew the textile business in North and South Carolina better than Lynard. In an empathetic way, I expressed to him, "No one could have responded, given the circumstances, better than you did, Lynard." This, in fact, was true. Lynard was trained in the Toyota production system and knew lean manufacturing "cold." No Wall Street ex-Washington OMB budget director could outsmart him, nor could David outsmart the team. We were well connected and respectful of one another; all were professionals in the automotive industry and in our individual disciplines. We were a tight group that was assembled under Wyler's leadership. The dinner was quite uneventful.

After returning to the Troy headquarters, later that week, the senior NAAIS staff was summoned to Nivens' conference room. We were advised that on the following Monday, Frank Brydon would be joining C&A as the president of the North American Auto Interior Systems group. Frank was coming to us from Lear-Masland, a competitor to NAAIS.

Frank was an interesting professional and a Scotsman. On appearance, Frank had high regard in the industry and was an individual who ascribed to lean manufacturing principles. The senior staff immediately took a liking to Frank, as did I. He was certainly a leader, and he demonstrated that every day.

Frank appeared somewhat inaccessible to me in the first couple of months of his joining. This was a strangely different atmosphere and culture to what I experienced with Gene Wyler. Gene was open, honest and a southern gentleman to all. It was often that, with our administrative assistant's nod, I would pop in and out of Gene's office regularly for business and otherwise, but mostly business. Gene was all about business.

Frank brought with him a new administrative assistant whose name was Penny Fillergrin. Penny was quite a different duck. She behaved like a royal guard to Frank's door and accessibility. Cold, unfriendly and off-putting, she would often run interference for Frank. This seemed quite strange to me. Again, another first in my career.

One day, Frank apparently had invited consultants in for a meeting. They consisted of a mid-40s or early-50s male who I understood to be a previous financial executive and a woman about the same age who was a financial systems specialist. I was curious as to why I had not received an invitation. They came, spent a couple of hours and parted from Frank with mutual smiles. With my background and career, I wasn't necessarily worried for my job, but the inaccessibility of Frank, the royal guard who essentially stood between Frank's door and I, and the visit of the "financial consultants" all had begun to make me think and feel a bit uneasy.

With Penny's off-putting approach being slightly less than collegial, I expressed to Frank that her dedication solely to him left me in somewhat of a lurch for administrative support. I also advised that this approach was completely contrary to the way that Gene and I operated previously and that my lack of administrative support was clearly getting in the way of my productivity.

He kindly suggested that I hire a person to provide my administrative support. Coincidentally, I learned that Penny had a friend from another employment experience who was looking for a job very similar to what I spec'd out. After a week of interviews, I had decided that as a proactive peace offering to Penny (with no necessity for one), I would select this person, Kim Paton, who would share our office and workspace, across an aisle from Penny.

As I was able to gain traction and favor with Frank and the C&A senior team, I was able to round out my staff, including a previously mentioned director of financial planning and analysis (Jeff Woodson) and a financial analyst (Debbie Priester). This was extremely helpful as the financial management of a $1.5+ billion manufacturing concern required support from a planning and analytics perspective.

Within the last week of the year—and with results not being near a point that Nivens would believe to be acceptable, seeing as he was in the middle of a deal with Stockman—Tom called a meeting to which I was summoned. Frank Brydon was out of the office at the time and I was to represent NAAIS in what was to become a beating of the profit drum to find more profit and strongarm tactics for better results (I really wasn't sure what could possibly change in the matter of a few days and with the Christmas shutdown[10] upon us, but I aggressively and assertively participated). It was Nivens and I in his office, along with Singh, and all of our remote business unit heads on a conference call.

This was to be a futile exercise, without substance. It really amounted to Tom not liking some of the guys' numbers and advising them of what they had to change their numbers to. Tom signs everyone's paychecks, including the business unit heads', so they would be unlikely to buck Nivens' direction. The numerous conversations went something like this:

Nivens to Business Unit (BU) head: Your fourth quarter forecast for this year is showing $X sales and $X of operating income. This is 15% less than last year's fourth quarter results and worse than your average quarter for this year. I need you to increase your operating income by $X.

BU head to Nivens: Tom, in theory you are correct, but when you consider increased energy costs of X%, material cost increases of X% and the price downs that we had to give GM to award us the Epsilon program, it's just not possible to get there. We have already baked-in all possible improvement.

Nivens to BU head: Yes, but what about all of the cost improvements that you have been touting about as a result of implementing the new machine that I approved? I would have never approved that appropriation request had I known that your results would have been this poor.

BU head to Nivens: But Tom, the improvements are taking hold and need time to ramp up to maturity. In the meantime, we've got all of this additional cost that we're dealing with and the price downs.

Nivens to BU head: That's neither here nor there. Your results are inferior, and I want you to go back and scrub your numbers and make them the best that they can possibly be. I need to know that results must improve by $X. Give me a range.

BU head to Nivens: (acquiescing) OK, minimum, we'll improve them by $X and $X on the top end.

I could not believe my ears; this was after all of the

coaching that I had done with the BU heads and controllers that we would not change numbers without substantive reasons that complied with GAAP. I left the meeting, feeling as though I lost control of NAAIS (and it fell into the control of Nivens). A bizarre handwritten message upon the compilation that one of Singh's financial managers pulled together from the meeting showed up the next day:

Can't Regulate This   D. J. Burgundy

12-21-00 14:01   THOMAS NIVENS   ID=84773! 1234   P.02

Collins & Aikman
4th Quarter Profit Improvements
$ in 000

	Original Forecast	Minimum Commitment	Maximum Commitment	Minimum Better / Worse than Original Forecast	Maximum
U. S. Carpet & Acoustics	7,776	8,500	9,000	724	1,224
Canada Carpet & Acoustics	5,400	5,200	5,400	(200)	0
Accessory Mats	3,100	3,500	3,800	400	700
N. A. Plastics	1,181	2,300	2,600	1,119	1,419
Eliminations	(2,700)	(2,700)	(2,400)	0	300
N. A. Division	(500)	(500)	(300)	0	200
Total NAAIS	14,257	16,300	18,100	2,043	3,843
Fabrics	1,665	2,400	2,700	735	1,035
Total Brydon	15,922	18,700	20,800	2,778	4,878

FAX / TO: Lynard Strong   Info. CC Frank Brydon
           Dan Pierott   Dinesh Singh
           Louis Langer   Ken Affinhoffer
           Gerald Jones   David Burgundy
           Mike Reagan

I thought we had really good sessions last week regarding pulling together an adequate financial performance for the 4th quarter. The above table lays out the commitments we made — I'm counting on us collectively hitting these numbers and closing off 2000 on a positive note. Each of your contributions is critical to this. Thanks, Tom Nivens

Nivens' persuasion for more fraud - table and note - 1 page

This was not about whether our existing financial statements were incorrectly under-reporting the company's income; this was additional fraud in the making. As this note and worksheet were written and sent via fax at 2:01 p.m. on December 21, 2000, with essentially no operations and minimal sales through the Christmas break, which were already forecast originally through the end of the year—where in God's creation was an improvement of $2.8 - $4.9 million going to come from four days before Christmas? Santa Claus?

What does "commitment" with no time before the end of the year have to do with putting bona-fide operational improvement in place to actually yield better financial performance? The heavy emphasis on "commitment" and the words "I am counting on us collectively hitting these numbers and closing off 2000 on a positive note" is the type of CEO intimidation that a subordinate does not want to cross. If s/he did, one would likely risk his own name and future with the company and therefore feel the need to be complicit in the fraudulent actions.

There was going to be some magic done by Dr. Fraud and I would have no part of it. As my process of enforcing that the right thing be done had manifested itself, I alerted my attorney about the "pump the numbers" process as he and I moved the company closer to the future publishing of the completed year 2000 financial statements which would be GAAP-compliant. I sent this 'Nivens proclamation' along with the note below to my attorney, Bill Waldon.

To: Bill Waldon 11/25/2001

Fr: Dave Burgundy

"Directions from our CEO
in the last week before
Christmas".

(How do you change your business
at the last moment to
create 2.8 million of [income])

Dave B.

Burgundy note to attorney Waldon (re: Nivens' fraud table and note) - 1 page

I had always believed that even though folks receive a paycheck for their help, services and support, a small token of my appreciation around the Christmas holiday is important. For the professionals, I would buy each of them a bottle of decent wine. I would not only do this for my staff, but for my boss and his supporting staff of VPs (marketing, supply chain, operations, etc.). For the support staff (administrative assistants in this case), I bought both Penny and Kim a $100 gift certificate to Macy's, or some facsimile thereof, along with a box of Godiva chocolates. Expecting nothing in exchange, Penny gave me a hug and a peck on the cheek and advised me that I didn't have to do that (I knew otherwise!). Kim's expression was far less friendly, but nonetheless was one of appreciation.

Christmas came and went, along with the relatively lengthy holiday away from work that was customary in the automotive industry and welcomed. This was much needed as we all were feeling the heat of "making the number"—me especially, given the knowledge of what falsehood existed in the financial statements. I knew I was going to have to make a decision and drive a hard line after months and months of politely trying to lead and cajole Nivens and Singh to the right decision of disclosing the large liability properly in the financial statements.

I had decided that upon returning in January, a night out of drinks and dinner with my immediate staff, including Penny, was warranted to let off some steam. The team knew the heavy weight that I was under as the ultimate decision maker, but they shared the pressure, especially those who knew the wayward way of Nivens and Singh and what the right thing to do actually was.

So just as we were sitting in the restaurant booth—three to a side with me sitting in the middle of Penny and Debbie, and Jim Tomkowicz, my hire for the plastics controller, Jeff Woodson and Kim sitting across the table—jokes and jocularity began to fly. Some of the jokes were about Penny's office demeanor; in fact she was the subject of the fun. While feeling kind of bad for her and her revealing backward ways, and being the leader of the group, I patted her leg, as she was sitting near, in a fashion that said, "It's okay, they can say what they want to say." This was done in a fairly open fashion and without discretion. I would come to regret this gesture, as you shall learn. As the collegial get together came to a close, and I sensed a stronger bond among us as a team, I had asked for the check. Tomkowicz, Debbie Priester and Jeff headed for the door. Penny and Kim, the two administrative assistants, hung back with me until the paying business was over with. We exited and conversed for a few minutes in the parking lot about what tomorrow might bring at C&A. Saying good night, I thanked them and gave each lady a friendly hug.

,An update: the fourth quarter press release was published to the world at large with the assurance that earnings would be at or near the prior estimates given, along with the announcement of the Heartland pending deal and its highlights *(Ignoring the earnings turbulence in the fourth quarter and the result of my pending recognition of the GMX-270 Deville door shade liability)*:

Collins & Aikman

News Release

FOR IMMEDIATE RELEASE
January 12, 2001

CONTACTS:
Analysts: Lauren Collins
(248) 824-XXXX
lauren.collins@colaik.com

Media: Tasha Robinson
(248) 824-XXXX
tasha.robinson@colaik.com

COLLINS & AIKMAN ANNOUNCES HEARTLAND INVESTMENT AND FOURTH QUARTER UPDATE

TROY, Mich – Collins & Aikman Corporation (NYSE: CKC) announced today that Heartland Industrial Partners, L.P. (Heartland) has agreed to purchase 25 million newly issued primary shares from the Company at a price of $5.00 per share, representing a cash investment in the Company, before fees and expenses, of $125 million. The purchase price also gives the Company a profit participation right of up to $.25 per share on certain future stock sales by Heartland. This transaction immediately provides Collins & Aikman with capital in order to enhance its long-term growth, and represents a key step in making the Company a stronger competitor and improving future stock liquidity.

The Company also announced today that its controlling shareholders – Blackstone Capital Partners, L.P. (Blackstone) and Wasserstein Perella Partners L.P. (Wasserstein) have entered into a definitive agreement to sell 27 million shares, or approximately 50% of their collective holdings in Collins &Aikman, to Heartland at a price of $5.00 per share, plus a profit participation right as previously described. The two transactions combined represent a $260 million investment in Collins & Aikman stock by Heartland and provide liquidity to the selling shareholders.

Commenting on the transaction, **Thomas E. Nivens,** Collins & Aikman's Chairman and Chief Executive Officer stated, "This deal is truly a transforming event for Collins & Aikman. I believe that with this infusion of new capital from Heartland, we should be able to significantly enhance the growth opportunities for our global business, subsequently maximizing value for our employees, customers, suppliers and shareholders. We enthusiastically welcome Heartland to our organization and, as evidenced by their significant investment in the automotive industry, we couldn't ask for a more supportive and strategically aligned partner. This transaction should position Collins & Aikman to be an even stronger player in our sector."

Highlights of the Transaction, Upon Completion, Include:

- Heartland purchases 25 million newly issued primary shares from Collins & Aikman at a price of $5.00 per share ($125 million before fees and expenses).
- Heartland purchases 27 million shares from Blackstone and Wasserstein at a price of $5.00 per share ($135 million).
- Transaction projected to close by mid-February, 2001, subject to certain conditions.
- Collins & Aikman's total shares outstanding increases from 62 million to 87 million.
- Blackstone & Wasserstein ownership percentage declines from 87% to 31%.
- Heartland ownership percentage in Collins & Aikman will be approximately 60%.

(more)

The Collins & Aikman Board of Directors, upon the unanimous recommendation of a Special Committee of independent directors has approved the transactions. The Special Committee was advised by UBS Warburg and the law firm of Morris, Nichols, Arsht & Tunnell. The transaction, which is expected to close by mid-February, is subject to certain conditions including bank and bondholder consent, the need to seek waivers of the change of control provisions in the Company's existing debt agreements (all of which are to remain outstanding), and the need to obtain Hart Scott Rodino clearance.

"Collins & Aikman represents an ideal growth platform for Heartland," stated David A. Stockman, founder and senior managing director of Heartland Industrial Partners. "Their strong senior management team, leading market share positions and global capabilities in acoustics and interior surface styling products all combine to make Collins & Aikman a perfect candidate for our industrial "build-up" investment strategy. We believe that with Heartland's support, Collins & Aikman will be better positioned than ever to capitalize on growth opportunities."

The Company also reported that recently announced additional fourth quarter North American light vehicle production cuts are currently expected to reduce the Company's fourth quarter sales by approximately 12 percent as compared to the fourth quarter of 1999. Prior to these most recent production cuts, the Company had expected fourth quarter sales would decline approximately eight to 10 percent versus the year ago period. The Company estimates that these additional production cuts will adversely impact fourth quarter operating income by approximately $6 million.

Additionally, the Company announced that its fourth quarter operating income would be negatively impacted by approximately $6 million, due primarily to the write-off of certain assets and the impact of additional European restructuring actions, including the layoff of approximately 25 staff employees and the relocation of Collins & Aikman's European headquarters from Wiesbaden, Germany to the Company's existing technical center in Heidelberg, Germany. These European cost cutting actions, in tandem with the asset write-offs and North American production cuts, are expected to put the Company's fourth quarter operating income in the $15-to-$20 million range.

"Given the current tough operating environment and the fact that Heartland Industrial Partners will be coming in as our new major shareholder these fourth quarter actions, though difficult, made good sense for our Company," stated **Thomas E. Nivens,** Chairman and Chief Executive Officer of Collins & Aikman. "Going forward, I believe we're well positioned to continue to drive costs out of our system, enhance our debt coverage and further leverage our leadership position in the products we provide."

(more)

Heartland Industrial Partners, LP is a private equity firm established to "invest in, build and grow" industrial companies in sectors ripe for consolidation and long-term growth. The firm has equity commitments in excess of $1.1 billion and intends to increase its commitments to $2 billion. Heartland was founded by David A. Stockman, a former partner of the Blackstone Group and a Reagan administrative cabinet officer; Lewis D. Spinetta, the former President and Chief Operating Officer of Penske Corporation; and Trev Steinem, a former Managing Director of Chase Securities.

Collins & Aikman, with annual sales approaching $2 billion, is the global leader in automotive floor and acoustic systems and is a leading supplier of automotive fabric, interior trim and convertible top systems. The Company's operations span the globe through 63 facilities, 13 countries and over 15,000 employees who are committed to achieving total excellence. Collins & Aikman's high-quality products combine industry-leading design and styling capabilities, superior manufacturing capabilities and the industry's most effective NVH "quiet" technologies. Information about Collins & Aikman is available on the Internet at www.collinsaikman.com.

Collins & Aikman will be conducting a conference call Tuesday, January 16, 2001, at 11 a.m. EST to discuss the transactions. Interested parties may either call (973) 628-9554, or access the web cast via the Company's web site at www.collinsaikman.com. If you are unable to attend, you may dial into the digital replay at: (402) 220-2919, pin number 22121.

This news release contains forward-looking statements within the meaning of the Private Securities Litigation Reform Act of 1995. Actual results may differ materially from the anticipated results because of certain risks and uncertainties, including but not limited to general economic conditions in the markets in which Collins & Aikman operates, fluctuations in the production of vehicles for which the Company is a supplier, labor disputes involving the Company or its significant customers, changes in consumer preferences, dependence on significant automotive customers, the level of competition in the automotive supply industry, pricing pressure from automotive customers, the substantial leverage of the Company and its subsidiaries, limitations imposed by the Company's debt facilities, charges made in connection with the integration of operations acquired by the Company, the implementation of the reorganization plan, changes in the popularity of particular car models or particular interior trim packages, the loss of programs on particular car models, risks associated with conducting business in foreign countries and other risks detailed from time to time in the Company's Securities and Exchange Commission filings including without limitation, in Items 1 and 7 of the Company's Annual Report on Form 10-K for the year-ended December 25, 1999, and Item 1 in the Company's Quarterly Report on Form 10-Q for the periods ended April 1, 2000, July 1, 2000 and September 30, 2000.

###

C&A Jan. 12, 2001 Press Release - earnings and Heartland - 3 pages

This press release, with an approximate erosion of $12 million of earnings, did not include any degradation in earnings due to the recognition of the liability owed to General Motors and attempted to place a significant amount of blame on reduced business volume, European restructuring actions in reducing corporate staff and incurring severance for 25 employees and the consolidation of the European headquarters into an existing engineering facility. The fact of the matter is that the business was not performing to the expectations that they set for current ownership and future ownership; they knew it and needed something to hide behind. On January 12, 2000, the realism of just how bad off the company was when we would eventually report the year 2000 results was not appreciated nor embraced by the CEO of the business. Through the wordsmithing, he was intent on marching toward the big payday in fine and unfettered fashion.

My relationship with Frank as president of NAAIS and I as VP of finance/CFO began to develop nicely as he was becoming a great deal more appreciative of what I had to bring to bear on to the situation. I wish I could say the same for my relationship with the door guard. Things didn't get better with Penny in the New Year; in fact they got worse—so worse, I felt compelled to place a note in my personnel file to the effect of the strange demeanor that she possessed and the strain it caused to our operation. This is the memorandum:

Can't Regulate This   D. J. Burgundy

Collins & Aikman
North America Automotive Interior Systems

---

*Interoffice Memo *** Personal and Confidential****

TO: **Greg Grinnell**   c: Personal File

FROM: **Dave Burgundy**

DATE: January 16, 2001

SUBJECT: Personnel Issue

For some unknown reason to me, there has been an issue with Penny Fillergrin's ability to work with me. I have confronted J. Penny on this and she will not provide the time to discuss any issues that may exist.

Since I detected this, I have gone out of my way to extend myself in kindness and I even have gone so far as to personally purchase gifts of flowers and candy as a peace offering gesture. At that point Penny hugged and kissed me on the cheek and said, "you really did not have to do this."

From that point things just deteriorated. Penny, will not share any part of Frank's schedule with me so that I can adquately plan when I can see him on key business issues. She has not facilitated Frank Brydon's accessibility to me and I am having to circumvent this roadblock to be effective with Frank. There are no known issues that I have with Frank F Brydon nd as late as this morning, in a related conversation, Frank advised me that he highly values my presence and input to our business process.

As a matter of record, I gave Penny a rather generous gift in the spirit of Christmas and to hopefully make a statement, again as a peace offering. Knowing that there would be talk and not wanting to show partiality, I gave the same gift to Kim (Paton my direct Administrative Assistant.

Penny's actions are contrary to the relationship that a Chief Operating Executive should have with his Chief Financial Executive. Penny will not so much as give me the time of day on any issue. I personally find this to be ineffective from a business perspective and I have never experienced this treatment after being in executive finance roles since in the late 1980's.

I personally believe that Penny may not be seasoned enough to fully understand the relationship that senior management should have in order to maintain effectiveness,

Greg Grinnell
Personnel Issue
January 16, 2001
Page Two

especially when Frank and I are purposely positioned in the office to foster a good and open relationship that facilitates effectiveness. I believe that she feels that I have breached the precious "security barrier" that she holds, perhaps in her mind, for Frank.

As of this morning, Frank Brydon and I have had a discussion about this and a few other staffing issues. Frank told me that Penny earlier advised him that she would like to be transferred because of this issue. Frank is committed to work out this issue, as I have been and will continue to be.

I am unclear as to where this is going but felt it appropriate to note it to you and in my personnel file.

Sincerely,

Dave Burgundy

Burgundy Jan. 16, 2001 letter VP-HR, HR issue - 2 pages

As time marched forward and with every Cadillac DTS manufactured, the liability grew in amount. Pressure continued to mount as we moved closer to the end of the year when my signature was required on the "management representation letter," which was a statement that, to the best of my knowledge, the financials were clean, accurate, without material (significant) mis-statement and absent of fraud. Knowing there was an eminent sale of the company, the consequences were paramount. Should the financials be misrepresenting of the truth on the count of an honest error or omission, that is one thing and certainly enough for someone (likely me) to lose my job—but there was something else going on here of a major magnitude. These guys were more interested in fabricating a story that did not exist to hit the big payday and I was implicated. I never expected this in my career, but here I was. I always professionally hung with guys that were interested in getting it right while creating value, rather than putting themselves and a big payday ahead of what was more important. That is how I am cut. I was 40 years old and quite concerned and unsure about my future. I am sure that my emotional response was similar to most people who are placed in such position. Some may even succumb to the higher-ups for fear of losing a paycheck, family security and, more broadly, the confidence and collegiality of the senior management of the company. Senior management's confidence and future job reference certainly is an important element of one's career and future success. These things certainly can confuse one's objectivity.

Part of my inner circle was Jim Tomkowicz, the person whom I brought in to C&A NAAIS to take the lead controller job for the plastic interior components business. I worked for Jim at the Masco family of companies where he was a "group controller." It was within Jim's business of NAAIS that this growing liability existed.

Jim was also surprised by this condition, but like I, he knew what the right answer had to be. While ultimately it was my decision, the decision would affect the reported results of Jim's business.

From time to time, in closing off a meeting, or in a spot of scant idle time, Jim would raise the issue to see how I was doing and to get a bead on where my head was with next steps and necessary actions. Jim was an individual who would cozy up to you, I learned over time, just to use information obtained to advantage himself. This gave me fair reason to appear somewhat ambiguous, even oblivious to the situation, as I was concerned that if Jim had learned what was going through my head, he may have used the information that may have injured himself in the process. I certainly did not want to be a conduit of consequential ill fate to come to Jim as a result of wrong doing by profiteers of such an engineered result of greed. Although, I'm not sure if Jim had the status or the "balls" enough to confront the situation head on and do what was necessary to get it done. Certainly, the intelligence about the subject matter in addition to understanding the consequences of both approaches—should either the right thing be done or the wrong thing—have large gravity.

There would also be political implications that would be career altering with either outcome. I am not sure if Jim, nor many, would be up to the risk involved in doing the right thing. Truthfully, while not offering any solutions when Jim would ask, "What are you going to do?" my simple and honest response was, "I don't know at this point." And that was the honest to God's truth. While I knew what had to be done, while I knew that the right numbers must be disclosed and booked into the financial statements, I hadn't engineered a way that would accomplish the two objectives.

First and foremost, the production of good, credible, accurate financial statements that were presented in accordance with Generally Accepted Accounting Principles and was absent of fraud, and second, providing myself enough protection and safety in enforcing that the company does the right thing "on my watch," were these prime objectives. Far less obvious at the time—it was proven to me (over and over) since—was that making the first objective happen was going to preserve and maintain my good name and my ability to continue with a flourishing career and take care of my family. You just don't see this when you are actually going through such a prolonged event. The stress, the uncertainty and the fear of what might happen is overwhelming.

Our NAAIS numbers were due to be reported to the holding company on Friday, January 10, 2001 for the 2000 reporting year. That morning, I had a joint venture status meeting with Mexican Industries, our JV partner's CEO and head financial person. Our joint venture company was known as ACAP (Aguirre, Collins & Aikman Plastics) and they produced the instrument panel for the Cadillac DTS, the same vehicle related to the significant liability owed to General Motors. Hank Aguirre, the ex-Detroit Tigers star Mexican player began Mexican Industries, a "minority-owned" automotive supplier [11] principally providing "cut and sew" interior products to the OEMs.

The JV status meeting was quite interesting. Although knowing that Mexican Industries was not flooded with cash, without our prior knowledge, I learned that Mexican Industries entered into an agreement with a restructuring firm to re-engineer the financial status of their company. The restructuring firm's employee was the acting CEO, so it was described to me. This situation placed C&A in a compromised position: forgetting that we had our own financial hurdles that were solvency obstacles, we had one of our highest visibility products being produced by a joint venture who was one-half potentially insolvent. This meant that we would need to step in and take full control of the production of the DTS instrument panel. We eventually did so.

Walking to my car, I decided to call Jim Tomkowicz. I asked Jim if there was anything new regarding the financial results. Jim mentioned that certain of the plastics' operating locations had reported, and the results were mixed. He then asked me if there was anything new on my front as it pertained to the financial results, meaning, had I made a decision about the liability and its disclosure? I advised Jim that we would be doing the right thing; however, without a clue as to the conditions under which this was to occur and in satisfaction of the two criteria set out above, I advised him that I would make a decision that same day and let him know.

In leaving the joint venture meeting, I set out in my car, headed for our company headquarters office which should have been about a thirty-minute trip. There were two routes that I could have taken, and as it was, I decided to drive the way that was most comforting to my soul, given the level of stress that I was under for the longest time and what I was about to face. This path took me past familiar places: my church, the street off of Woodward Avenue on which I lived, among other favorite places. As I exited the freeway, about one mile later I came upon my church. I was bewildered, not knowing the next steps that I would take. As I passed the church, I pulled to the side of the road and burst into tears from the pressure. I had to do something immediately, right then and there, as part of my motivation came from the need to preserve my ability to sit across from my loved ones at the dinner table and advise them to do the right thing. Should I not uphold my values in my own life and career, how could I give that strong advice with meaning?

I picked up my mobile phone and called Gil Rochieux. Gil was an attorney who headed Rochieux, Waldon and Stein, a notable law firm in the area and the one that Masco (my prior respected employer) used in important labor related legal instances requiring counsel and advice. The gravity of the situation must have come through in my voice as Gil's assistant asked me to wait on the phone for one moment as she was about to patch me into his phone at his Florida vacation home. Once we were connected, I dispensed with the courtesies of how he was, how his family was, etc., and then got to the meat of why I was calling. I described the situation to Gil, as best as I could, and he asked me to hold on for a moment so that he could queue his "subject matter expert" attorney up on the phone. He did so and returned to our conversation during which he advised me that I was not to return to my office today, but instead meet with attorney Bill Waldon and describe the situation in totality so that we could devise next steps and what needed to be done. The goal was to create a solution that would allow me to make the proper financial disclosure and claim safety during the process and subsequently thereafter. I felt somewhat relieved in that I was talking to a trusted confidante. This was in addition to knowing there was a route to doing the right thing and getting to a safe place. I would learn that this was not to come without significant incremental work and exponential stress.

Home was on the way, so I stopped to regain some composure. I jumped back in the car and pointed it in the direction of the law firm to meet with the person who I would later call one of my best friends in life. I arrived at their Troy offices which coincidentally were located in the same high-rise office building that once housed C&A's corporate office in transition when the company was in the process of moving its headquarters from Charlotte, NC, to Troy, MI. I pressed the "9" button in the elevator and arrived at the firm which occupied both the ninth and tenth floors. After the receptionist called Bill to tell him of my arrival, I was advised to move up one floor where Bill was housed in his office. We first met in a conference room and Bill introduced himself to me, and then introduced me to Mickey Teague, one of his colleagues in the firm. Mickey was a business law attorney and also part of the family who owned and operated Teague Stadium, the historic home location of the Detroit Tigers. The day in and of itself was full of awe for me and, had it been any other day—having been a childhood fan of the Tigers—I would have been more appreciative of meeting Mickey and been inquisitive of the events he experienced as being a member of the family who owned the real estate of the Detroit Tigers.

The meeting kicked off with my scoping the issue about the undisclosed liability owed to General Motors. I took them through the story of Stuart and his close colleague coming to my office to share this sensitive and potentially scary topic, their display of evidence and the resulting over-billing condition that existed as C&A was charging GM for something that our company clearly was not providing. Having heard such stories and potentially negative assertions about CEOs and other senior managers, and being quite financially astute, they poked around the facts and tested me on whether or not there was some "grey area" that would make this overbilling a justified condition.

After hearing them out and very well understanding the need for their "discovery phase" to flush out the true facts before the firm was to take on any case, I complied with further compelling discussion that demonstrated the simple fact that either the rear door has a sunshade or it does not and that the company was billing each rear door unit as if it had a sunshade which was erroneously built into the price for each and every door that was shipped to General Motors. Because this lawyer visit was totally unexpected as I started my day, one would think that I had none of the documents demonstrating the fraudulent billings with me. It just so happened that I did. With the gravity of this situation being so great, I carried the evidence with me in my briefcase wherever I went. I did not want to part with these documents as I was concerned that the same paper trail could never be recreated, especially having disclosed this situation to Singh and Nivens, for I did not know what to expect from them. I only knew that the past nine months were a passionate but respectful, thoughtful and collegial fight for me to get them to do the right thing, but to no avail.

After producing the documents and upon their inspection, they concluded that there in fact was no grey area in this matter—quite to the contrary—and that the issue was black and white. Upon their conclusion, again I was relieved by the fact that other sane and perhaps more intelligent people than I believed this to be an issue, such an issue to warrant caution and correction. We wrapped up the meeting and it was approximately 3:00 p.m. In closing, Bill advised that he would call me a little later that day with next steps and a short term game plan.

The call from Bill came just ahead of 5:00 p.m. that same day. He advised the next steps as being a weekend full of research that he and his legal team would conduct, on my behalf, that would involve exploring the "Whistleblower Law," how it applied to this specific situation and how Michigan statute interrelates with the Whistleblower Law; clearly, because C&A was a Delaware corporation and the stock of C&A was traded on the NYSE open market, both state and federal laws applied. I expressed my full appreciation and knew that there was no turning back. I also had to immediately explain that I had just built a home and that excess cash to invest in his firm's endeavor on my behalf would be non-existent. Bill, the guy that he is, told me not to worry about that and that we'd work it out on the back end of the ordeal. I had to place my full, undivided trust in Bill, as I had no one other than him to help me get through this messy debacle. Further, Bill advised that he would contact me on Monday and advise what our game plan would be.

As Monday approached, I was confident with knowing that I took the right steps that would ultimately deliver an appropriate result to C&A's stockholders, third party investors, lenders and commercial banks that had a stake in the results of the company. The reporting deadline for year 2000 results came and left with the past Friday. As it was left and to the best of my knowledge, our pre-tax income and Earnings before Interest, Taxes, Depreciation and Amortization (EBITDA), a measure by which investors judge the value of a company in multiples thereof, was overstated by an approximate $4 million dollars, or roughly five-percent. Five-percent is a significant number when independent accountants (CPA firms) assess the accuracy of a company's financial statements. I took no action, at this point, to correct the fraud related to the undisclosed liability, in the financial statements. I was confident that the right time would come.

One of the first things that I did that morning was to get with Frank Brydon and advise him of the actions that I had taken on Friday. Frank was extremely relieved. Frank, as president of NAAIS, would be a party to signing the management representation letter, along with myself. Up until this point, given the ambiguity that I had to deal with in finding resolve to the situation, plus the risk of letting anyone into the knowledge of how I was to handle such a situation, I had to act in a stealthy manner. This was a situation where my strength of character would prevail and I was the only one who had conviction enough to deliver the right results; I also had a great deal to lose: a: CPA certification, a flourishing career where I knew the greater parts were yet to come, but most of all the confidence of my family lest I acquiesce and allow these periled lies to persist, thereby losing my integrity.

Frank's relief manifested itself in a newfound relationship with him. Somehow, he was checking with me on what was going on, what I was up to, what next steps were in the process of bringing C&A (Nivens and Singh) to the higher ground of truthfulness. Not that we had a bad working relationship immediately prior to my news and actions, but the bond strengthened just as two combat comrades sink into a fox hole just before the fire fight. Frank was as concerned about this liability as I was, as I had educated him into the implications and specifics. He wanted the right results to show in our financial statements as much as I did.

At this point, the "ice lady" door guard barrier began to melt and we were actually beginning to function as an executive team. Although there was much (professional) stress in my life at this time, this gave way and eased the operating environment on a day-to-day basis. I advised Frank that Bill was to come back to me with his directive counsel and advice by the close of the day and upon that, I would get a hold of him and let him know what Bill had to say. Frank also mentioned that he had sought some legal advice on the subject, not near to the extent that I launched into, and asked my permission if he could talk with Bill. I gave my full cooperation to Frank and encouraged him to call Bill.

I wanted badly to have this resolved and begin to live life normally, once again, as if there was a quick exit ramp, but there wasn't a quick off to this one. I heard from Waldon a little later that day. He explained that our approach needed to be as follows:

- *You must go to work every day as if nothing has happened and do your job,*
- *You must take and thereby demonstrate the necessary measures to cause the company to publish the financial results in accordance with Generally Accepted Accounting Principles,*
- *We must communicate often and regularly regarding your progress,*
- *Should your efforts prove unsuccessful, we shall author a series of letters addressed to Singh and/or Nivens that explain:*

   1. *You are aware of certain inconsistencies in the company's financial statements that cause them not to be*

in accordance with GAAP,

2. You have tried to work with the company to achieve the proper result which is the publication of financial statements in accordance with GAAP,

3. While your efforts are clearly motivated to cause the company to do the right thing, Nivens / Singh have restrained you from doing so, and

4. Should Nivens / Singh continue to restrict the financial statement integrity, we shall notify a number of regulatory bodies that shall impose strong consequences on the company and its initiatives.

I must say that I was disappointed with the approach and with what would be required to get this across the goal line. I felt that at this point, I had done enough and would have rather turned it over to Bill and let him duke it out, but it wasn't going to be that way. I had not only to prove the case—as I had done for the last ten months—but effectively I was required to get Singh and Nivens to deny me doing the right thing. The only official lever that I had would be the management representation letter.

I set a meeting with Singh for later in the week, a couple of days away. My approach was to discuss the liability, discuss the rep letter, provide some options that may be amenable to Singh in reflective verbiage in the form of a "disclaimer" footnote with the hope that he would get a statement from me saying that "all but for this, the financial statements presented are expressed in accordance with GAAP." I mocked up the management representation letter and advised Singh that Frank and I would be prepared to sign this document:

COLLINS & AIKMAN CORPORATION
DIVISION REPRESENTATION LETTER
FOURTH QUARTER AND 53 WEEK PERIOD ENDING DECEMBER 31, 2000

DIVISION:_North America Automotive Interior Systems

January 23, 2001

Dinesh Singh, Executive Vice-President and CFO
James Slowinski, Vice-President of Finance and Corporate Controller
Collins & Aikman Corporation
5755 New King Court
Troy, Michigan 48098

Dear Mr. Singh and Mr. Slowinski,

We represent and certify that the following internal control procedures have been performed in conjunction with preparing the financial statements for the period end indicated above:

1. All bank accounts (including payroll) have been reconciled to the general ledger.
2. Accounts receivable, accounts payable and inventory subsidiary ledgers have been reconciled to the general ledger.
3. The date of the last physical count of inventory occurred on various (mainly Sept. 30 and Nov. 4. The general ledger balance for inventory has been adjusted to reflect the results of that physical count.
4. Inventory has been reviewed for excess, obsolete and slow moving items. Proper accruals have been recorded to reduce inventory-carrying values for these items.
5. All purchases of fixed assets and any fixed assets placed into service during the fourth quarter and throughout fiscal 2000 have been capitalized and depreciated in accordance with Company policy.
6. Tooling costs incurred after December 25, 1999, in excess of amounts reimbursed have been expensed unless a written contract which allows for "the non-cancelable right" to use the tool has been obtained. Tooling reimbursements after December 25, 1999, in excess tooling costs incurred (tooling gains) are being amortized into earnings over the life of the platform's production run.
7. Tooling is properly classified in the balance sheet between Current Assets and Long Term Assets in accordance with Company policy. A customer purchase order or other appropriate third party documentation supports amounts capitalized as Reimbursable Tooling.

Can't Regulate This   D. J. Burgundy

8. Engineering, research and development costs and all costs associated with starting up production on a new product during the fourth quarter and throughout fiscal 2000 have been charged to expense unless a written contract for reimbursement from the customer has been obtained.
9. No significant changes in business conditions have occurred indicating an impairment of long-live assets (i.e. fixed assets).
10. Purchase discounts have not been recorded without a written, contractual agreement from the vendor.
11. All price reduction agreements, rebate agreements and other allowance arrangements have been reviewed and the proper liability has been fully accrued.
12. Customer deductions (residing in accounts receivable) have been reviewed and have been fully reserved where necessary. Also, actions for recovery have been initiated where appropriate.
13. Accounts receivable has been reviewed and proper reserves for bad debt have been provided.
14. All product shipments have been properly invoiced to the customer.
15. No shipments have occurred without written, authorized purchase orders. The purchase orders include the most current price.
16. All reserve amount changes during the fourth quarter and fiscal 2000 are fully documented for the following: the change in facts which occurred causing the change in the reserve requirements, a calculation and support for the amount of the change and comments relating to the need for remaining reserve balances.
17. All intercompany transactions have been recorded in accordance with Company policy and are in balance with affiliate operations.
18. All restructuring related costs have been either billed back to Corporate Accounting (if part of the approved 1999, restructuring program) or have been expensed in the fourth quarter and throughout fiscal 2000.

In connection with the financial statements of **North America Automotive Interior Systems** as of December 31, 2000 and for the 53 weeks then ended, to be included in the Collins & Aikman Corporation Annual Report on Form 10-K to be filed with the Securities and Exchange Commission, we hereby certify that as of that date and the date of this letter, to the best of our knowledge and belief:

1. The financial statements fairly present the **North America Automotive Interior Systems'** financial position and the results of operations in accordance with generally accepted accounting principles, on a basis consistent with that for the 52 week ended December 25, 1999.

Can't Regulate This   D. J. Burgundy

DIVISION REPRESENTATION LETTER

Page 3

2. We have made available to Arthur Andersen all financial records and related data.

3. We acknowledge our responsibility for the maintenance of an adequate system of internal accounting controls. We believe that the system of internal accounting controls presently in existence provides reasonable assurance that transactions are properly executed and recorded, and that assets are controlled and safe-guarded.

4. There have been no:

    a. Irregularities involving management or employees who have significant roles in the system of internal accounting controls.

    b. Irregularities involving other employees that could have a material effect on the financial statements.

    c. Communications from regulatory agencies concerning non-compliance with, or deficiencies in, financial reporting practices that could have a material effect on the financial statements.

    d. Violations or possible violations of laws or regulations.

    e. Other material liabilities, unasserted claims, or assessments, or gain or loss contingencies that are require to be accrued or disclosed by Statement of Financial Accounting Standards No. 5. [See note (1)]

5. We have no plans or intentions that may materially affect the carrying value or classification of assets and liabilities.

6. Inventories are carried at the lower of cost or market and where appropriate, excess or obsolete items in inventories have been reduced to net realizable value.

7. There are no:

    a. Related party transactions and related amounts receivable or payable, including sales, purchases, loans, transfers, leasing agreements and guarantees which have not been properly recorded or disclosed.

DIVISION REPRESENTATION LETTER

Page 4

- b. Capital stock repurchase options or agreements or capital stock reserved for options, warrants, conversions or other requirements

- c. Arrangements with financial institutions involving compensating balances or other arrangements involving restrictions on cash balances and lines-of-credit or similar arrangements.

- d. Agreements to repurchase assets previously sold.

8. The accounting records underlying the financial statements and year-end reporting package accurately and fairly reflect, in reasonable detail, the transactions of the Company.

9. The company has satisfactory title to all owned assets, all liens and encumbrances on such assets have properly reflected on the appropriate schedules of the annual Financial Reporting Package; and no assets have been pledged.

10. We have complied with all aspects of contractual agreements that would have a material effect on the financial statements in the event of non-compliance.

11. There are no material losses to be sustained in the fulfillment of, or from inability to fulfill any sales commitments.

12. There are no material losses to be sustained as a result of purchase commitments for inventory quantities in excess of normal requirements or at prices in excess of the prevailing market prices.

13. No underwriter, promoter, director, officer, employee or principal holder of equity securities other than affiliated, have an aggregate indebtedness to the company for amounts in excess of $100,000 at December 31, 2000, or at any time during the 53 weeks ended December 31, 2000.

14. No events have occurred subsequent to December 31, 2000, which would require adjustments to, or disclosure in, the financial statements.

Can't Regulate This   D. J. Burgundy

DIVISION REPRESENTATION LETTER

Page 5

Note (1):

We are aware of an unrecorded liability that is the result of a customer purchase order pricing error. This pricing error which was detected in April 2000 relates to Collins & Aikman NAAIS receiving payment from General Motors for an option (sun shade) on a automotive rear door that does not exist on that particular product. During the remainder of the year, NAAIS senior management was interpreting the problem and strategizing as to the correct position to be taken with external parties to Collins & Aikman. As of December 31, 2000, our financial books and records do not reflect this liability to General Motors and thereby, our sales and earnings are overstated for year 2000. The amount approximates $3.0 million.

Over the course of year 2000, we have experienced two focused tool audits by Ford Motor Company. As of October 2000, we have closed one of these audits resulting in an approximate $350,000 liability owing to Ford Motor Co. Another Ford tooling audit is soon to be closed with a probable amount owed to Ford approximating $450,000. These amounts are not reflected within our statement of financial position as liabilities to Ford Motor Company.

DINESH SINGH
W/

Jan 23, 2001
Date Signed

David J. Burgundy

NAAIS Vice President, Finance

———————
Date Signed

Frank J. Brydon

NAAIS President and Chief Operating Officer

DRAFT LETTER AS DISCUSSED

Proposed Management Rep Letter from Burgundy - 5 pages

I sincerely did my best and pleaded my case with Singh about the necessity of this disclosure. The meeting produced the result I needed to press enforcement forward.

Denied!

Singh was not about to let me stand in the way of his and Nivens' premium payday! I expressed to Singh that in that case, I was unwilling to provide him the clean management representation that he required and immediately left his office. I now knew what needed to develop over the next few weeks. I was nearly going out of my mind. This is a big number and could not be swept under the rug. I was on the phone with Waldon with nearly every development, calling him sometimes seven or eight times within a day. I was quite nervous about the situation, the company's destiny, and the malfeasance being committed against shareholders and creditors, some of whom are pension funds, and—just as importantly—the employees who were so deserving of leadership. I felt bad for Bill Waldon and my nuisance calls, but I had no one else to provide counsel and advice at the time.

A short time later, I began receiving Wall Street Journal articles from Bill that described my situation to a "T," but the financial executives who fell victim to such circumstances had extremely poor outcomes because they did not proactively address how they must protect themselves. Luckily, I had the foresight. The one story that really sticks with me is a Xerox finance executive who bucked the inside trend to over-report earnings and the associated outcome for the perpetrator. I guess this one stuck with me because Xerox was such a household name that I naively believed that it was as good as American Pie. The February 5, 2001, article describes how "James F. Bingham" was blackballed inside of Xerox because of his fair and proper initiatives to report the correct and true numbers that pertained to revenue recognition at Xerox. If not corrected, the financial statements would over report the revenues and profits of Xerox. There were further unwanted, adverse and unjust circumstances that came to Mr. Bingham, just for the want of doing the right thing and telling the truth.

These articles did little to provide me comfort and solace during one of the most difficult periods of my life. What they did do, though, was to give me a sense that there are other folks out there who are wanting to do the right thing and are having to fight the fraudsters. I was fortunate to seek protection from knowledgeable legal professionals ahead of driving my case home with the force that would be required.

I informed Frank of Singh's denial. Frank wasn't surprised, and while Frank was reserved and always a polite gentleman, you could see the "ire" build in this Scotsman. His anger was subdued by my quiet calm in that I had a plan and I was confidently executing it. The plan—which leveraged the management representation letter between Singh, Nivens and Frank and I—was going to protect us by preserving the integrity that we brought to this company. Together, we sought to create value for the company, shareholders, lenders, employees and their families and, last but not least, ourselves.

I also finally connected with Bill. I told him of Singh's denial, which, if my proposal was accepted, would have cut my $18,000 legal bill by a magnitude. Yes, $18,000 of my own cash that I put up to stand up to the company and numerous characters supporting the fraud. I guess that is the price that an executive in such a leadership position will pay to get the right things done. Bill and I conversed further about next steps and the timing required for them. As it was now just past mid-January with no complete financial statements for NAAIS, the largest business unit of the company making up about 75% of its entirety. And with time pressure on Singh to report numbers, he could only flash preliminary numbers to Stockman and Blackstone. We knew that without my approval and representation on the numbers for NAAIS, Singh could not report any final results to the current nor prospective owners. My position remained: "It's either done right, or it's not done at all."

Wondering when we would pull the trigger, I called Bill Waldon the next morning. My thought was such that, since I received Singh's denial, that the letters would start flying. Placing utmost trust in the counsel and advice of Bill, his direction was contrary. I am guessing that Bill's negotiation experience had told him that those who are desperate will act first and that it would be better to react to their action than provide them a position to respond to. I followed his lead.

The following day, I received a meeting invitation from Singh for a meeting to commence at 2:00. It was disclosed that the topic of the meeting would be the GMX 270 - Deville Door; however, it was not disclosed that there would be others at the meeting. In preparation for the meeting, I pulled the documents that were provided by Stuart Blumenthal for a once-over and also scanned them and sent them to Singh in advance of the meeting. I wanted to be completely assured that his disclosure denial was based 100% off of the facts, with no ambiguity involved. Below is the most compelling of the "telling" documents. It is a price/cost listing used to develop customer pricing:

Can't Regulate This   D. J. Burgundy

GMX-270 Pricing Sheet - Smoking Gun - 1 page

You can readily see that the column handwritten with the title "NO SHADE," to the contrary, includes the cost of the sunshade. This is clearly the issue that had led to the incorrect yet unknown billings for the rear door of the Cadillac DeVille. Knowing this, and without correction, would constitute a fraudulent billing which would lead to fraudulent financial statements should no liability be recorded. The evidence is black and white!

I chose to knock on Frank's door and tell him what was up. As I pulled a chair closer to Frank's desk, with him sitting across from me and behind his desk, he chose to relocate himself and sit next to me. He complimented me for hanging tough and getting the right thing done. He also gently let me know that at one time early in his position with Collins & Aikman, he was in the process of replacing me (recall the two "financial consultants" that came to visit with Frank, exclusively?). Yes, Frank did admit that, but he also stated that I proved myself to him in my daily activities and my interaction with him and the other senior managers of NAAIS. He was glad that he did not replace me and felt that would have been a big mistake on his part.

Frank also delicately alerted me to a "sexual harassment investigation" that had been undertaken by C&A corporate HR department which was against me. The only thing I can think of that would lead to such nonsense was when I tapped Penny's leg, stimulated by the ribbing she was taking from Tomkowicz about her office manner. This must have been reported to Singh and Nivens. Someone had an inside line as to what was going on and a direct connection to Singh and Nivens at that cold January evening dinner.

By discrediting me in such a claim, this would discredit me across the board and given them cause to fire me and allowing them to sail on to their big payday without any complication from me.

Upon learning this, I assured Frank that there must be some misunderstanding here and that this is a fabrication. Frank, our spouses and I socialized together so he knew I would not stoop to such a level. Frank said that upon his learning of this from corporate HR, he asked that this matter be paced in his hands for ultimate resolve, to get to the bottom of the issue and set things straight. **DENIED!** Corporate HR advised him that this was an HR matter and no one else is invited into the process (Nivens signed the corporate VP of HR's paycheck, too!). I thanked Frank for his confidence, his honesty and sincerity and excused myself after informing him of my 2 p.m. meeting with Singh.

I truly felt threatened. My relationship with Penny had been ice cold from the point of her entrance and it appears that she misunderstood my actions guided by my openness and kindness to try to break through the ice. I am not even sure that she was involved in lodging or aiding the complaint. She acted as if she wasn't involved, but her involvement was compelled by the C&A senior management. I immediately advised Bill Waldon of this crap. Bill immediately knew what they were up to—B.S.!

Two o'clock rolled around, and I entered Singh's office, expecting no one other than himself. What I found was about ten individuals surrounding his conference room table. This was a very interesting manner to conduct a meeting that would take a black and white issue and attempt to color it grey. I learned that we were going to debate whether or not the GM rear door liability truly existed. Around the table were none other than Dinesh Singh's lieutenants, the "yes men,"—the "Bobble-Heads" as I call them—Ken Affinhoffer, corporate director of financial planning and analysis; Tim Peters, corporate senior financial analyst; David Racik, corporate financial analyst; Jay Torrell, corporate financial systems administrator; Jim Slowinski, corporate controller (the buck stops with him on GAAP accounting); Dinesh Singh himself and yours truly, VP of finance / CFO, NAAIS.

I sat at one end of the table and Singh at the other, with the individuals filling in around. To my immediate right was Jim Slowinski, the corporate controller who was my advanced accounting teacher at Walsh College. At the time, Jim worked for Touche Ross, a "big six" accounting firm. When in college, I aspired to be as knowledgeable and accomplished at accounting as Jim Slowinski one day. He was very instructive about the rules and regulations of the Financial Accounting Standards Board (FASB), who was responsible for developing GAAP, and you had only to believe that he walked the walk. What I didn't understand at the time is that it mattered to Jim which side of his bread was buttered. I later learned that after teaching and the public accounting career, he went on to be corporate controller of TRW which is where a lot of these guys named on the above meeting roster hooked up and got to know each other. Their relationship obviously carried forward.

This was quite an interesting show! How is it that you debate and interject opinion into a matter that is black and white? Well, in any case, this is what we did. Dinesh conducted the meeting and proceeded to go around the table and ask each participant whether or not they believed the situation gave rise to a liability in which C&A owed General Motors approximately $4 million.

The answers to the questions, not surprisingly, were

as follows:

Ken Affinhoffer, corporate director of financial planning and analysis:

After considerable mealy-mouthed bullshit justification, in trying to pitch a case that would satisfy his boss and his boss' boss—who once was his direct boss—his answer was, "No, not a liability."

Tim Peters, corporate senior financial analyst:

In Tim's congenial and good-natured way, he pointed to the very fraudulent documents themselves as if to give sanction to them, claiming that the price is valid just because it is written on the paper. To satisfy Singh, his answer was, "No, not a liability."

Halfway through this mocked charade of a meeting, Tom Nivens, CEO, stepped into the room and wanted to know what was going on, --*as if this wasn't rigged*, also. In response to Nivens' query of, "What's going on, Dinesh?" Singh responded, "We're sitting here debating David's $3 million issue."

"What do you mean $3 million issue?" Nivens questioned.

"The GMX-270 door issue and its potential impact on NAAIS profit for year 2000," Singh recanted.

Nivens face grew redder by the second. "No, not in addition to the $3 million blow in Europe in missing their forecast," he said. "We can't have it. Not with all the work and traction that we have gained with the investors and the street, [this will cave the deal.] We cannot have this, and we won't!" His next words, in his "madness," were, "Over my dead body!" as he stormed out after giving an icy stern look to the members of the meeting scattered around the table.

The meeting continued.

David Racik, corporate financial analyst:

David couldn't recognize a bona fide liability if it jumped up and bit him in the ass. In any case, his answer was, "No, not a liability."

Jay Torrell, corporate financial systems administrator:

I felt the equivalent of Racik's credence toward Jay; in any case, his answer was "No, not a liability."

Jim Slowinski, corporate controller (the buck stops with him on GAAP accounting):

The guy who really counted and mattered to me, as if I paired his intellectual capacity to his honesty and selfless judgment—his answer was, "No, not a liability." (*Oh my God,* I thought, *this is the guy I looked to for instruction at a tender young age!*)

Dinesh Singh, himself:

Singh had clearly felt that he had won and looked to me. In conclusion, he intimated that my esteemed colleagues believe there is no liability, so how could I?

and

Me, VP of finance / CFO, NAAIS.

I responded by stating facts of the matter and the absurdness of turning a factual issue into one of opinion. I expressed that I had had enough and immediately rose from the table and left all of them sitting there around that big conference room table that would later be auctioned off in bankruptcy.

Immediately after, I reported what had happened in this meeting to both Frank Brydon and Bill Waldon, not to their amazement. Bill knew that the fun was only beginning. I learned from Frank that he was beginning to negotiate his way out of this mess and was seeking the level of severance that was agreed to by Nivens when Frank joined on. Two years! I clearly could not fault Frank for this; after all, it was Nivens who was in breach of Frank's deal.

By now the news of my abstinence from being one of the "bobble heads" was making rounds in not only my organization, but also the areas of the business for which I was not responsible. Given Frank's and my broad management backgrounds, prior to these fine events, we were tapped to oversee another business unit, "C&A Fabrics." The "fabrics" operation was about a $200 million business headed by Gerald Jones, vice president and general manager, and Controller Paul William. Well, my phone began to ring with Paul William and Gerald calling at the suggestion of Frank.

What I learned in this phone call was once again astounding and another first in my career. Bill had told me that he had been directed to (financially) ignore quality claims against C&A Fabrics, hide telephone and utility bills and leave them unrecorded and hide tooling invoices and supply stores requisitions from the supply crib. These, in fact, were Paul's words.

I had asked for Paul to send me a list of all of the aberrations. He complied and faxed over a remarkable document. We took them one by one:

The quality claim: There was $1 million of product that Magna (a customer and integrator of our products) rejected due to quality reasons. Normally, customers will either return for credit the products that are bad or, with the approval of the supplier (in this case C&A), scrap the bad stuff at their location and charge the supplier—again, C&A—for the value of the bad stuff. The diligence process involves the quality organization of the supplier to affirm that the "stuff" is indeed bad. I then started on my diligence in the conversation with Paul:

Me: Paul, are the goods in fact bad or not to specification?

Paul: Yes, they are bad.

Me: Was your quality organization involved in that determination and was an RMA (Return Material Authorization) granted by them?

Paul: Yes.

Me: Has Magna debited and charged you back for the goods?

Paul: Yes, and they deducted the value from their remittances.

Me: So, effectively they already have the cash?

Paul: Yes.

Me: How did you not reflect this in your financial statements?

Paul: Tom (Nivens) told us, "Place the quality rejection in dispute and do not allow the value to hit your P&L statement," and that is what we did.

Me: So you stuck it on your balance sheet, and it hasn't yet hit your P&L number yet?

Paul: That's correct.

Me: Paul, well, you are going to book it and tell them I said that you were to book it. You'll be fine. I know that I am the fall guy for this, with everything that I have learned and am enforcing, and I will be out! If you tell them that it was me who gave you that direction, you should be fine.

Paul: OK, David, we'll do that.

In fact, the total amount of Fabrics' problems was north of $3.5 million dollars! With my GMX-270 door shade issue, we're now clocking the fraud at $7.5 million

+/-. My advice to Paul, after performing my similar diligence as it pertained to the remaining $2.5 of the $3.5 million, was again to "book all of the items and tell them that I directed you to do so."

Below you will find a listing of all of the fraudulent items that existed at Fabrics, prior to my involvement and ultimate correction:

Can't Regulate This   D. J. Burgundy

FABRICS GROUP
2000/2001 FINANCIAL IMPACT

	FARMVILLE	ROXBORO	TOTAL

YEAR-END POSITION   DEC

1. Deferred Performance

Kept in WIP - did not Ship — In-Plant 2nds — 442 / 84 / 526
HELD SUPPLY REQUISITIONS — Supply Room Issues — 62 / 124 / 186
HELD/HID INVOICES — Phone Bills — 25 / 11 / 36   *March*
                                        $ 529 $ 219 $ 748   748

2. Reserve Requirements

50% DEC. ISSUES External Quality Issues — 140 / 108 / 248   124
550$ Rox, 340 Questioned Magna Deductions 3Q 2000 — 890 / / 890   *accrued*
Excel Deductions 3Q 2000 — / 603 / 603   *10 mos.*
                                        $ 1,030 $ 711 $ 1,741

PULLED INTO 2000

39, trice led Pull Ahead Unifi Rebates *12 mo's,* $ 210 $ 490 $ 700
Ford Rebate Deferred $ 330 $ 330   330
                                $ 210 $ 820 $ 1,030

TOTAL IMPACT $ 1,769 $ 1,750 $ 3,519   1200

1Q	2Q	3Q	4Q
748			
174	510	510	510
90	250	250	250
~~10+2~~ 1200	760	760	760

**List of C&A Fabrics' Group Financial Fraud, 2000 and 2001
- 1 page**

Well, I bet you can guess where my next call was!

-148-

Bill Waldon? Yup! After Bill understood the gravity of what I was telling him, he emphasized that since I had knowledge of this, and given that the Fabrics business was just coming under my span of control and authority, I was responsible to see it through so that the right financial statements were published for the Fabrics business unit. I knew this, and, with or without his advice, I would have had it no other way, as you well know.

The next morning, I got a very special visit from Mr. Hester (Kraig), my director of information technology. He knocked and entered, less concerned about the political implications of doing so and more concerned with what he was about to say. In a very brief, succinct manner, Kraig delivered his message: "David, I don't want to know the whys or wherefores about what's going on, but you need to know that they're listening and they're watching."

Astounded with another career first, I asked, "What? What does that mean?"

Kraig responded, "They're listening to your phone conversations and they are monitoring your emails." *Oh my God*, I thought. I was clearly not safe here and began to wonder about my general safety; after all, a big deal in the hundreds of millions of dollars was about to go down and I may be its Achilles' heel! "What might desperate people do in a desperate situation?" I thought to myself. It was obvious that they would go to great lengths to preserve their large payday. "So large that could I pay the ultimate price for causing the company to do the right thing?" I had begun to question.

Kraig asked me, "Do you wish for me to put a stop to their surveillance activity?"

I said "absolutely" and asked that he provide evidence that he had done so. It took some time for Kraig to work through the wrinkles on this, but he eventually shut access to my email down to those who shouldn't have it. Below you shall see who had access to viewing my emails along with the associated time frames. Pauline Chilcut was on the other side and was monitoring my emails on Singh's and Nivens' behalf.

Kraig produced the image from the computer system's administrative agent showing who was accessing my email, the time frame and when access was denied to those individuals who should not have access.

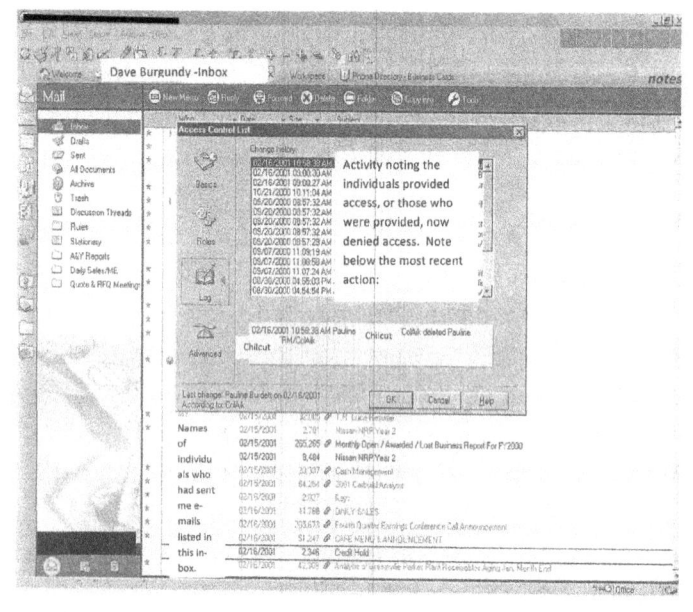

Proof that C&A CEO-CFO were spying on me with company devices - 1 page

As I was very cautious and deliberate with my actions, in my time of peril, I never used my office phone when conversing with Bill Waldon, nor my email. Thus,

Nivens and Singh had no knowledge of the privileged attorney-client communications.

That night, and for every night thereafter for a year, I slept with a loaded .38 caliber "police special" pistol within arm's reach of where I slept.

Entering the last week of January 2001, I knew the pressure was mounting on Singh to produce final numbers for Stockman, Heartland Industrial Partners, Blackstone and the remaining stakeholders. Early in the morning on January 25, I used my cell phone and called Waldon. Bill had asked if I had my arms around the numbers and what it would take for me to sign-off on the financial statements. My usual diligence caused me to keep a list. Below, you shall find that list after I reviewed and re-reviewed it with all concerned parties in the effort to get it right:

1/25/2001

To: Bill Waldon   **Fr: Dave Burgundy**

2 PGS

~~(REVISED)~~

Bill   PRELIM. FINAL

This is the sum total of the change that I need effected for comfort on my representation letter.

David B.

Can't Regulate This — D. J. Burgundy

COLLINS & AIKMAN
YEAR 2000
ADJUSTING JOURNAL ENTRIES

FINAL

FABRICS PROBLEMS	~~(1670)~~ ~~(1690)~~	(1815°)
TOOLING @ PLASTICS	(1000)	(1023.0)
DOOR SHADE @ MANCH.	~~(3000)~~	(3277.4)
DN OVERPAYMENT @ ST.CL.	~~(250)~~	(371.4)
LOSS ON INVENTORY @ MANCH	~~(1000)~~	(948.0)
INVENTORY ALLOW ADJ @ ALB/PK (& MISC ADJ'S.)	900	800.°
OVERACCRUED SALES (INCORRECT PRICING)	(400)	(350.°)
TOTAL	$(6440)	~~$(6859.8)~~
		$(6984.8)

> Fabrics Adj's.
>
> DJB
> 1/29/2001
>
> Inventory Write-down
> on Quality Issues $500.º +/-
>
> Supply Stores Issues (Unrecorded)   186.º
>
> Unrecorded Accounts Payable   36.º
>
> Reserve Requirements for
> Quality Rejections   1093.º
>
> Total Adj - Fabrics $1815.º
>
> Please follow-up w/ PAUL WILLIAM
> (336) 503- xxxx

**Note to Waldon, atty along with List of C&A Interiors Group
Financial Fraud, 2000 and 2001 - 3 pages**

When excluding the favorable $800,000 adjustment

to inventory allowances at the Albemarle operation, or negating it out of the adjustment, there was nearly $8 million of fraud that would have been incorporated into the financial statements. With a business being sold for a multiple of six-times earnings, this is nearly a $85 million erosion of total enterprise value. That in effect is a major fraud on the stock transaction that effectively would transfer (sell) the ownership of 60% of the company!

Later that morning, at about 11 a.m., I received a call from Affinhoffer, Singh's director of financial planning and analysis, on my office phone! Affinhoffer said, "Dinesh says to go ahead and book the adjustments. He doesn't like it, but he said go ahead and book them." I advised that we would go ahead and book the Fabrics' unit adjustment as well and that we would need access to their ledger via their computer code and sign-on. Affinhoffer said, "We would rather you work with Paul William to accomplish that. He and his staff can put those adjustments through."

Bill Waldon's plan worked. As I was the boots on the ground executing Waldon's orders of fervently staying the course, the combination of letters advising Singh and Nivens that the next action was a call to the SEC served as the smelling salts causing them to wake up.

I immediately contacted the appropriate individuals on my team to affect the change required in the financials and that I would require them to demonstrate that the proper entries were made by demonstrating to me the "before and after books" clearly depicting the change. It took approximately two hours, but we got it done and the change was demonstrated.

I advised Bill Waldon of this and although we accomplished our mission, the heat was not yet off of me. I still had my own skin to protect, and all I had to rely on was the fact that I engaged a great attorney and the trail of evidence that lead to my C&A demise (immediate dismissal, perhaps). I called Frank to let him in on the good news and that we had done our proper job. He was happy to hear that. Apparently, he was out of the office due to medical reasons and was hanging in there due to the legal advice I am sure that Bill provided him.

The next morning, I entered my office to open my email and learned of a company-wide email which was sent from Dinesh Singh that thanked me for my services as VP of finance / CFO of the North America Automotive Interiors Systems business and that I was now "special projects vice president." I immediately picked up my office phone, called Dinesh Singh and advised him that I do not accept the assignment of "special projects vice president" and fully remain "vice president of finance / CFO of the North American Automotive Interior Systems." This did not meet with Singh's plans, as I am sure that my next step as "special projects vice president" was out the door!

To this effect, within a couple of days, I sent this letter—jointly authored by Bill Waldon and myself—to Singh:

Can't Regulate This   D. J. Burgundy

January 29, 2001

Dinesh Singh,
Executive Vice-President and CFO
Collins & Aikman Products Co.
5755 New King Court
Troy, MI 48098

Dear Mr. Singh,

As soon as our financial statements reflect my recommended adjustements, I am prepared to sign the management representation letter for the North America Automotive Interior Systems (NAAIS) division. One of these significantly material items is proper recognition of liability to General Motors related to the absent sunshade on the rear doors of the Cadillac DeVille (GMX 270) supplied out of our Manchester operation. So that there is no misunderstanding, I wish to recount some of the events which lead up to the inclusion of these entries in the NAAIS financials. In addition, I want to again raise issues related to the Fabrics Group.

As the supplier to General Motors of the rear door, some doors are ordered with a sunshade; some are not. However, the Company has charged GM for the sunshade, even on doors that do not have one. There is no basis by which the Company can claim it is entitled to the money. Mr. Stuart Holtshauser, in an internal report of February 24, 2000 regarding the situation, concluded that the amount of the overcharge, as of the end of January 2000, accumulated to approximately $1.5 million.

As the Vice President of Finance for North America Automotive Interior Systems, I concluded that the amount owed GM was a liability that must be reflected on the Company's financial statements. I was repeatedly instructed not to include it on the Company's interim financial statements since the Company was evaluating its position in terms of response to our customer. In any case, my personal and full intent was to include this in our financial statements, independent of any customer related outcome. As you know, this liability was included in our fourth quarter forecast. Understanding your pressure to keep reported financial results elevated for purposes of any pending stock transaction, you directed that this liability be ignored and that we would provide for this over the twelve months of 2001. At the end of 2001, the liability would grow to $5.3 million ($3.3 million as of Dec. 31, 2000, plus an additional $2.0 million for calendar year 2001).

My draft management representation letter regarding our year 2000 financial statements was prepared in accordance with Generally Accepted Accounting Principles (as of December 31, 2000) and properly included disclosure of this liability along with the disclosure of an item of lesser materiality to the statement of financial position. This draft management representation letter was rejected by you.

Following a number of meetings with various executives where I indicated the disclosure must be made (and if not made, I would report it to the Securities and Exchange Commission and other appropriate public bodies), the Company has agreed to include these liabilities along with appropriate disclosures in the December 31, 2000 Statement of Financial Position and Operating Results for the twelve months ending December 31, 2000.

Mr. Dinesh Singh
Year 2000 Financials
January 29, 2001
Page Two

To my surprise, while a number of people have supported my decision, I have also been told by Mr. Tom Nivens, CEO and Chairman, that my insistence on telling the truth would be a "threat to the pending transaction with Heartland, tarnish all of the work that we have done with the "street", not to mention that this will have negative impact with our lenders." Tom further advised that because of all of the above, "our (fourth quarter) number cannot drop beneath $15 million. We just cannot have that and we won't, whatever it takes."

There are also issues related to the Fabrics Group. About 10 days ago Paul William advised me of a number of misstatements that were contained within his year 2000 financials that approximated $3.5 million. Paul's purpose for calling me was to ask my direction on how to integrate these items into his quarterly 2001 forecast. As the discussion progressed, I pondered on how I could most help Paul Gerald Jones Group Vice President – Chief Operating Officer of the Fabrics Group. That led me to ask Paul whether or not he disclosed these items in his management representation letter. He told me that he did not. I asked why and he advised me that he was directed to give a "clean" representation, as I was for the NAAIS group.

While the Fabrics Group was not included in NAAIS for 2000, and therefore does not require my review for our audit, my actual knowledge of these misstatements required me to insist that they either be included and properly stated in our consolidated financial statements, or disclosed to our auditors via taking exceptions within Paul's management representation letter. Without such disclosure, I would be required to report this information to the Securities and Exchange Commission and other appropriate public bodies. In addition, the Fabrics Group has become part of NAAIS as of January 1, 2001 and is now my responsibility. I can not allow these misstatements to continue where I had actual knowledge of them, not to mention that they are now part of my division.

I trust that the appropriate financial recognition and disclosures will be made regarding all known items to management, including the GM sunshade issue and the misstatements within the Fabrics Group.

Sincerely,

David J. Burgundy

Burgundy letter of advisement to Dinesh Singh - 2 pages

Can't Regulate This D. J. Burgundy

Apparently, this letter received the proper level of attention as the below summary representation of the company's consolidated financials was delivered to me for my verification:

Can't Regulate This   D. J. Burgundy

Corroborating Evidence Schedule that the proper financial adjustments were made - 2 pages

As you can see, after incorporating the correct numbers into the NAAIS financials, we produced approximately $87.7 million of Earnings Before Interest and Taxes, or 79.7% of our $110 million target as set by Nivens. With this, I then provided this "clean" management representation letter signed by Frank Brydon and I along with the accompanying letter.

Can't Regulate This   D. J. Burgundy

January 31, 2001

Dinesh Singh,
Executive Vice-President and CFO
Collins & Aikman Products Co.
5755 New King Court
Troy, MI 48098

Dear Mr. Singh,

Enclosed is the management representation letter which I have signed, now that North America Automotive Interior Systems (NAAIS) financial statements, contain relevant and significantly material entries. One of these significantly material items is proper recognition of liability to General Motors related to the absent sunshade on the rear doors of the Cadillac DeVille (GMX 270) supplied out of our Manchester operation. So that there is no misunderstanding, I wish to recount some of the events which lead up to the inclusion of these entries in the NAAIS financials. In addition, I want to again raise issues related to the Fabrics Group.

As the supplier to General Motors of the rear door, some doors are ordered with a sunshade; some are not. However, the Company has charged GM for the sunshade, even on doors that do not have one. There is no basis by which the Company can claim it is entitled to the money. Mr. Stuart Holtshauser, in an internal report of February 24, 2000 regarding the situation, concluded that the amount of the overcharge, as of the end of January 2000, accumulated to approximately $1.5 million.

As the Vice President of Finance for North America Automotive Interior Systems, I concluded that the amount owed GM was a liability that must be reflected on the Company's financial statements. I was repeatedly instructed not to include it on the Company's interim financial statements since the Company was evaluating its position in terms of response to our customer. In any case, my personal and full intent was to include this in our financial statements, independent of any customer related outcome. As you know, this liability was included in our fourth quarter forecast. Understanding your pressure to keep reported financial results elevated for purposes of any pending stock transaction, you directed that this liability be ignored and that we would provide for this over the twelve months of 2001. At the end of 2001, the liability would grow to $5.3 million ($3.3 million as of Dec. 31, 2000, plus an additional $2.0 million for calendar year 2001).

My draft management representation letter regarding our year 2000 financial statements was prepared in accordance with Generally Accepted Accounting Principles (as of December 31, 2000) and properly included disclosure of this liability along with the disclosure of an item of lesser materiality to the statement of financial position. This draft management representation letter was rejected by you.

Following a number of meetings with various executives where I indicated the disclosure must be made (and if not made, I would report it to the Securities and Exchange Commission and other appropriate public bodies), the Company has agreed to include these liabilities along with appropriate disclosures in the December 31, 2000 Statement of Financial Position and Operating Results for the twelve months ending December 31, 2000.

Can't Regulate This
D. J. Burgundy

Mr. Dinesh Singh
Year 2000 Financials
January 31, 2001
Page Two

To my surprise, while a number of people have supported my decision, I have also been told by Mr. Tom Nivens, CEO and Chairman, that my insistence on telling the truth would be a "threat to the pending transaction with Heartland, tarnish all of the work that we have done with the "street", not to mention that this will have negative impact with our lenders." Tom further advised that because of all of the above, "our (fourth quarter) number cannot drop beneath $15 million. We just cannot have that and we won't, whatever it takes."

There are also issues related to the Fabrics Group. About 10 days ago Paul William ised me of a number of misstatements that were contained within his year 2000 financials that approximated $3.5 million (resolved at $1.8 million). Paul's purpose for calling me was to ask my direction on how to integrate these items into his quarterly 2001 forecast. As the discussion progressed, I pondered on how I could most he Paul nd Gerald Jones, Group Vice President – Chief Operating Officer of the Fabrics Group. That led me to ask Paul ether or not he disclosed these items in his management representation letter. He told me that he did not. I asked why and he advised me that he was directed to give a "clean" representation, as I was for the NAAIS group.

While the Fabrics Group was not included in NAAIS for 2000, and therefore does not require my review for our audit, my actual knowledge of these misstatements required me to insist that they either be included and properly stated in our consolidated financial statements, or disclosed to our auditors via taking exceptions within Paul's management representation letter. Without such disclosure, I would be required to report this information to the Securities and Exchange Commission and other appropriate public bodies. In addition, the Fabrics Group has become part of NAAIS as of January 1, 2001 and is now my responsibility. I could not allow these misstatements to continue where I had actual knowledge of them, not to mention that they are now part of my division.

I trust that the appropriate financial recognition and disclosures will be made regarding all known items to management, including the GM sunshade issue and the misstatements within the Fabrics Group.

Sincerely,

David J. Burgundy

Can't Regulate This   D. J. Burgundy

COLLINS & AIKMAN CORPORATION
DIVISION REPRESENTATION LETTER
FOURTH QUARTER AND 53 WEEK PERIOD ENDING DECEMBER 31, 2000

DIVISION:_North America Automotive Interior Systems

January 31, 2001

Dinesh Singh,
    Executive Vice-President and CFO
James Slowin ski, Vice-President of Finance and Corporate Controller
Collins & Aikman Corporation
5755 New King Court
Troy, Michigan 48098

Dear Mr. Singh and Mr. Slowinski:

We represent and certify that the following internal control procedures have been performed in conjunction with preparing the financial statements for the period end indicated above:

1. All bank accounts (including payroll) have been reconciled to the general ledger. [See note (1)]
2. Accounts receivable, accounts payable and inventory subsidiary ledgers have been reconciled to the general ledger.
3. The date of the last physical count of inventory occurred on various (mainly Sept. 30 and Nov. 4. The general ledger balance for inventory has been adjusted to reflect the results of that physical count.
4. Inventory has been reviewed for excess, obsolete and slow moving items. Proper accruals have been recorded to reduce inventory-carrying values for these items.
5. All purchases of fixed assets and any fixed assets placed into service during the fourth quarter and throughout fiscal 2000 have been capitalized and depreciated in accordance with Company policy.
6. Tooling costs incurred after December 25, 1999, in excess of amounts reimbursed have been expensed unless a written contract which allows for "the non-cancelable right" to use the tool has been obtained.
7. Tooling is properly classified in the balance sheet between Current Assets and Long Term Assets in accordance with Company policy. A customer purchase order or other appropriate third party documentation supports amounts capitalized as Reimbursable Tooling.
8. Engineering, research and development costs and all costs associated with starting up production on a new product during the fourth quarter and throughout fiscal 2000 have been charged to expense unless a written contract for reimbursement from the customer has been obtained.

9. No significant changes in business conditions have occurred indicating an impairment of long-live assets (i.e. fixed assets).
10. Purchase discounts have not been recorded without a written, contractual agreement from the vendor.
11. All price reduction agreements, rebate agreements and other allowance arrangements have been reviewed and the proper liability has been fully accrued.
12. Customer deductions (residing in accounts receivable) have been reviewed and have been fully reserved where necessary. Also, actions for recovery have been initiated where appropriate.
13. Accounts receivable has been reviewed and proper reserves for bad debt have been provided.
14. All product shipments have been properly invoiced to the customer.
15. No shipments have occurred without written, authorized purchase orders. The purchase orders include the most current price.
16. All reserve amount changes during the fourth quarter and fiscal 2000 are fully documented for the following: the change in facts which occurred causing the change in the reserve requirements, a calculation and support for the amount of the change and comments relating to the need for remaining reserve balances.
17. All intercompany transactions have been recorded in accordance with Company policy and are in balance with affiliate operations.
18. All restructuring related costs have been either billed back to Corporate Accounting (if part of the approved 1999, restructuring program) or have been expensed in the fourth quarter and throughout fiscal 2000.

In connection with the financial statements of **North America Automotive Interior Systems** as of December 31, 2000 and for the 53 weeks then ended, to be included in the Collins & Aikman Corporation Annual Report on Form 10-K to be filed with the Securities and Exchange Commission, we hereby certify that as of that date and the date of this letter, to the best of our knowledge and belief:

1. The financial statements fairly present the **North America Automotive Interior Systems'** financial position and the results of operations in accordance with generally accepted accounting principles, on a basis consistent with that for the 52 week ended December 25, 1999.

DIVISION REPRESENTATION LETTER

Page 3

2. We have made available to Arthur Andersen all financial records and related data.

3. We acknowledge our responsibility for the maintenance of an adequate system of internal accounting controls. We believe that the system of internal accounting controls presently in existence provides reasonable assurance that transactions are properly executed and recorded, and that assets are controlled and safe-guarded.

4. There have been no:

    a. Irregularities involving management or employees who have significant roles in the system of internal accounting controls.

    b. Irregularities involving other employees that could have a material effect on the financial statements.

    c. Communications from regulatory agencies concerning non-compliance with, or deficiencies in, financial reporting practices that could have a material effect on the financial statements.

    d. Violations or possible violations of laws or regulations.

    e. Other material liabilities, unasserted claims, or assessments, or gain or loss contingencies that are require to be accrued or disclosed by Statement of Financial Accounting Standards No. 5. **[See note (2)]**

5. We have no plans or intentions that may materially affect the carrying value or classification of assets and liabilities.

6. Inventories are carried at the lower of cost or market and where appropriate, excess or obsolete items in inventories have been reduced to net realizable value.

7. There are no:

    a. Related party transactions and related amounts receivable or payable, including sales, purchases, loans, transfers, leasing agreements and guarantees which have not been properly recorded or disclosed.

DIVISION REPRESENTATION LETTER

Page 4

    b. Capital stock repurchase options or agreements or capital stock reserved for options, warrants, conversions or other requirements

    c. Arrangements with financial institutions involving compensating balances or other arrangements involving restrictions on cash balances and lines-of-credit or similar arrangements.

    d. Agreements to repurchase assets previously sold.

8. The accounting records underlying the financial statements and year-end reporting package accurately and fairly reflect, in reasonable detail, the transactions of the Company.

9. The company has satisfactory title to all owned assets, all liens and encumbrances on such assets have properly reflected on the appropriate schedules of the annual Financial Reporting Package; and no assets have been pledged.

10. We have complied with all aspects of contractual agreements that would have a material effect on the financial statements in the event of non-compliance.

11. There are no material losses to be sustained in the fulfillment of, or from inability to fulfill any sales commitments.

12. There are no material losses to be sustained as a result of purchase commitments for inventory quantities in excess of normal requirements or at prices in excess of the prevailing market prices.

13. No underwriter, promoter, director, officer, employee or principal holder of equity securities other than affiliated, have an aggregate indebtedness to the company for amounts in excess of $100,000 at December 31, 2000, or at any time during the 53 weeks ended December 31, 2000.

14. No events have occurred subsequent to December 31, 2000, which would require adjustments to, or disclosure in, the financial statements.

DIVISION REPRESENTATION LETTER

Page 5

Note (1):
Due to the change of banks in the middle of the year of 2000, there has been an unreconciled balance of $42,000 at our Scarborough operation since this time. As of the end of 2000, I have been advised that the December bank statement is reconciled all but for this $42,000.

Note (2):
Relating to our employee incentive compensation plan (EICP), while we believe that we have met certain of the performance criteria involved in the computation of management bonus, we have been advised by corporate management that the bonus plan will be subject to our Chairman and CEO, Tom Nivens' discretion. We understand that in exercising his discretion, Mr. T Nivens decided that there will be no bonus granted to the participants of the EICP, except for those individuals guaranteed of a bonus, specific to the issue of year 2000 financial performance. Our understanding is that the corporate accounting group is managing the bonus accrual account and reflecting the adjustments somewhere within our financial reporting system. This decision has not been communicated to the participants of the EICP program.

Jan. 31, 2001
Date Signed

David J. Burgundy

NAAIS Vice President, Finance

31st January 2001
Date Signed

Frank Brydon

NAAIS President and Chief Operating Officer

Burgundy Confirming Letter to Singh along with properly executed Management Rep Letter - 7 pages

Being that the Heartland / Blackstone deal was eminent, the financial audit immediately commenced. I found it very interesting that Carmella Sotor, the lead audit manager of Arthur Andersen, then C&A's auditor, came to visit me and ask how I had found these liabilities and expenses. I explained the situation and how things evolved. It is ironic that there no longer exists an Arthur Andersen audit firm as the result of Enron; of course, the Enron debacle had not materialized and the C&A situation was in no way Enronian in proportion. To be totally fair, and part of the reason for writing this book, is that it is likely that these items would not have been detected in audit. "Conscience is D-E-A-D" for some financial individuals when talking with auditors. I had the heart and soul of everyone who wanted to do right in C&A, and that is the reason that these liabilities and expenses were revealed to me. Money is to be made the right and old-fashioned way: by earning it. Not by cheating.

Shortly after, Penny had a change of heart. She was either influenced by the truth or by the common sense of Frank and the general situation. She submitted this letter that put it back in the face of Nivens, Singh and Corporate HR: With Frank essentially gone, pushing toward the severance arrangement, I felt like the Lone Ranger with no Tonto. Having enforced the right thing, it was now just me and the counsel of Bill Waldon against Singh, Nivens, their disciples of (potential) fraud and the Human Resources Department to figure my safe way out of this mess.

Can't Regulate This	D. J. Burgundy

February 1, 2001

Mr. **Greg Grinnell**
Mr. **Bill Short**
Ms. **Joyce Johnson**
Collins & Aikman
5755 New King Court
Troy, MI 48098

Dear Greg, Bill and Joyce:

I have given thought to your request this morning. I decided in December not to make a formal complaint against N   David Burgundy. Nothing has changed. My problem with David   was short lived and not of such a serious nature so as to justify any further discussion. For this reason I decline to make any written statement other than this. Thank you for your concern.

Sincerely,

Penny Fillergrin

Feb. 1, 2001 Fillergrin letter to HR recinding their offer to enforce a false claim of harrassment - 1 page

Shortly thereafter, I was approached for a meeting

by Mr. Greg Grinnell, VP of HR and his sidekick, Rod Banks. These guys were going to try to browbeat me, profess there was no wrongdoing by Nivens and Singh and convince me that I should take the role of the special projects vice president, or a small token severance for my trouble, upon leaving the company and signing off on a release. Greg Grinnell told me that Frank had a model that he regularly used for collecting severance and then move to another company. "This is the second time that Frank has done this." "Frank looks for ways to collect his severance and move on to new jobs."

They took me down the path of interrogation and intimidation. White light, small room, no air conditioning—these guys were getting too up close and personal for my liking. I had no other response than to ask, "What does this have to do with the facts?"

Grinnell responded, "Everything."

I responded, "Nothing," and then schooled Grinnell on the applicable GAAP, telling him that anything he has to say absolutely could not change my mind.

Adhering closely to Bill Waldon's advice, I rolled up to the C&A address every morning and dreaded it. Time could not move more slowly. Although I did not accept the new but empty assignment and title of VP of special projects, Singh and Nivens had adjusted the organization so that they would circumvent my influence and involvement in the business of North America Automotive Interior Systems. As I was now relieved of the day to day management of the business, I read the Wall Street Journal for most of the day and fielded my subordinates' questions, as well as those from Singh's staff, for my opinion of how they should handle certain situations, both professional and otherwise. Bear in mind that since these developments, it was highly unpopular to visit with me.. I am quite sure that Singh's and Nivens' lieutenants were watching who was coming and going.

With no need to be concerned about my attire—as I no longer was visiting with executives, investment bankers, or had to give the "executive" persona—I had donned clothes of black, regularly, sometimes black jeans with a black mock turtleneck, a black leather coat, gloves and shoes. Frank was rolling in with casual attire, sometimes blue jeans, while he was managing the activities toward his exit from the company. We would get together from time to time and just talk about how things were going and other more important topics of life.

With no other work on the docket, Frank and I forged forward in trying to setup a new life. We had done the right and noble thing for the company, its shareholders and other stakeholders, including its employees. Now we had to go to work for ourselves, otherwise these bastards would have hung us out to dry.

Frank was in and out of the office—mostly out—while he was negotiating his proverbial final "OUT." Covering himself, as advised by counsel, he would keep communicating about himself and his progress and initiatives to continue to deliver value to the company. Before mid-February, Frank was gone and received his two-year severance package. That was his protection.

At the time of my joining C&A, I did not negotiate a severance and therefore I was likely subject to a six-month severance that was standard, except in this case. As a result of the prior events, I would hold out and negotiate to the best of my ability to get near Frank's exit deal.

As the results became known to Stockman, Heartland and Blackstone, the major adjustment that I enforced and brought into being was dubbed "The David and Frank Adjustment." As it was increasingly more difficult to roll up to the C&A headquarters on a daily basis, I'm not sure if this notoriety made me feel any better, but at least I could chuckle about it!

Now that the deal was all but done and announced, the big payday was in the making for Nivens and Singh. While 87% of the outstanding stock of C&A was owned by private equity firms (Blackstone and Wasserstein-Perella), it was a public company traded on a public stock exchange. This made press releases necessary that were focused on earnings and other important developments of the company.

In the following press release, pay particular attention to Nivens' explanation as to the major miss being explained as "one-time adjustments and write-downs." This is fallacy, false and should have been called upon by Arthur Andersen as this press release—in and of itself—is misleading to investors. Used properly, a one-time adjustment and asset write-down does not generally affect the ongoing revenues and profits of a business. Nivens and Singh were living in some la-la land as (while they cite these financial recognitions as "one-time adjustments and write-downs"), nearly every one of them affected the ongoing run rate of the business. LIES!

Can't Regulate This   D. J. Burgundy

Collins & Aikman

News Release

For Immediate Release
February 21, 2001

Contacts:
Analysts: Lauren Collins
(248) 824-XXXX
lauren.collins@colalk.com

Media: Tasha Robinson
(248) 824-XXXX
tasha.robinson@colalk.com

COLLINS & AIKMAN ANNOUNCES RESULTS FOR THE FOURTH QUARTER AND YEAR ENDED DECEMBER 31, 2000

TROY, Mich. – Collins & Aikman Corporation (NYSE: CKC) today reported fourth quarter and annual results for its fiscal period ended December 31, 2000. For the current fiscal quarter, the Company reported sales of $436.8 million, operating income of $2.0 million and a net loss of $15.9 million, or ($.26) per diluted share. Operating income in the quarter was impacted by approximately $18.0 million in one-time costs and write-offs, the majority of which were non-cash related.

Recent Highlights Include:

- First step of Heartland Industrial Partners, L.P. (Heartland) investment in Collins & Aikman announced – **Significant capital infusion to enhance global growth opportunities.**
- Introduced AcT™ (Acoustically Tuned Technologies) – **Revolutionary industry development for acoustically tuning vehicles.**
- Completed acquisition of COMET™ Acoustic Software – **Leadership in acoustic modeling and predictive capabilities further enabling "bumper-to-bumper" NVH solutions.**
- Announced new business awards in Europe with Renault, GM and Chrysler – **Continuing to enhance European presence.**
- Received Toyota Quality Alliance Gold Supplier Award and KIA Most Valued Partner Award - **Strong commitment to providing excellent service, quality, value and delivery.**

Commenting on the Company's fourth quarter results, Collins & Aikman's Chairman and Chief Executive Officer, Thomas I. Nivens stated, "Although our fourth quarter operating income was impacted in total by approximately $18.0 million in one-time costs and write-offs, our reported financial performance in the quarter was disappointing. Despite the benefits realized from our restructuring actions, the current operating environment has caused our customers to ratchet production down far quicker than expected and simultaneously toughen their positions on a variety of commercial issues. To offset this, we are taking an aggressive stance on all spending, including limitations on all discretionary expenses and implementation of a global hiring freeze. Additionally, we are actively assessing our entire organizational structure and associated staffing levels, and anticipate quickly taking some significant actions to further lower our costs. In terms of capital spending, we are realigning our capital spending initiatives so as to further enhance productivity. Although these actions are difficult, we will continue to vigorously respond to market conditions and position Collins & Aikman to achieve the growth, debt coverage and cash generating goals to which we remain committed."

- more -

Can't Regulate This   D. J. Burgundy

Fourth Quarter Performance Highlights

For the fourth quarter 2000, the Company reported a net loss of $15.9 million, or ($.26) per diluted share. In the fourth quarter of 1999, the Company earned net income of $6.6 million, or $.11 per diluted share, excluding a pre-tax restructuring charge of $13.5 million, or $.15 per diluted share after-tax.

Operating income for the fourth quarter 2000 was $2.0 million, which in addition to lower vehicle production and an unfavorable business mix, was negatively impacted by approximately $18.0 million in one-time costs and write-offs. In the fourth quarter of 1999, operating income was approximately $35.6 million, excluding the previously mentioned restructuring charge, or $22.0 million as reported. Free cash flow for the quarter was $50.8 million, compared to $87.3 million in the 1999 fourth quarter, which also excludes the previously mentioned restructuring charge. For the quarter ended December 31, 2000, the Company had approximately 62.0 million shares outstanding on a weighted average diluted basis, versus 62.5 million in the year ago period, excluding the restructuring charges.

Net sales for the 2000 fourth quarter were down 14 percent to $436.8 million, as compared with $505.6 million in the fourth quarter of 1999. Relative to the fourth quarter 1999, fourth quarter 2000 sales were negatively impacted by approximately $38 million due to a change in the Company's fiscal calendar and by approximately $14 million due to the negative impact of foreign currency translation. Net sales were also negatively impacted by a six percent decline in North American light vehicle production and a three percent decline in European light vehicle production. As a result, sales for the Company's North American Automotive Interior Systems Division decreased approximately 15 percent to $267.1 million, while in Europe, sales declined 21 percent to $65.4 million, as compared to $82.9 million in the fourth quarter of 1999. Sales for the Company's Specialty Automotive Products Division decreased three percent to $104.3 million, versus $107.0 million in the fourth quarter of 1999.

- more –

Year-To-Date Performance Highlights

For the twelve months ended December 31, 2000, the Company earned net income of $4.5 million, or $.07 per diluted share; reflecting a net loss from continuing operations of $1.4 million, or ($0.03) per diluted share, net income from discontinued operations of $6.6 million, or $.11 per diluted share and an extraordinary charge for early debt retirement of $.7 million, or ($.01) per diluted share. For the twelve months ended December 25, 1999, the Company earned net income of $20.1 million, or $.32 per diluted share, excluding 1999 pre-tax restructuring charges of $33.4 million, or ($.34) per diluted share after-tax, and the cumulative after-tax effect of a change in accounting principle of $8.9 million, or ($.14) per diluted share.

Operating income for the full year 2000 was $108.1 million, as compared to twelve month 1999 performance of approximately $131.9 million, excluding the previously mentioned 1999 restructuring charges. Despite the decline in operating income, year-to-date free cash flow of $168.5 million, exceeded 1999's performance of $167.7 million, which excludes the previously mentioned restructuring charges. For the twelve months ended December 31, 2000, weighted average diluted shares outstanding were 62.4 million, unchanged from a year ago, excluding restructuring charges and the cumulative effect of a change in accounting principle.

Year-to-date, consolidated sales for 2000 were relatively flat with the prior year at approximately $1.9 billion. Strong sales during the first half of the year were partially offset by an eight percent sales decline in the second half of the year. Overall, sales for the North American Automotive Interior Systems Division rose two percent to $1.2 billion, while sales for the European Automotive Interior Systems Division decreased seven percent to $284.5 million. Sales for the Specialty Automotive Products Division were $441.7 million versus 440.5 million the prior year, as higher fabric sales offset a 30% decline in Chrysler Sebring convertible volume.

- more -

Nivens continued, "Despite current industry conditions, I believe that Collins & Aikman is better positioned than ever for future growth, and with Heartland's investment, we have another highly supportive capital partner to assist us in this regard. Our acoustic resources and customer offerings have been substantially enhanced through our new global technology structure, the recently announced family of AcT™ acoustically tuned technologies and the completion of our Comet Acoustics acquisition. Additionally, we're aggressively tackling cost cutting throughout the Company and our business backlog remains solid. Telematics and systems integration continue to accelerate, and we view these long-term industry trends as important drivers for our growth. In summary, although we remain cautious in the short-term, the long-term outlook for Collins & Aikman remains quite bright."

Collins & Aikman, with annual sales approaching $2 billion, is the global leader in automotive floor and acoustic systems and is a leading supplier of automotive fabric, interior trim and convertible top systems. The Company's operations span the globe through 72 facilities, 13 countries and approximately 15,000 employees who are committed to achieving total excellence. Collins & Aikman's high-quality products combine industry-leading design and styling capabilities, superior manufacturing capabilities and the industry's most effective NVH "quiet" technologies. Information about Collins & Aikman is available on the Internet at www.collinsaikman.com.

This news release contains forward-looking statements within the meaning of the Private Securities Litigation Reform Act of 1995. Actual results may differ materially from the anticipated results because of certain risks and uncertainties, including but not limited to general economic conditions in the markets in which Collins & Aikman operates, fluctuations in the production of vehicles for which the Company is a supplier, changes in the popularity of particular car models or particular interior trim packages, the loss of programs on particular car models, labor disputes involving the Company or its significant customers, changes in consumer preferences, dependence on significant automotive customers, the level of competition in the automotive supply industry, pricing pressure from automotive customers, the substantial leverage of the Company and its subsidiaries, limitations imposed by the Company's debt facilities, charges made in connection with the integration of operations acquired by the Company, the implementation of the reorganization plan, risks associated with conducting business in foreign countries and other risks detailed from time-to-time in the Company's Securities and Exchange Commission filings including without limitation, in Items 1 and 7 of the Company's Annual Report on Form 10-K for the year-ended December 25, 1999, and Item 1 in the Company's Quarterly Reports on Form 10-Q for the periods ended April 1, 2000, July 1, 2000 and September 30, 2000.

- more -

COLLINS & AIKMAN CORPORATION AND SUBSIDIARIES
CONSOLIDATED BALANCE SHEETS
(In thousands)

ASSETS	(Unaudited) December 31, 2000	December 25, 1999
Current Assets:		
Cash and cash equivalents	$ 20,862	$ 13,980
Accounts and other receivables, net	196,451	233,819
Inventories	131,720	132,625
Other	75,852	84,942
Total current assets	424,885	465,366
Property, plant and equipment, net	434,147	443,526
Deferred tax assets	97,314	86,235
Goodwill, net	245,509	256,362
Other assets	78,435	97,401
	$ 1,280,290	$ 1,348,890
LIABILITIES AND COMMON STOCKHOLDERS' DEFICIT		
Current Liabilities:		
Short-term borrowings	$ 3,835	$ 3,088
Current maturities of long-term debt	84,302	27,992
Accounts payable	178,483	198,466
Accrued expenses	123,109	132,709
Total current liabilities	389,729	362,255
Long-term debt	799,677	884,550
Other, including post-retirement benefit obligation	245,870	253,206
Commitments and contingencies		
Common stock (150,000 shares authorized, 70,521 shares issued and 62,024 shares outstanding at December 31, 2000 and 70,521 shares issued and 61,904 shares outstanding at December 25, 1999)	705	705
Other paid-in capital	585,481	585,484
Accumulated deficit	(636,639)	(641,117)
Accumulated other comprehensive loss	(42,925)	(33,260)
Treasury stock, at cost (8,497 shares at December 31, 2000 and 8,617 shares at December 25, 1999)	(61,608)	(62,933)
Total common stockholders' deficit	(154,986)	(151,121)
	$ 1,280,290	$ 1,348,890

- more -

Can't Regulate This   D. J. Burgundy

COLLINS & AIKMAN CORPORATION AND SUBSIDIARIES
CONSOLIDATED STATEMENTS OF CASH FLOWS
(Unaudited, in thousands)

	Quarter Ended		Twelve Months Ended	
	December 31, 2000 (13 weeks)	December 25, 1999 (13 weeks)	December 31, 2000 (53 weeks)	December 25, 1999 (52 weeks)
OPERATING ACTIVITIES				
Loss from continuing operations	$ (15,878)	$ (2,515)	$ (1,437)	$ (1,365)
Adjustments to derive cash flow from continuing operating activities:				
Impairment of long-lived assets	—	7,768	—	13,361
Deferred income tax expense (benefit)	(10,398)	2,567	(8,545)	(6,800)
Depreciation and amortization	21,744	19,530	76,436	71,474
Decrease in accounts and other receivables	40,412	1,601	78,214	1,826
Decrease in inventories	7,727	22,866	905	20,215
Increase (decrease) in accounts payable	3,722	38,890	(19,983)	28,658
Increase (decrease) in interest payable	(12,812)	(13,645)	3,434	946
Other, net	(1,510)	(11,443)	8,089	(28,455)
Net cash provided by continuing operating activities	33,007	65,619	137,113	99,860
Net cash provided by (used in) discontinued operations	(1,872)	(10,984)	357	(16,770)
INVESTING ACTIVITIES				
Additions to property, plant and equipment	(24,810)	(31,218)	(75,120)	(86,430)
Sales of property, plant and equipment	3,711	173	5,543	10,126
Other, net	—	1,717	—	(1,225)
Net cash used in investing activities	(21,099)	(29,328)	(69,577)	(77,529)
FINANCING ACTIVITIES				
Issuance of long-term debt	—	—	—	100,000
Repayment of long-term debt	(7,298)	(5,272)	(67,343)	(20,607)
Proceeds from (reduction of) participating interests in accounts receivable	—	—	—	2,000
Net borrowings (repayments) on revolving credit facilities	(32,476)	8,100	(34,046)	(35,293)
Increase (decrease) in short-term borrowings	22,806	(27,691)	38,405	(7,405)
Dividends paid	(4,336)	(8,610)	1,581	(50,198)
Reissuance (purchase) of treasury stock, net	—	(505)	392	(2,097)
Other, net	475	(1,736)	—	(1,736)
Net cash used in financing activities	(20,829)	(35,714)	(61,011)	(15,336)
Net increase (decrease) in cash and cash equivalents	(10,793)	(10,407)	6,882	(9,775)
Cash and cash equivalents at beginning of period	31,655	24,387	13,980	23,755
Cash and cash equivalents at end of period	$ 20,862	$ 13,980	$ 20,862	$ 13,980

- more -

Can't Regulate This   D. J. Burgundy

COLLINS & AIKMAN CORPORATION AND SUBSIDIARIES
FOURTH QUARTER 2000 – SUPPLEMENTAL SCHEDULE
(Unaudited – in millions, except CPV)

SALES DATA:

DIVISION:	Quarter Ended December 31, 2000 (13 weeks)	Quarter Ended December 25, 1999 (13 weeks)	Twelve Months Ended December 31, 2000 (53 weeks)	Twelve Months Ended December 25, 1999 (52 weeks)
North American Automotive Interior Systems	$267	$316	$1,176	$1,152
European Automotive Interior Systems	66	83	284	306
Specialty Automotive Products	104	107	442	440
Total	$437	$506	$1,902	$1,898

OPERATING INCOME (LOSS)(a):

DIVISION:	Quarter Ended December 31, 2000 (13 weeks)	Quarter Ended December 25, 1999 (13 weeks)	Year-to-Date December 31, 2000 (53 weeks)	Year-to-Date December 25, 1999 (52 weeks)
North American Automotive Interior Systems	$10	$34	$ 87	$ 89
European Automotive Interior Systems	(8)	(5)	1	2
Specialty Automotive Products	3	7	23	40
Other	(3)	-	(3)	1
Total	$ 2	$36	$108	$132

STATISTICAL DATA:

	Quarter Ended December 31, 2000 (13 weeks)	Quarter Ended December 25, 1999 (13 weeks)	Twelve Months Ended December 31, 2000 (53 weeks)	Twelve Months Ended December 25, 1999 (52 weeks)
EUROPEAN CPV	$13	$16	$ 14	$ 15
N. AMERICAN CPV	$88	$91	$ 89	$ 88
EBITDA (a)	$24	$55	$185	$203
CAPITAL EXPENDITURES	$25	$31	$ 75	$ 86
FREE CASH FLOW (b)	$51	$87	$169	$168

(a) 1999 Excludes restructuring charges.
(b) Free Cash Flow equals EBITDA (excluding restructuring charges) less capital expenditures, plus/minus the operating change in accounts receivable, accounts payable, and inventory.

###

Feb. 21, 2001 C&A Press Release - 4Q & full year 2000
Financial Results - 9 pages

What a work of art on Nivens' and Singh's part, as well

Can't Regulate This D. J. Burgundy

as their complicit staff. This just goes to show that men and women of this stature can make any set of numbers sing a tune that serves their purpose. Quite frankly, I wasn't quite sure if this was Washington, D.C., or Troy, Michigan!

Then, the conclusion of the deal and the announcement of its details:

Collins & Aikman — News Release

FOR IMMEDIATE RELEASE
February 26, 2001

CONTACTS:
Analysts: Lauren Collins
(248) 824-XXXX
lauren.collins@colaik.com

Media: Tasha Robinson
(248) 824-XXXX
tasha.robinson@colaik.com

COLLINS & AIKMAN ANNOUNCES CLOSING DETAILS OF HEARTLAND INVESTMENT

TROY, Mich – Collins & Aikman Corporation (NYSE: CKC) announced today that it has completed the sale of 25 million shares of its common stock to Heartland Industrial Partners, L.P. (Heartland). The company also announced that its former controlling shareholders, Blackstone Capital Partners, L.P. (Blackstone) and Wasserstein Perella Capital Partners L.P. (Wasserstein) completed the sale of 27 million shares of common stock to Heartland. As a result of this transaction, Heartland will own approximately 60 percent of the outstanding shares and Collins & Aikman has obtained an equity infusion of $125 million before transaction fees and expenses. These funds will initially be used to pay down the Company's revolving credit facility and in the long term, will be used to fund corporate growth initiatives.

Commenting on the transaction, Thomas Nivens, Collins & Aikman's Chairman and Chief Executive Officer, stated, "As we previously indicated, having Heartland as part of our team is a "win-win-win" for Collins & Aikman, our customers and our investors. We're very pleased to have this transaction completed, and I'm confident that it should be a significant enabler for Collins & Aikman to further strengthen its product offerings and market positions."

Other Transaction Highlights Include:

- 16,510,000 of the 25 million common shares sold by the Company to Heartland were in the form of a non-voting convertible preferred stock, which will be convertible into common stock upon shareholder approval at the Company's March 6th special meeting of shareholders.
- Due to the change in control resulting from the transaction, Collins & Aikman's existing bank debt facilities have been renegotiated which has resulted in substantial flexibility in existing bank debt covenants.
- The Company has established a new $50 million term loan (tranche D) at an effective interest rate of LIBOR plus 4-1/4 percent, which will be used to retire the Company's 11-1/8 percent JPS senior notes, due June, 2001.
- As the Company's former controlling shareholders – Blackstone and Wasserstein – have agreed to vote in favor of the shareholder proposals, a favorable shareholder vote is assured at the Company's March 6th special meeting of shareholders.

- more -

Following the Company's special shareholder meeting, the Company's Board of Directors will expand to 13 members, composed as follows: Thomas Nivens, Chairman and CEO – one seat, Heartland – seven seats, Blackstone – one seat, Wasserstein – one seat, and independent directors – three seats.

Commenting on the transaction, David Stockman, founder of Heartland Industrial Partners, L.P. stated, "With this transaction now finalized, we look forward to helping Collins & Aikman realize its long-term growth potential. On behalf of Heartland, I'd like to thank the Company's bank group and bondholders, Blackstone, Wasserstein and the entire Collins & Aikman management team for their very strong support."

Collins & Aikman, with annual sales approaching $2 billion, is the global leader in automotive floor and acoustic systems and is a leading supplier of automotive fabric, interior trim and convertible top systems. The Company's operations span the globe through 72 facilities, 13 countries and nearly 15,000 employees who are committed to achieving total excellence. Collins & Aikman's high-quality products combine industry-leading design and styling capabilities, superior manufacturing capabilities and the industry's most effective NVH "quiet" technologies. Information about Collins & Aikman is available on the Internet at www.collinsaikman.com.

Heartland Industrial Partners, L.P. is a private equity firm established to "invest in, build and grow" industrial companies in sectors ripe for consolidation and long-term growth. The firm has equity commitments in excess of $1.1 billion and intends to increase its commitments to $2 billion. Heartland was founded by David A. Stockman, a former partner of the Blackstone Group and a Reagan administrative cabinet officer; Lewis D. Spinetta, , the former President and Chief Operating Officer of Penske Corporation; and Trey Steinem, a former Managing Director of Chase Securities.

This news release contains forward-looking statements within the meaning of the Private Securities Litigation Reform Act of 1995. Actual results may differ materially from the anticipated results because of certain risks and uncertainties, including but not limited to general economic conditions in the markets in which Collins & Aikman operates, fluctuations in the production of vehicles for which the Company is a supplier, labor disputes involving the Company or its significant customers, changes in consumer preferences, dependence on significant automotive customers, the level of competition in the automotive supply industry, pricing pressure from automotive customers, the substantial leverage of the Company and its subsidiaries, limitations imposed by the Company's debt facilities, charges made in connection with the integration of operations acquired by the Company, the implementation of the reorganization plan, changes in the popularity of particular car models or particular interior trim packages, the loss of programs on particular car models, risks associated with conducting business in foreign countries and other risks detailed from time to time in the Company's Securities and Exchange Commission filings including without limitation, in Items 1 and 7 of the Company's Annual Report on Form 10-K for the year-ended December 25, 1999, and Item 1 in the Company's Quarterly Report on Form 10-Q for the periods ended April 1, 2000, July 1, 2000 and September 30, 2000.

###

Feb. 26, 2001 C&A Press Release - "C&A Announces Closing Details of Heartland Investment" - 2 pages

I absolutely could not believe it! Former Director of the United States Office of Management and Budget,

David Stockman, did this deal for the initial price and without any adjustment to the purchase price based on the significantly eroded earnings!

In between the earnings release and the deal announcement, the Evan's "Organizational Realignment" announcement was made. Frank Brydon, obviously not with the company any longer, apparently was the only deletion with the business unit heads reporting directly to Nivens. The timing of this almost seemed conditional on the results and the conclusion of the deal. The typical thing for Singh to do at this point was to follow with a similar "Finance Organization Reporting Structure," which he did within a short time. You can guess that it was patterned nearly identical to the Nivens' announcement. I followed with a note to Bill Waldon, as I was completely nonexistent on the organization chart.

Can't Regulate This					D. J. Burgundy

Lots of Boxes, Titles and Names- None of Which Was Mine!

Collins & Aikman *Internal Correspondence*

DATE: March 5, 2001

TO: All Global Employees

CC: Tom Nivens, Greg Grinnell

FROM: Dinesh Singh

SUBJECT: **Finance Staff Reporting Structure**

Per Tom Nivens February 28th organization realignment announcement, the senior division financial executives will have a dual reporting responsibility to the Office of the CFO and their respective manufacturing operations leader. Each Vice President of Finance will report either to Ken Affinhoffer, or me (see attached organization chart). The business unit controller will continue to report to their respective Vice President of Finance and each plant controller will report to their respective business unit controller.

The new reporting relationship is crucial to properly defining and aligning the priorities and roles and responsibilities of finance personnel throughout Collins & Aikman.
The reporting structure will enhance the level of service that the finance organization provides to operating management and will facilitate the execution of Collins & Aikman's vision of reducing transactional processing costs. Additionally, this change will redirect the flow of work toward more consistent and valuable types of analysis which will assist in achievement of the Company's operational and financial objectives.

Under the new reporting relationship, the CFO and his designates will provide functional guidance in all aspects of accounting and finance including the following:

1. Interpretation and application of the Company's financial accounting policies and procedures.
2. Efficient transaction processing and simplification.
3. Business reporting and analysis.
4. Budgeting and forecasting.
5. Strategic planning support.
6. Treasury and cash management.
7. Tax compliance and management.
8. Internal control objectives and activities.
9. Development of cost standards.

All personnel actions relating to hiring, transferring, promotions, etc. at the plant controller level and above should receive joint approval of the CFO and their respective COO. I look forward to the opportunity to work closely with each of you to enhance the overall teamwork environment that Collins & Aikman values.

If you have any questions about the new structure, please feel free to call Ken or myself.

Sincerely,

Dinesh Singh

Can't Regulate This — D. J. Burgundy

Collins & Aikman Corporation Finance

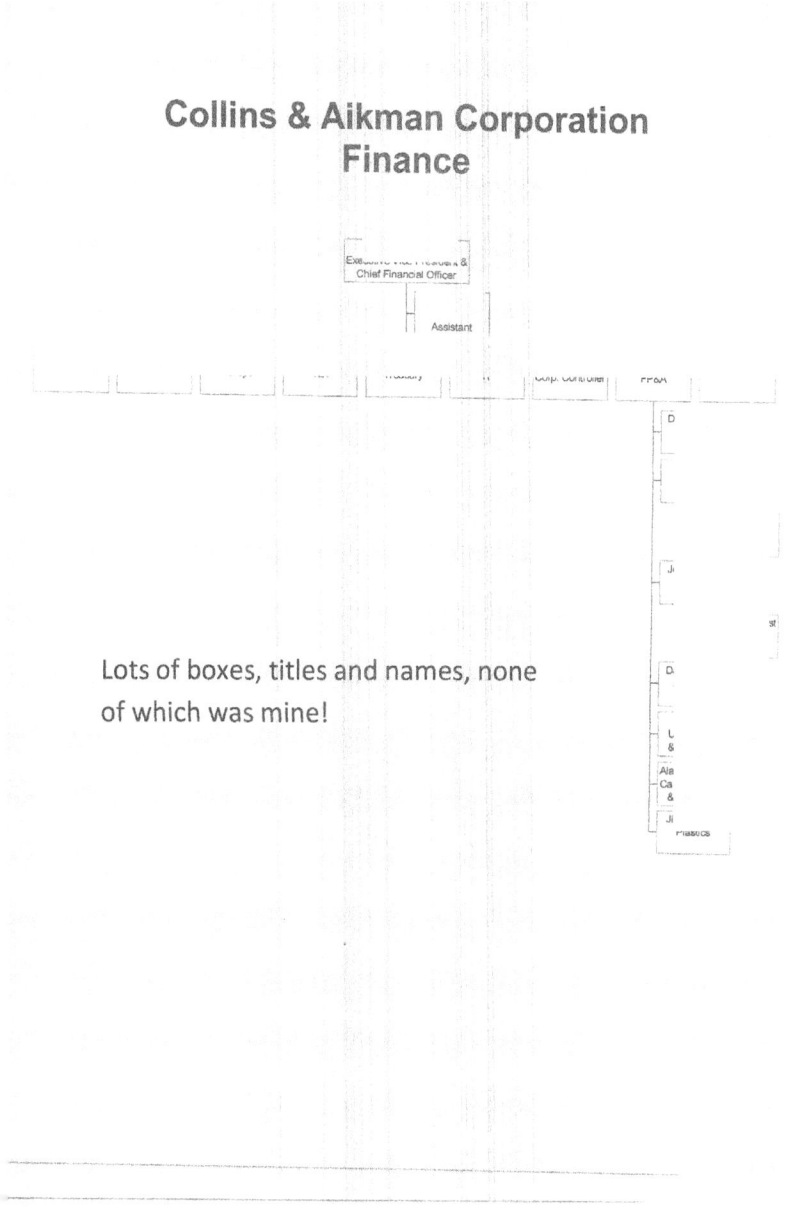

Lots of boxes, titles and names, none of which was mine!

March 5, 2001 Singh announces new finance org structure with org chart - 2 pages

After the sizable financial adjustment to the fourth quarter financials, the audit committee of Collins & Aikman requested of Arthur Anderson that a "forensic audit" be performed of the year 2000 results. This whole thing was so damn incestuous with cross fertilized motivations that because this deal had to be done, you couldn't tell who was on which end of the transaction; therefore, how would it be possible to hold anyone or any party responsible for the chain of events that led up to the major correction? Certainly, each person was going to have their own story and that story was likely that they had no idea of what was going on and at the end of the day, the proper numbers were recorded; so long as it could be spun that they were not directing otherwise, they likely would come out "safe."

The forensic audit was very interesting. It consisted of Arthur Andersen conducting closed door meetings with a broad range of pertinent individuals: Nivens, Singh, all of Singh's finance staff, my finance staff, some of the operational leaders whose business results were affected by the adjustments and of course, me. I would do nothing without Bill Waldon by my side, so he arrived, and I greeted him in my office shortly before we were summoned to the inquisition.

As we were summoned, we calmly walked upstairs and found the conference room where the Arthur Andersen team assembled. Bill and I sat at the table. We were requested to state who we were and the position we held. I explained who I was, as did Bill. Silence. Bill then asked for everyone to introduce himself or herself; after all, there were about six to eight individuals in the room with two Polycom conference call devices sitting on the table. They started with the attendees in the room. While

I cannot recall exact names, I am going to use fictitious placeholders to demonstrate the relevance of the attendees. Bill Tomkins, Arthur Andersen ("AA") Detroit; Susan Smith, AA Detroit; William Williams, AA Chicago; Tom Andrews, AA Cleveland; and John Jenkins, AA Cleveland. "And who's on the phone?" Bill asked. Andrew Johns, AA New York; Charles Chumming, AA New York; Carl Cannes, AA Toronto; and Randolf Dalter, AA Toronto. Bill proceeded to ask if there were "any other non-Arthur Andersen oversight in the meeting." The answer was "no." One would think that someone other than the company's auditor, who is normally paid to express an opinion on the financial statements—from the same audit firm who had no knowledge of the major errors contained in the financial statements of a business that was in the midst of a change of ownership where several hundreds of millions of dollars were involved—would not be the only one in the room. Now their work was suspect as well as the company's. This certainly was the proverbial case of "the fox watching the hen house." A better approach would have been to have peer audit firms perform this forensic review; however, the cards were stacked a certain way to achieve the certain desired result.

As we proceeded into the questions, it was obvious that they were engineered to produce a desired result. The questions were very vanilla:

"Do you recognize these financial statements to be those for the business which you are responsible, the North American Automotive Interior Systems Group?"

"Do they contain any material misstatements?"

I wanted to climb all over this situation, but Bill kept me in check. There were absolutely no questions that were relevant to the intent of the senior two executives of C&A or their willful direction to restrict the proper recognition of the financial affairs of the company. What a sham!

The next few days were especially difficult for me. The company wanted me gone. It was as if I was in head to head combat with Grinnell, the HR vice president and Banks, the managerial sidekick. Their mission was to treat me as the special projects vice president, which I refused. My conscience told me that I should ask to meet with Singh to see if there actually was such a job of substance. After repeated attempts, and Singh's repeated cancellation of said meetings, I concluded that there really wasn't a job. I shared this with the HR duo. They then advised me that I would be subject to receiving a severance of six months compensation, since I refused to take the role.

I told them that I should be treated fairly and that is all I wanted. I advised them that since Frank Brydon received two-years of severance pay, I should, too, since we were both subject to the same circumstances. The discussions turned very heated and Banks, who had a hand in my hiring, was red-faced and sweating. I wasn't about to let them push me around. As a result of this undeserving treatment, Bill and I authored a letter to Singh that described just how unfairly I had been treated during the course of events.

Can't Regulate This   D. J. Burgundy

March 12, 2001

Dinesh Singh,
Executive Vice-President and CFO
Collins & Aikman Corporation
5755 New King Court
Troy, Michigan 48098

Dear Mr. Singh,

This letter is in response to recent events at Collins & Aikman and meetings I have had with either you or Greg Grinnell or both.

In January, I refused to sign a letter to our auditors stating that the financial records of the company were "clean," when you, Tom E Nivens, Frank Brydon myself and others knew there were a number of large liabilities amounting to many millions of dollars which had not been posted. Only after my meetings with you and others were these liabilities properly placed on the books on January 25. My letter to you of January 31 sets forth many of those facts in greater detail.

Regrettably, since that time, you and the company have breached my employment agreement, defamed me, and retaliated against me in violation of the law. These events to which I am alluding include the following:

- About February 1, the company tried to intimidate, Penny Fillergrin my administrative assistant, into an unfounded and fabricated sexual harassment claim against me. After leaving the meeting (very upset I understand), she later delivered a signed letter to Greg Grinnell in Human Resources stating that the company's allegations were not true. I have since learned that this unfounded charge has been repeated to at least one person outside the company. The attempt to pressure Ms. Fillergrin in this fashion could only be motivated by the hope of developing a pretext to fire me in retaliation for the issues I have raised, and the spreading of this false rumor constitutes defamation of my character.

- On February 26 and February 27 two very important company strategy meetings were held.

Dinesh Singh,

Executive Vice-President and CFO
Collins & Aikman Corporation
March 12, 2001
Page 2

I was not invited to either. I understand the purpose of these meetings was to commence the relationship with Heartland Industrial Partners as majority owners of the company and to announce a "realignment" of the organization. The only apparent "realignment" consists of the removal of Frank Brydon, President of North America Automotive Interior Systems and Fabrics (NAAIS) and myself as Vice President of Finance NAAIS. Not coincidentally, we are the individuals responsible for telling the truth about the company's finances.

- On February 28, you and Greg Grinnell advised me that my position as Vice President of Finance NAAIS "no longer existed." You advised me that I would have responsibility for "special projects" (a "responsibility" similar to that given to Frank Brydon, a few days earlier), and my new title was Vice President for Special Projects. This position had not previously existed, had no defined duties and you could not tell how long it would last. You both advised me that I should begin to look for a new job. This "special projects" title not only breaches my contract, but also seriously damages my future employment prospects, since the change in duties will imply to any future employer that I had not performed my duties properly, and the title is essentially a clear code word indicating that I am being put out to pasture.

- On March 2, you published a company memorandum announcing a new "Finance Staff Reporting Structure." My name is completely absent from that memorandum and organizational chart. As you know, my employment agreement states that I am the Vice President of Finance NAAIS.

- On March 5, I was following up on the one and only "special project" that was assigned to me (regarding Mexican Industries). I was advised by the company's lawyer, Ron Howell that the project was being taken away from me, I was no longer authorized to work on this project and that you were handling it.

In addition, the company has continued to take action to hide the true nature of the liabilities at issue and to deflect responsibility for the problems which have arisen. Specifically:

- The company announced earnings for the 4th quarter and year-end that were approximately $18 million less than the January 12 guidance provided to the public. In the announcements regarding the 4th quarter and year-end, both Mr. Nivens and you advised the public that all or most of the $18 million short fall was a result of one-time adjustments and write-offs and that

-190-

Dinesh Singh,
Executive Vice-President and CFO
Collins & Aikman Corporation
March 12, 2001
Page 3

---

the profitability run rate of the business was unaffected by the contents of the fourth quarter short-fall. This was not true.

- The company hired its own auditors, Arthur Anderson, to perform a superficial investigation into the contents of my letter. I understand that Arthur Anderson concluded that while the failure to book the liabilities that I insisted be booked was improper, "upper management" had not instructed that these liabilities be kept off the books. The conclusion was obviously predetermined and an effort to cover up these improprieties. Arthur Anderson clearly had a conflict of interest and was not independent, but rather wanted to protect its account with the company worth many hundreds of thousands of dollars a year. The conclusion is also absurd in light of the organizational structure of the company, the statements of myself and Fran Brydon regarding instructions from you and Tom Nivens and the memo of Stuart Blumenthal from last February.

Mr. Singh, I insisted on telling the truth to the public and our shareholders about the company's finances, as required by law. Because I followed my legal duty and did the right thing, you and Collins & Aikman have breached my agreement with the company, retaliated against me and defamed me. I insist that I be restored to the position of Vice President of Finance for NAAIS with full responsibilities (with the appropriate announcement made to the company's employees) and that the company retract the defamatory statements about me. In the absence of a satisfactory resolution of the matter, within three days, I will have no alternative but to first bring this to the attention of our new owner, Heartland, and if no resolution is reached, then to take legal action against the company to right these wrongs.

Very truly yours,

David J. Burgundy

March 12, 2001 Burgundy letter to Singh - hard stand - 3 pages

Well, that started the volley. Apparently, with this letter, Bill and I were beginning to get some attention. On the fourth day, this came from Grinnell, the HR vice president:

Collins & Aikman

Internal Correspondence

DATE: March 16, 2001
TO: Dave Burgundy
FROM: Greg Grinnell

In an attempt to respond to your letter (see attached) of March 12, 2001, I need to <u>once again</u> inform you that the company's position remains that you have the opportunity to be fully employed as the Corporate Vice President of "Special Projects". As you are aware, the company is moving rapidly towards several major acquisitions which are expected to result in significant integration and "special project" activities. It is unfortunate that you are presently rejecting the "special projects" opportunity that we have provided (at your normal full pay, bonus and benefits level) following the company's restructuring of the NAAIS organizational structure.

If this arrangement is not acceptable to you, we stand ready to work actively and constructively with you to leave the company and pursue another career direction beyond Collins & Aikman. However, <u>also unfortunately,</u> you have chosen to write a totally unfounded letter setting forth serious false allegations against the company and its management.

- With respect to your allegations regarding the company's earnings announcement, your letter of January 29, 2001 and the investigation conducted by Arthur Andersen, the company is confident that the financial information it has reported is accurate and that the investigation was properly conducted.

- The Company did nothing to instigate a sexual harassment claim against you. Instead, the company took the appropriate steps, in accordance with company policy, to investigate a complaint which was brought to the attention of the Vice President of Human Resources.

- You are currently an at-will employee of the company and there is no employment agreement between you and the company guaranteeing you any particular job for any period of time.

- The company made a business decision to eliminate an unnecessary level of management. Effective February 27th, it was determined that

NAAIS Operations and Sales & Marketing functions would report directly to Tor Nivens and that the NAAIS Division Controllers and CFO function would report to Dinesh Singh. The changes were made to increase efficiency and to allow all units to improve their focus on meeting Company performance objectives and future business growth.

Your letter and false accusations have been accompanied by your repeated unreasonable demands for excessive (well beyond any reasonable levels) severance package benefits in exchange for dropping your threatened claims. The Company will not be pressured to accept your demands for extraordinary payments based on unsupported allegations and threats of litigation.

By Monday, March 19, 2001, I need to know your decision relative to either your diligently going to work as the Vice President of "Special Projects" or accepting a reasonable severance package and related outplacement program. I am available today and throughout the weekend (home phone # - (704)-(xxx-xxxx cell phone # (704 xxx-xxxx to discuss this matter with you. Hopefully, we can find a way to satisfy both the best outcome for yourself, your career going forward and the company.

Regards,

Greg Grinnell

C: Ron Howell
Tom Nivens
Outside Legal Counsel

March 16, 2001 HR rebuttal to Burgundy - 2 pages

As I was experiencing such fun, my newest and best friend, Bill Waldon, kept sending me Wall Street Journal articles of similar situations. Every outcome for each of the victims was unfavorable due to their poor and improper planning of next steps.

The thugs from HR weren't through with me. As they were attempting to impose only six months' severance on me, I knew that this was worth more. Also, in a normal situation, pursuing and securing a position such as the one I was leaving takes at least one to two years.

This treatment lasted for about ten more days with red faces and heated arguments. Finally, we met in the middle and agreed on one year of severance and benefits. It was done, FINALLY!

I am proud to say that on my watch, the company did the right thing. I could sit across the dinner table from my family and tell my loved ones to do the right thing and it would actually mean something! Thanks to Bill Waldon (and my backbone, as well as the spirit my Mom placed in me), I could do this and hold my head up.

Thank Bill. Thank God.

After signing the severance agreement and tendering my resignation on March 23, 2001, I immediately went to work for Gene Wyler and R. J. Bamraulia. R. J. was about to acquire a major operation from General Motors that needed a bunch of tender loving care and I got the nod to be the EVP and CFO.

After I left the company, C&A and the cast of characters continued to make the news. One article of particular interest came in spring of 2003 from the Detroit Free Press which was titled "Collins & Aikman changes auditor." Well, if this wasn't a sign! It is a pattern for companies doing financial misdeeds to change auditors to keep them off balance.

The article stated that the company dismissed PricewaterhouseCoopers LLP, the highly credible auditor that I brought with me to C&A, in favor of the cheaper KPMG LLP. Could the real story be, as the article highlights, that, "In its 2002 audit, PricewaterhouseCoopers reported conditions related to timely cash account reconciliations, nonstandard journal entries, revenue accounting and currency translation at foreign locations, and compliance with accounting policies and procedures, according to the filing. Collins & Aikman said it plans to correct all the conditions during 2003"?

Well, I have taken you through that which I endured over the course of my 1-3/4 years at C&A. Just as I did throughout my years of making my mark in my career at Masco's automotive forgings business, I led a large-scale business to create intrinsic value via improving operations, negotiating good deals on both the supply and sales sides of the business, driving the team to work hard while mentoring them on the "how to" aspects of transforming a business to excellence and treating all with mutual respect. I upgraded the finance function in a manner such that it became a respected entity at C&A. I corrected systems, implemented new ones, corrected accounting methods and enforced that the company will play its game "inside the white lines." After my departure, the company's leadership returned to its illicit behavior of concealing the financial truth of the company. Ford was a major customer of C&A. A day came in 2005 whereby certain economic and Ford specific conditions led to a rating agency downgrade of Ford's securities. A downgrade of Ford indicates more risk on those doing business with Ford. Already struggling to service its already gargantuan debt, C&A's strong dependency on Ford caused an increase in C&A's financing cost (interest), due to the downgrade of Ford, to the point where C&A could no longer meet its debt obligations. You can't argue with cash: you've either got it, or you don't. C&A didn't. This took all of the ambiguity out of the gamesmanship the (then) leadership of C&A injected into its financial statements. As you have read, C&A entered bankruptcy in 2005. Only then did the lies stop.

Indictments were handed out a few years later. Among those named in federal court documents were Stockman, of course, Galante and Gerald Jones. Gerald Jones was a colleague in charge of the Fabric's division who I mentored into doing the right thing in the 2000–2001 timeframe. My name was not on that list.

Footnote Explanations

(7) Remember Arthur Andersen? They were Enron's auditor. That obviously didn't go so well for them, but this was pre-Enron, pre-Tyco and long before anything like Sarbanes-Oxley.

(8) Prior to Heartland acquiring MascoTech, MascoTech was a large-scale, publicly-traded metalworking company, possessing a wide ranging product portfolio and vast technology in the cold, warm and hot forging and extrusion segment of the automotive supply industry.

(9) As cited in "The King of Capital," the story of Blackstone and Steven Schwarzman's continuing and overwhelming success in private equity, Collins and Aikman was a subsidiary of Wickes, a conglomerate that Blackstone purchased.

(10) It is typical in the automotive industry for companies to shut down operations from Christmas Eve through New Year's Day and for five to ten days with the celebrated Independence Day holiday, depending upon customer demand.

(11) In the 1990s and well into the first decade of the 21st century, it was quite in vogue in the automotive industry for the OEMs to procure value in terms of parts/products from minority-owned enterprises. This gave the OEMs government status and clout, not to mention the appearance of wanting to do the right thing for minorities in society. Often what would happen is that the OEM would make introductions of individuals who were of a minority status to mega suppliers and ask the supplier to work with the minority in such a manner so that they can provide a value to the OEM. This would most likely be

in the realm of assembly of modules that would later be sequenced in order of car production, this due to the fact that most assembly processes are less complicated and capital intensive. This would allow the supplier to share some of the positive accolades. The OEMs would also measure and monitor the amount of dollar content that would flow through minority enterprises. This turned out to be a convenient way to claim minority credit because what it amounted to was the supplier selling their products to the minority enterprise who would add little value and then turn to sell it to the OEM who would claim the whole value as minority content—kind of a sham, so to speak. This was the most significant C&A minority relationship and it had high visibility given the level of content and the car that this instrument panel was to be installed into.

Can't Regulate This	D. J. Burgundy

Old habits die hard.

U.S. SECURITIES AND EXCHANGE COMMISSION issues *Accounting and Auditing Enforcement Release No. 2581, March 26, 2007. (filing civil suit against perpetrators).*

U.S. SECURITIES AND EXCHANGE COMMISSION

Litigation Release No. 20055 / March 26, 2007

Accounting and Auditing Enforcement Release No. 2581 / March 26, 2007

Securities and Exchange Commission v. Collins & Aikman Corporation, David A. Stockman, J. Michael Stepp, Gerald E. Jones, David R. Cosgrove, John G. Galante, Elkin B. McCallum, Paul C. Barnaba, Christopher M. Williams and Thomas V. Gougherty, United States District Court for the Southern District of New York, SEC v. Collins & Aikman Corporation, et al. Civil Action No. 1:07-CV-2419(LAP) (S.D.N.Y. March 26, 2007)

Washington, D.C., March 26, 2007 - The Securities and Exchange Commission today filed civil fraud charges against auto parts manufacturer Collins & Aikman Corporation ("C&A"), David A. Stockman ("Stockman"), who served as C&A's former Chief Executive Officer and Chairman of the Board of Directors, and eight other former C&A directors and officers.

The SEC's complaint alleges that between 2001 and 2005, Stockman personally directed fraudulent schemes to inflate C&A's reported income by accounting improperly for supplier payments. In furtherance of those schemes, the complaint alleges that Stockman and other defendants obtained false documents from suppliers designed to mislead C&A's external auditors. According to the complaint, when aspects of the schemes were discovered in March 2005, Stockman embarked on a public campaign to mislead investors, potential financiers and others by minimizing the extent of the fraudulent accounting and hiding C&A's dire financial condition. During the time Stockman was engaged in this fraudulent conduct, he was collecting millions of dollars of the management fees C&A paid Stockman's private equity fund, Heartland Industrial Partners. The other former officers, including the Chief Financial Officer, Corporate Controller, and Treasurer, and a former member of C&A's Board of Directors, are alleged to have participated in the accounting schemes or the campaign to mislead investors. The SEC and C&A have agreed to settle the charges against the company.

In addition to Stockman, the other former C&A directors and officers charged in the complaint are:

1. J. Michael Stepp, the former Chief Financial Officer of C&A and Vice-Chairman of its Board of Directors;
2. Elkin B. McCallum ("McCallum"), a former member of C&A's Board of Directors;
3. David R. Cosgrove, the former Corporate Controller of C&A;
4. John G. Galante, the former Treasurer of C&A;
5. Christopher M. Williams, the former Executive Vice President of C&A's Business Development Group;
6. Gerald E. Jones, the former Chief Operating Officer and Executive Vice President of C&A's Fabrics Division.
7. Paul C. Barnaba, the former Vice President and Director of Purchasing for C&A's Plastics Division; and
8. Thomas V. Gougherty, the former Controller of C&A's Plastics Division.

The Commission's complaint alleges that between late 2001 and early 2005, the defendants engaged in multiple fraudulent schemes and made materially false and misleading statements concerning C&A's financial condition and operating results in, among other things, filings with the Commission, offering documents, and press releases. The allegations include the following.

- Between the fourth quarter of 2001 and the first quarter of 2003, Stockman and other defendants negotiated a series of "round-trip transactions" with McCallum. These transactions were structured to give the appearance that C&A was receiving rebates that would increase C&A's income from a company McCallum owned. In fact, because C&A repaid McCallum or his companies for each purported rebate, the transactions should have had no impact on C&A's income statement, and C&A's use of these transactions to inflate its income was improper.

- From at least as early as the second quarter of 2002 until the scheme was discovered in early 2005, C&A accounted improperly for actual rebates it received from its suppliers. Some of these rebates were recognized in income prematurely, while others should never have been recognized in income at all. At the direction of Stockman and other defendants, C&A's Purchasing Department solicited and received false confirmation letters from suppliers that purported to justify the immediate recognition of rebates in income, and were intended to mislead C&A's outside auditors if they questioned these transactions.

- Between the round-trip transactions and the improper accounting for rebates, C&A fraudulently and materially increased its reported income by over $49 million. As a result, C&A overstated its reported pre-tax operating income (or reduced its loss) by ten percent or more in eight different quarters.

- In March 2005 questions from its outside auditor forced C&A to publicly acknowledge the improper accounting for supplier rebates. However, Stockman, in concert with other defendants, engaged in a campaign to reassure investors, analysts and others that C&A was still economically viable, when in fact the company was on the verge of bankruptcy. In press releases, an earnings call and a presentation to potential bond investors, Stockman, and other defendants, concealed C&A's liquidity crisis and made unreasonable financial projections. As a result of these false and misleading statements, C&A obtained additional financing. But when a more accurate picture of C&A's financial condition emerged a month later, C&A was forced to declare bankruptcy.

C&A simultaneously settled the charges, without admitting or denying the Commission's allegations, by consenting to the entry of a final judgment permanently enjoining it from violating Section 17(a) of the Securities Act of 1933 ("Securities Act") and Sections 10(b), 13(a), 13(b)(2)(A) and 13(b)(2)(B) of the Securities Act of 1934 ("Exchange Act") and Exchange Act Rules 10b-5, 12b-20, 13a-1, 13a-11 and 13a-13 thereunder. The settlement is subject to the approval of the United States District Court for the Southern District of New York.

The Commission's complaint alleges that the individual defendants violated and/or aided and abetted C&A's violations of the federal securities laws as follows:

- Stockman and Stepp violated Section 17(a) of the Securities Act; Sections 10(b) and 13(b)(5) of the Exchange Act and Exchange Act Rules 10b 5, 13a-14, 13b2-1, and 13b2-2 thereunder, and aided and abetted C&A's violations of Sections 13(a), 13(b)(2)(A), and 13(b)(2)(B) of the Exchange Act and Exchange Act Rules 12b 20, 13a-1, 13a-11, 13a-13 thereunder;

- McCallum and Galante violated Sections 10(b) and 13(b)(5) of the Exchange Act and Exchange Act Rules 10b 5, 13b2-1, and 13b2-2 thereunder, and aided and abetted C&A's violations of Sections 13(a), 13(b)(2)(A), and 13(b)(2)(B) of the Exchange Act and Exchange Act Rules 12b 20, 13a-1, 13a-11, 13a-13 thereunder;

- Cosgrove violated Section 17(a) of the Securities Act; Sections 10(b) and 13(b)(5) of the Exchange Act and Exchange Act Rules 10b 5, 13b2-1, and 13b2-2 thereunder, and aided and abetted C&A's violations of Sections 13(a), 13(b)(2)(A), and 13(b)(2)(B) of the Exchange Act and Exchange Act Rules 12b 20, 13a-1, 13a-11, 13a-13 thereunder;

- Williams violated Sections 10(b) and 13(b)(5) of the Exchange Act and Exchange Act Rules 10b 5 and 13b2-1 thereunder, and aided and abetted C&A's violations of Sections 10(b), 13(a), 13(b)(2)(A), and 13(b)(2)(B) of the Exchange Act and Exchange Act Rules 10b-5, 12b 20 and 13a-11 thereunder;

- Jones, Barnaba and Gougherty violated Sections 10(b) and 13(b)(5) of the Exchange Act and Exchange Act Rules 10b 5, 13b2-1, and 13b2-2 thereunder, and aided and abetted C&A's violations of Sections 10(b), 13(a), 13(b)(2)(A), and 13(b)(2)(B) of the Exchange Act and Exchange Act Rules 10b-5,12b 20, 13a-1, 13a-11, 13a-13 thereunder;

As to all of the individual defendants, the complaint seeks permanent injunctions against future violations of these provisions, officer-and-director bars, disgorgement of ill-gotten gains, with prejudgment interest, and civil penalties.

Today the U.S Attorney's Office for the Southern District announced parallel indictments against Stockman and others. The Commission acknowledges the assistance and cooperation in this investigation of the U.S. Attorney's Office for the Southern District of New York and the U.S. Postal Inspection Service.

The Commission's investigation is continuing.

> SEC Complaint in this matter

http://www.sec.gov/litigation/litreleases/2007/lr20055.htm

Home | Previous Page   Modified: 03/26/2007

Sent from my iPad

March 26, 2006 US SEC issues Acctg and Audit Enforcement (suit against C&A perpetrators) - 3 pages

Following the now public violations sited in the SEC documents, Crain's Detroit Business published on April 20, 2010, "Ex- Collins & Aikman CEO David

Stockman to pay $7.2 million to settle SEC lawsuit." As noted in the above SEC documents, the U.S. Securities and Exchange Commission lawsuit claims that he misled investors while running now-defunct Southfield-based automotive components maker Collins & Aikman Corp. While Stockman neither admitted nor denied liability in the settlement, his $7.2 million payment will be partly offset by $4.4 million that Stockman previously paid to settle investor lawsuits. This settlement ended a case that began where Stockman and four other ex- Collins & Aikman executives were indicted for intentionally defrauding investors. Later, the indictments were dismissed by Federal prosecutors and the SEC dropped its claim that Stockman knowingly misled investors.

"The criminal indictment has been dropped, the knowing fraud claims have been dropped," Andrew Weissman, Stockman's lawyer said in an April 20, 2010 interview with Crain's. "What is left is an effort by Mr. Stockman to get on with his life," Weisman continued.

The $7.2 million included a $400,000 civil penalty; the remainder was disgorgement and interest. The Crain's article continued, "The SEC alleged in its lawsuit that Stockman, the company and others inflated earnings between the fourth quarter of 2001 and early 2005." [WHEN I LEFT THE COMPANY IN MARCH 2001, THE COMPANY REPORTED THE TRUE AND CORRECT NUMBERS FOR YEAR 2000, AS WELL, AND UP UNTIL I LOST MY POWER AND AUTHORITY OVER THE COMPANY'S REPORTING EARLY IN THE FIRST QUARTER OF 2001]

Can't Regulate This					D. J. Burgundy

CRAIN'S DETROIT BUSINESS
Detroit and Southeast Michigan's premier business news and information website

April 20, 2010 10:37 AM

Ex- Collins & Aikman CEO David Stockman to pay $7.2 million to settle SEC lawsuit

By Bloomberg

David Stockman, a former budget director in the Reagan administration, will pay $7.2 million to settle a **U.S. Securities and Exchange Commission** lawsuit claiming he misled investors while running now-defunct Southfield-based auto-parts maker **Collins & Aikman Corp.**
Stockman, who was chief executive officer of the company, neither admitted nor denied liability in the settlement, which was made public today in a filing in Manhattan federal court.
The $7.2 million payment will be partly offset by $4.4 million that Stockman previously paid to settle investor lawsuits. The settlement of the SEC's allegations against Stockman and four other ex-Collins & Aikman executives ends a case that began with a criminal indictment claiming the defendants intentionally defrauded investors. Federal prosecutors later dismissed the indictment, and the SEC has dropped its claim that Stockman knowingly misled investors. The settlement involves lesser claims.
"The criminal indictment has been dropped, the knowing fraud claims have been dropped," Stockman's lawyer, Andrew Weissman, said in an interview today. "What is left is an effort by Mr. Stockman to get on with his life."
The $7.2 million payment is made up of $6.8 million in disgorgement and interest, and a $400,000 civil penalty.
The SEC alleged in its lawsuit that Stockman, the company and others inflated earnings between the fourth quarter of 2001 and early 2005. Collins & Aikman said in March 2007 that it settled the SEC claims by agreeing not to violate securities laws. The company paid no fine and admitted no wrongdoing.
Collins & Aikman shut down in October 2007 as part of its Chapter 11 bankruptcy liquidation. Stockman served as Reagan's director of the **Office of Management and Budget** from 1981 to 1985.

Apr. 20, 2010 Crain's Detroit Article - David Stockman settles SEC lawsuit for $7.2 million - 1 page

Collins & Aikman operations shut down in October, 2007, and are no longer under Collins & Aikman control as part of its Chapter 11 bankruptcy liquidation.

One has to wonder that something other than the potent evidence that the SEC and regulators had regarding what was perpetrated at Collins and Aikman between the time that I left and its bankruptcy led to the dropping of charges; I believe the phrase used in the January 9, 2009, New York Times article was, "After a renewed assessment of the evidence," Lev Dassin, acting United States attorney for the Southern District of New York, said in a statement, "The government has concluded that further prosecution of this case would not be in the interests of justice." As noted in the Crain's April 20, 2010, article, four of the nine individuals received a pass from the original charges; however, what happened to the remaining five indictments? It also mentions that the company admitted no wrongdoing and paid no fine. The remaining five had to be the "fall-guys." The government had to make something stick to someone. That's just how it works. Stockman and his closest people were probably saved due to Stockman's service to the Senate and the Reagan administration.

Without my strong ethics and character, along with my own $18,000, this would have been me. It was in 2008 or 2009 when I met a recruiter who called out my history at C&A. He asked me, "Were you indicted?"

My passionate response was, "Absolutely not! On my watch, C&A, the company did the right thing in booking nearly $10 million dollars of corrected frauds to its P&L. It then took me two months and nearly $20,000 of my own to enforce it and to negotiate a fair out!"

He responded that he met with either Galante, Gougherty or Crossgrove to review an employment opportunity. When either one of them responded "yes" to whether or not they were indicted, he stopped the meeting and pitched their CV into the trash bin.

Someone once told me that you don't get a second chance to preserve your integrity.

Simply, do the right thing.

The reason I took you through all of the lengthy detail of the C&A experience is to demonstrate the conviction that one must have to endure and withstand bosses that are concerned about their own well-being to the exclusion of all else and direct others to commit fraud and put themselves, shareholders and employees at risk. I would have never guessed that I would have to actually go through all that I have shared with you. Doing things right just takes strength and fortitude.

Consider a middle-aged, dominant Iranian who is a technically savvy engineering type and who is placed in charge of a noncore business (U.S. subsidiary) owned by a Euro multinational German based company who wishes to spin-off this non-core business into a 50-50 merger of global equals and do so while optimizing enterprise value as the contributory consideration to the joint venture. This individual has strong short-term and long-term financial incentives to accomplish this mission, whatever it takes. He really wants to make a name for himself among the Euro hierarchy and run the combined business in North America.

The

BestRideAuto

A subsidiary of Heidelstat Group
Experience

In February 2008, I entered as chief financial officer of BestRideAuto, the wholly owned U.S. subsidiary of the Heidelstat Group of Germany. The business consisted of the manufacture and supply of components designed to dampen the noise, vibration and harshness ("NVH") associated with the engine, drivetrain and chassis of the vehicles produced within the light vehicle automotive segment. This includes light trucks (SUVs, pickup trucks, vans, etc.). The product lines of the company are: air springs, Microcellular Urethane (also known as "MCU," (road vibration absorbers made of alternate materials to traditional rubber), chassis components, torsional vibration dampers and engine mounts. This U.S. business, because of its historical poor performance, was treated like the "stepchild" of the Heidelstat Group. I learned that the prior finance manager, who had migrated to another Heidelstat company, had had enough with trying to turn this company around. Also, he openly didn't care for the president of BestRideAuto, "Balkahi-Tar" as a person and leader.

As with all prospective employers during the interview process, I detailed my professional experience and brought out the appropriate and fitting highlights. There are reasons for moving on from each stop in one's career. The relatively short stop at Collins & Aikman gets a lot of attention in such an interview process. I have absolutely nothing to hide about my experiences there; in fact, I made significant progress in the initiatives I sought and I am proud to tell that story. I am also proud to demonstrate my professional and personal ethics. Taking someone through the closing chapter of my C&A experience clearly demonstrates my character. It is very interesting that—after giving this sermon about the experience—Ghorbani Balkahi-Tar, the president of BestRideAuto and my boss, gave me complete and total assurance that never would any such thing happen at the Heidelstat Group of companies. You are about to find out just how interesting this assurance proved to be (re: the ease of lying for some when a premium payday is in the offing).

Upon my entry, the bottom line was negative 9.8% on roughly $100 million of sales; in other words, for every $10 of sales, we were losing about $1. The president of BestRideAuto and my boss, Ghorbani Balkahi-Tar, was an Iranian immigrant, held a Ph.D. in the science of microcellular urethane and, as I learned relatively early in my tenure of approximately four years, was a micro-manager, making all decisions by himself, keeping all important information about the company to himself for his own use. He was also a hoarder of credit for anything good that happened, resentful, a finger-pointer in the event that something unfavorable were to happen, and a very poor manager who chose to use negative motivational tactics (the stick, rather than the carrot). After spending in excess of four years with him, I learned that those were probably his good qualities.

Within my first few months of joining, I had learned from sources other than Balkahi-Tar that the ultimate goal, given the right set of conditions, was for BestRideAuto to be first in market share within the NVH market segment and to undertake an initial public offering ("IPO"). An acceptable alternative to that would be for the Heidelstat to take a minority ownership position in the company through a sale or merger. One would think that the president of the company would share this important information with his CFO at or near the CFO's inauguration period.

The company was performing poorly from a financial perspective, so Balkahi-Tar sought to treat his customers—just like he treated his employees—with a sharp poke in the eye. In this case, the poke was aggressively laid price increases. Upsetting customers is not a good thing when you want to grow a company and win new business.

I'll take a moment to briefly and better explain how BestRideAuto's business was put together along the lines of business:

1. AirSprings—This was a 2005 acquisition of "States" AirSprings business and was located in Lerma (Toluca) Mexico. Highly profitable, the products consisted of gas filled rubber canisters that are part of the shock absorbing system on premium SUVs and high-end light duty passenger vehicles.

2. Rubber to metal parts (a broad category of products where rubber is adhered to the steel via adhesive, including chassis components, suspension bushings, driveline dampers, engine mounts, torsional vibration dampers and miscellaneous other products). These products are common in most any light duty passenger and utility vehicles.

3. MCU (this goop, which is coagulated during the manufacturing process, replaces the rubber in applications where adherence to the steel is not mandatory for the part to take the vibration out of the vehicle). Jounce Bumpers (going on the top of shock towers to take the rough ride down) and "body mounts" were the primary products manufactured and sold in that business unit. Price versus performance was the debate with customers for this product line. The OEM customers may consider

the price premium to be worth the above average ride that this substance produces.

The rubber to metal parts were financially the poor performers. A significant amount of the price increases were to occur in the rubber to metal products. It was that or ask the customer to re-source the products to those suppliers who can make money at the prices that the customer was willing to pay.

Ligonier, Indiana, in the heart of Amish country, was BestRideAuto's center of rubber to metal production. With two plants, one, a company known as Motion Control Technologies ("MCT"), a joint venture partnership where BestRideAuto had 49% ownership and the other, a wholly owned entity of BestRideAuto, these plants sat right across the street from each other. MCT, a joint venture business, exclusively produced Torsional Vibration Dampers, or "TVDs" (a.k.a. engine dampers), and was making significant operational improvements and were marginally profitable. The problem here was that this was a core product line to the NVH market, but we only owned 49% of it. Cash flow for the business was a problem and the other side of the joint venture, the 51% ownership, was not willing to put any further cash into the business to fund working capital requirements while it was improving and developing sales growth.

The other operation which was wholly owned by BestRideAuto was far worse off. It was here and on this plant's behalf that the majority of the pricing actions, if successful, would take hold. There were much greater problems hitting this facility, however. Attracting talented engineering and manufacturing help to Ligonier, Indiana, is no small feat as professionals are non-existent in or near the small town. Fort Wayne is approximately 65 miles away and flushed with businesses in the manufacturing space providing ample demand for the supply of labor in the immediate area.

From the very beginning, it was quite evident that Balkahi-Tar disliked most people and had to work hard to overcome that element of who he was. In fact, he only treated his superiors and fellow "Ph.D.s" with respect for the simple reasons that his superiors could directly affect his status and fellow Ph.D.s could better fertilize his intelligence. Balkahi-Tar, now in his 50s, never figured out the key to leadership and that properly incentivizing and rewarding his subordinates would ultimately lead him to greater heights and rewards in his career. He did not have a genuine fiber in his body. Balkahi-Tar's poisonous management style, like a cancer, metastasized throughout the organization. Colleagues and Balkahi-Tar's other subordinates would confide in me their lack of understanding of the man along with their genuine hate for him. Balkahi-Tar himself was a transference of culture. He and his management style were toxic to the collaborative leadership style yielding success in the U.S..

Speaking of culture, allow me to set the stage. I think you pretty much get what the culture of BestRide-Auto was, but we also had to simultaneously deal with the "Heidelstat" culture. In this German Heidelstat Company, it ordinarily took years to make a decision. There were "management boards" who reported to "management boards." After issues were addressed at many levels, it was finally decided on by the actual Heidelstat Board of Directors. In addition, their focus was quite narrow. They only endorsed and agreed to use German-based ideas. It appeared as if that if it wasn't invented in Germany, it either didn't exist or it was no good.

Early in 2008, it was clearly apparent to me that the 100% owned operation in Ligonier, Indiana, needed fixing—or closing. I had learned that there were several resource intense initiatives to "fix" it over the years, to no avail. So this was my number one priority!

Second, there was MCT, the 49% owned joint venture that had no business being a joint venture. The product that was produced there was a substantial part of the engine compartment, and since we were the owner of the technology and the real "face" of the technology to the customer, the benefits of ownership ought not be shared. In Europe, this product, its production and sales were a core business that was highly profitable in the mother German operations in Nurnberg.

Although manufacturing process, geography, markets, automobiles and customers in Europe were different, this product line, currently marginally profitable as a joint venture in North America, should be nicely profitable through the sharing and implementation of best practices. This was a $40-$45 million revenue business with an approximate 5-7% pretax profit. EBITDA was somewhere around 10-12%. These numbers should be one and one-half times that level.

Over the course of a year, pertaining to the wholly-owned business—as the price increases which were proposed to customers on the rubber to metal product line had mixed to no results and in many cases were shunned by the customer—I had proposed that we instead decide to reduce the number of products produced and sold by asking the customers to re-source the business to our competitors. Actually, the customers had already begun to pull and re-source the business which received no pricing relief. The other piece of my proposal was to move the remaining production to a location neighboring our successful AirSprings Mexican business in Lerma (Toluca), Mexico.

My analysis yielded that moving this product line to Mexico would produce a near break-even result (a far better condition than the significant losses due to high fixed cost and inefficiency in Ligonier). After successive failed attempts at fixing this Amish country business, the proposal went to the Heidelstat Board. About three months later, it was finally approved, and we proceeded to move forward with transfer of production and closure of the facility. Believe it or not, three months was seen to be a record for such a review and approval process in the Heidelstat Group of companies.

Reacquiring the 51% of MCT, the minority joint venture, proved significantly more challenging to receive approval to move forward. A convenient feature was that the company was entering a phase of new launches and was consuming its cash flow on capital expenditures and working capital. Unfortunately, this revealed itself in lagging payments for the raw materials supplied by BestRideAuto for MCT's manufactured product. What was really required was a capital infusion by both partners such that the 51-49 ownership proportional relationship could be maintained. This would then fund the growth requirements. Unfortunately, the 51% owner, an African American decorated war veteran, was unwilling to do so and continued to stretch out MCT's timing of payments for that raw material. I learned of this and fired an email requesting that the 51% owner right such an unjust wrong in using BestRideAuto's cash to fund its operations. The email also questioned the 51% owner's integrity in not advising / confronting his partner about the joint venture's liquidity problems and the need for stretching out MCT's account payable to its partner. My goal, with that correspondence, was to stimulate discussion about reacquiring the 51% as I knew for the business to provide optimum value to the company shareholders, that was what was needed. After all, it was BestRideAuto's technology and BestRideAuto's cash that was fueling the business. The 51% owner was not contributing—to the contrary, he was utilizing our cash to fund his future benefit.

Although I was chastised for that correspondence by Balkahi-Tar and the Germans (as CFO, I did not believe that I needed board authorization to communicate a hard line). Reacquiring the 51% approximately two years later (2011), indeed was the end result, under my leadership and with deep involvement. This re-established this important product line as core to the BestRideAuto company. This was requisite for the major event that was to occur in 2012.

While the pricing activity continued to piss customers off, it was marginally successful in aiding the company's bottom line. In 2009, we entered into launching a new product for General Motors (jounce bumper) in the MCU product line. As such, we were required to provide "prototypes" for a period of time for product trial purpose on test vehicles. Ordinary production prices for jounce bumpers were between $1 and $3 dollars, depending upon the size and configuration of the product. Prototypes, because they involve new (trial) tooling and experimental processes, require an increase in pricing for a limited launch time period. The price for the prototypes was set at $17. The incremental cost for the prototype was far less than that—say $6—and this cost diminished over time as we became more efficient and productive in the manufacturing of these products as they neared production status at the higher production volumes.

There is a review and qualification for products to leave the prototype phase and enter the production mode with pricing that is significantly reduced as appropriate. Everything from product characteristics, functionality, performance specification, material, etc., right down to the product "packaging" is reviewed and must be approved. For the majority of the year 2009, General Motors was lax in approving the packaging of the product. Because of this, they were reluctant to remove the prototype status and pricing even though the product itself functioned and performed as intended and their "take rates" for these products were at the estimated production volume. Over the course of 2009, GM remitted approximately $4 million more than they actually had to. All it would have taken was the approval of the packaging, which was not substantially or substantively different from the version that ultimately was approved: a costly mistake on the part of GM but what a windfall of profit for BestRideAuto!

While I knew this was a minor change to the product fit, form and function, I was financially cautious (conservative), as chief financial officer, protecting both our P&L and balance sheet. You see, just as in the case with Collins and Aikman, the customer (in both cases GM) could have easily deducted the aggregate amount of overpayment (production prices were agreed to and contractually enforceable) and done so with justification. Knowing this, I recorded a liability for this amount because it was probable that GM would come back and deduct the overages from remittances, given the minor insignificant change that was required to get the prototype packaging approved and revert to a production price. After all, we were selling them the production part that they were using in the production vehicles, but it was just labeled "prototype" due to this slight packaging issue. The amount grew to nearly $3 million. I had decided to hold on to this "reserve" for approximately six months, then began to roll it into the revenue and income stream.

The triggering event for revenue recognition would not be the sale of the product, but it would be enough time passing such that by absence of GM actions to reduce payments, this would sanction BestRideAuto in keeping their (GM's) overly generous remittances. (Even though the contracts were written with the higher prices, GM could claim that changes in the mere packaging could not necessitate such premium pricing, given that all else was equivalent to a product in production. Thus, the production pricing of approximately $3 is all that is justified.) BestRideAuto had the legal right to bill for and collect the higher level of pricing as this was the contract. The onus was on GM to pull the lever to change the pricing from the ~$17 prototype price to the ~$3 production price. Absent this, the contract pricing of ~$17 dollars stood and was enforceable. This contrasts with the C&A situation because in fact, C&A was fraudulently billing GM for a part of the product that did not exist. (They were priced as if the doors contained a sunshade—a $50 option—when they did not actually have a sunshade.)

Sometime in 2010, when it appeared that GM would not claim for the lower price (enough time had passed), I took pro rata chunks of this beginning six months out and this spanned well into the next year, dividing the amount evenly over the number of months. This was quite a boon for our financial results and helped immensely with self-funding our transition from Ligonier to Mexico.

Since October, 2009, we confidentially had been working on the pending merger of BestRideAuto with the noise, vibration and harshness dampening business of Greesson, our largest competitor. As I had mentioned earlier, with the Heidelstat desire to be number one in NVH and to hold less than 100% interest in the business, the merger was both a convenient and lucrative avenue to achieve these dual objectives. In 2010, Balkahi-Tar and I found ourselves in the middle of due diligence, disclosing sensitive information to the other party and receiving the same. As it were, we were about to reveal high profit 2010 results and 2011 projections for BestRideAuto North American operations, which would be rolled into the BestRideAuto global results and analyzed by Greesson while used in setting the enterprise value upon which this major event would be transacted. To give a size of company perspective—with the full integration of the 51% share of the minority joint venture, which would occur in January 2012—our sales revenue was nearing $145 million in North America. Our European BestRideAuto sister (deemed the headquarters for BestRideAuto global) recorded revenues nearing $600 million at 2010/11 foreign exchange rates. Greesson on the other hand was the exact opposite mirror image of BestRideAuto. They were about $500 million in revenues in North America and approximately $150 million in Europe. The merger would likely displace a number of BestRideAuto individuals due to duplicative resources after the businesses combined, including myself; that's for a later discussion.

BestRideAuto North America 2010 results were shaping up to be quite good. Preliminary indications, upon re-forecast, were showing north of 10% return on sales at the pre-tax income line. With the restructuring (the closure of the Ligonier plant and move of production to Toluca, Mexico), the pricing actions with customers and the recognition of the prototype pricing uplift on production parts, these items all attributed to our exceptional results.

In 2011, while the business was clipping along on a consistent basis, the business was showing diminished profitability—when compared to 2010—moving into the new year on a forecast basis. This, mostly because of the large windfall of prototype price recognition which put nearly $3 million into 2009's bottom line, would not be there in 2011. The 2011 full integration of MCT, which was the prior 49% joint venture, would result in a dilution of profitability while increasing sales. This meant that 2011 profitability was projected to be around 5% on $140 million in sales revenues.

This presented an interesting dichotomy. The premium profit of North America BestRideAuto, when compared to Greesson's, was going to cause Greesson to pay significant cash to the Heidelstat Group, BestRideAuto's parent and owner, to merge the two companies. The fact that our four to five point erosion in return on sales profitability percent, year to year, would not bode well for the enterprise value from which the cash payment was to be established. Just explaining the differences in 2011 profitability, when compared to 2010, would not be enough. The BestRideAuto and Heidelstat senior managers who would be paid a success bonus based upon how much cash would be paid to Heidelstat were looking to maximize the enterprise value to secure a big pay day. (Déjà vu?)

As time was approaching for BestRideAuto to consolidate results for 2010 (ten months of actual results, two months of forecast) and 2011, Balkahi-Tar would have regular and exclusive meetings with the Heidelstat CFO. It was always interesting to me that Balkahi-Tar, always "the smartest guy in the room," would have financial related meetings with our owner's senior management, CEO and CFO, without including me, the BestRideAuto CFO, on special sensitive topics. "Interesting," but not surprising given his modus operandi as described earlier.

What I am about to describe to you is again a first in my career—a first in "form," but not in substance. Balkahi-Tar was always a dark person with a strong, broad, rigged and strained brow, thick with Iranian black hair, except when he wanted something from you. Then would come his attempt at smiling and brightness. This guy was intent on imposing his culture on the organization and that was it. A difficult place to spend any time.

It was the end of the day sometime early in the fourth quarter, and Balkahi-Tar—just getting back from one of those special meetings with Ralf Laggen, the Heidelstat CFO—comes to my door. With that false smile and attempted bright persona, he requested that I meet him in his office at 6:00 a.m. the following day (November 9) for a special meeting on a confidential topic. I did not even have to guess what this was going to be about.

I was quite concerned that if I did not comply with the directive that I knew I was about to receive, I most likely would be fired. Balkahi-Tar would rather run for cover than address a certain circumstance constructively.

Fully understanding the risk of my noncompliance, but not yet fully knowing what was going to be discussed that early morning, I recalled a small recording device that my musician son, David Jr., introduced me to some time ago. This item could be easily concealed, and the recording quality was especially good, if not excellent. I had a convenient memory about this. I stopped at a Radio Shack on my way home and they had one.

At dinner, I talked with my wife about what the day held and what tomorrow was likely to bring. I also told her of how I prepared myself to protect our income should an illicit direction be given to me which I would be unwilling to comply with. Our dinners were usually tense while Balkahi-Tar was my boss. I completely disliked the man. I hated the thought of what would come the next day.

I excused myself from the dinner table as I had to test the recording device and learn how to work it. I was about to record this sensitive conversation because I feared for my and my family's economic future. I cleared this through my attorney and good friend, Bill Waldon, and he advised me that "recorded" evidence without the permission of all parties to the conversation is admissible as valid evidence in a court given the circumstances. Should I deny the directed actions and be fired, this would be a smoking gun toward a wrongful dismissal.

Balkahi-Tar typically always arrived at work at 5:30 a.m. I was not going to beat him to work. If I did, he would know something was "up." I arrived at 6:00 a.m., greeted him in his office and advised him that given all the coffee so early in the morning, that I needed to excuse myself to the bathroom and would be back as soon as possible; little did he know that I was turning a "wire" on. Here is a transcript of the actual conversation:

- Minutes 0:00 through 19:00 plus: I reviewed some exposure on accounts receivable collections with

Balkahi-Tar, the (related) BMW business was a difficult business that required my deep intervention and analysis with respect to the non-collection of a few hundred thousand dollars of payments. Done right, we would get the majority of the amounts owed to us.

- The review of exposure also included shared expenses with the parent company. Balkahi-Tar, with his exclusion to anyone else in negotiating these deals, cannot believe the bad news that is bestowed upon him (if only he would include others in the business process…). He would go off and do deals with VW and other customers and keep the details to himself. The P&L effect of his activities would be as much a surprise to me, his CFO, as it would be to him (the guy who did the deals in his own world!).
- We then moved to my balance sheet review in preparation for the fourth quarter closing.
- Further explanations about how financial recognitions occur. Balkahi-Tar, in his cavalier approach, was wanting full understanding of how some double counting of income occurred.
- Further discussion about overall performance of the Lerma, Mexico, business occurred related to the business with customer BMW.
- Balkahi-Tar discussed the trading of numbers to hit the expected numbers.
- Balkahi-Tar shares his perspective of how Mexico accounting is not comprehensive. Balkahi-Tar says "black-eye" for all of us after Jose Luis, his chosen controller, who he personally chose for hire (against my recommendations) who later resigned.

At 31:42 of the recording, Balkahi-Tar changes direction, but still being in command of the financials…

- Further discussion entailed my buttoning up 2010, along with a major program launch explanation, to essentially cover his ass. We're at 35:19.
- 37 minutes is where the direction to commit fraud occurs....
- Balkahi-Tar is trying to develop a repoir with me that never existed... in set-up to facilitate his fraud.
- At 37 minutes, you can hear how BestRideAuto can increase 2011 return on sales at operating profit to 5.5% where as we currently have a return of 4.7% of sales.
- Ralf after discussions is "comfortable" that we could keep $1,000,000 as risk to pricing and collection from GM. (Recall that this is the item for which BestRideAuto already collected the cash. Concerned that GM would come back at us and deduct this cash from product payments, I chose to await time that would indicate we would keep the cash and GM would not admit their mistakes and ask for the cash back. I then recognized this income in a piecemeal and conservative fashion.) Hence, I counted all of that income in 2010 already and to reverse a portion of it would be contrary to my assumptions related to GM not coming back after BestRide Auto for the unjust increased pricing.
- I advised Balkahi-Tar that we have received cash already for this. This would be a very strange proposition to reclaim conservatism after dumping it into our income number (they wished for me to now remove the favorable affects from our P&L) after an ample period had passed such that we could safely claim the income... and then to reverse that decision. This would immediately be suspect to anyone, especially our auditors!
- You can actually hear my heart beat escalate (the

wire was on my chest) in the meeting as a result of this fraud proposition.

- I again relate that since we have received the cash with a valid purchase order and execution of a deal, but Balkahi-Tar shares that he doesn't know the mechanics that would require us to keep the "profit reserve" of at least $1,000,000. Nonetheless, he is directing me to create 5.5% income in 2010 when the correct number is 4.7%.
- I go out of my way to advise him and share a perspective that I am all for everyone's desire to do good on behalf of the company and that I will confer with Ralf (the Heidelstat CFO) on these items (even though I know their approach does not hold any merit whatsoever).
- Balkahi-Tar is rehashing results with the direction to mold them to an acceptable level for the big payday. A financial engineering feat that he can claim the fame to...

My full workday was already in by 8:00 am that morning!

- Balkahi-Tar, without the facts, references his discussions with "Ralf" and begins to mandate the numbers as how they need to be portrayed in the financial results. Balkahi-Tar's approach is bogus, and I try to prove to him that it is just not holding water as to his walk to the promise land profitability. Keep in mind, it will be his way and only his way. That is how the Iranian dictator operates.
- He continues to recite numbers to me, his CFO, about how the numbers will take shape. Keep in mind that the German company Heidelstat endorses his approach to engineering the financials.
- I leave the meeting, giving Balkahi-Tar a level

of assurance that I will visit with Ralf, understand their joint proposal (to cook the books) and that at the end of the day, I will make every effort to increase the following year's ROS for BestRideAuto by the 0.8%. The two words that I left off of my closing were "legally and ethically." In my mind, those words are implied when the prior sentence is spoken by a CFO.

Here's the interesting thing. I've come into the company of Ph.D.s and Harvard graduates several times in my career and in the case to be presented to you next, a "GE" manager. Most all of these people think that they are the smartest people in the room, even though the subject matter has no remote connection to their expertise. So, if Balkahi-Tar was actually as smart as he gives himself credit for, he would have asked me to think about how it is possible to move the income/EBITDA numbers by almost an aggregate 1% of sales value. Eight-tenths of one percent of sales value, in this case $140,000,000, is $1,100,000.

Let's do the math:

5.5% return on sales is what Laggen and Balkahi-Tar were after,

4.7% return on sales is where the business prospectively was to perform in 2010

0.8% is the difference on sales to make up.

$140,000,000 is the 2011 projected sales revenue of BestRideAuto

$1,120,000 (One million, one hundred, twenty thousand) is the gap. This is a significant amount in relationship to the company and its revenue size.

So instead of asking me what can be done and how we get the numbers to be more acceptable in 2010, the following year, Balkahi-Tar and Laggen provided me the answer of where to go on the profit increase, which would have been fraudulent in manifesting their desires. So they did not ask; they just assumed that there is nowhere to go (legally) to achieve their objective; therefore, they choose to go the dark side to achieve their big payday objective!

How did I solve this dilemma without getting fired and by operating within the rules? Being the CFO of the business, I was acutely aware of prior years' (originally prior to my watch) audit exceptions that the auditors brought forth to management to either refute or to correct. The process is such that an unadjusted difference, if relatively small and disputable on the case of judgment, is identified. One such item related to the shipment of goods from our Lerma (Toluca), Mexico, operation to a Hamburg, Germany, warehouse from where BMW would pull this product for use in its vehicle making process. This was a consignment inventory, meaning that we (BestRideAuto) owned the inventory until such time as BMW pulled it from the European warehouse and placed it into production. Upon such action, notice should be given to the BestRideAuto Finance staff and an invoice would be created and electronically sent to BMW Europe at which point the related sales revenue would be recognized.

One of the prior years' audit exceptions was that Lerma/Toluca pre-recognized the revenue (upon shipment from our Mexico location) to the consignment warehouse. Their prior years' audit position was to recognize the sales and resulting income domestically, within the BestRideAuto North American operations, upon shipment of the product to Hamburg. This was incorrect. The contract with BMW, the customer, was such that the customer would not take possession of the goods until they are pulled from the Hamburg warehouse. OEMs use this tactic to bolster their cash flow and reduce their investment in inventories. The payment terms clock does not start ticking until they actually installed the purchased items (our product) on their vehicle. Cash to cash, this is at least 30-45 days benefit, sometimes more, especially when dealing with an overseas customer.

As a result, whatever the value of inventory in the Hamburg warehouse was in its entirety, it was accounted for as if it had already been sold and not held in BestRideAuto's inventory until such time as BMW took possession of the goods. Being new to the situation, I was happy to step up and correct this issue.

Essentially, the directive from Balkahi-Tar and Laggen was to arbitrarily erode earnings in the current year, 2010, and increase earnings in the following year 2011 by $1,100,000. Their mission was to show that the company had sustainably good earnings, on a continuum, to keep the enterprise value of BestRideAuto high and cause Gleeson to pay BestRideAuto's owner more than they otherwise would have, if the numbers were left in a status quo. This is quite easy to do—if one were to fraudulently make-up entries and stories to support their entries—which is what they were suggesting. It is much more difficult to find a reality that would cause these entries to be legitimately made.

The sales value of the goods in the Hamburg warehouse, after discounting it for obsolete inventory, was $2.0 million. The gross margin on these items was near 25%, but since we would not be adding any fixed cost to realize these sales (being as it was just a paper entry), the "incremental/variable" margin on these items approached 40%. To be somewhat conservative on this estimate, I elected to use the demonstrated incremental profit impact on the $2.0 million, thus yielding $800,000. Doing this would correct a prior years' problem and bring this value stream in compliance with Generally Accepted Accounting Principles. A big win for me!

I had another $300,000 to solve. This stuff just doesn't materialize in front of your eyes!

2010 was a very good year because of GM's quality procedure causing premium prototype pricing to be paid to BestRideAuto for production parts. Effectively, we knocked the cover off of the baseball when compared to our original profit forecast / budget. Our incentive compensation targets were set on achievement of our forecast budget. Because of this, lots of bonus money likely would be due to many employees—so much bonus compensation that it potentially could be 100% above typical years, if staying with the standard bonus formulae.

Since at the end of the day, the Heidelstat CEO had full discretion over bonus compensation, in fact, if he desired and decided (hopefully for good and credible reasons), it is possible that no bonus would be paid. In addition to this, the BestRideAuto culture coming from Balkahi-Tar was one that caused all bonus eligible associates to fight for their rightful bonus amounts as Balkahi-Tar would push hard on soft measures and individuals' performance to minimize any potential bonus paid. Hence, even though the formula indicated that $ XX was eligible to be paid, the company may actually pay on 50% or 70% of that total eligible amount. That being said, under Generally Accepted Accounting Principles, a liability is recorded when it is "probable" to be paid and "estimable" (or the amount can be determined or calculated). In this case, we met both criteria to increase the full bonus accrued into the current year results. If, in fact all of the bonus that was estimated and reflected in that year's financials was not fully paid, the residual amount would be reclaimed as income in the following year when the payments are actually made, as long as the difference is not "significant".[12] So long as the estimate would be near $300,000 greater than the actual payments made in the following year, the reclaimed income in that year of $300,000 would accomplish the goal of moving the full $1,100,000 of income from year 2010 to year 2011. These were legitimate adjustments: (1) correcting prior years' revenue accounting errors and (2) recording bonus compensation eligibility via the formula calculation.

After performing some rough calculations in support of what I believed payments should be, I supplied them to the Heidelstat CEO (of course through Balkahi-Tar) and asked for a letter from the CEO citing the exceptional financial performance of the BestRideAuto subsidiary and stating that at this point, the estimate provided the best basis for inclusion in the year's financial results and that any bonus payments are at the full discretion of the CEO.

In a meeting with Balkahi-Tar and Laggen, I was asked to arbitrarily make changes to the year 2010 and 2011 financials without any basis for making such adjustments. I advised them that I had a plan to accomplish the legitimate income transfer of approximately $1,100,000 from year 2010 to year 2011. They had no idea that this was possible.

I reviewed this scenario about both adjustments with Balkahi-Tar and Laggen and they bought off on the adjustments (unlike the C&A situation to where more was never enough!). Once I had this okay, I gave my approval to incorporate these results, which were in accordance with Generally Accepted Accounting Principles, into the forecast for the full year of 2010 and prospective results for year 2011.

Now here's a fine comparison:

Option one (their option as sited in the transcripts of the recording):

Unjustly, unjustifiably, unconscionably and illegally reverse the correct accounting on the financial position taken related to the premium pricing on the GM production parts, long after the cash had been collected and now safely taken to income (In essence, blow bullshit up the auditor's asses and potentially get written up and be unsuccessful due to the circumstances, facts and the customer's binding contracts) or

Option two (my option that corrected prior errors and stated the numbers accurately):

Justly, justifiably, conscionably, legally and correctly record revenues and recognize (likely and probable) expenses in accordance with Generally Accepted Accounting Principles; sleep well at night and never have to keep looking over your shoulder.

Either way would (probably) get the job done. Only one way is the right way.

2010 and 2011 were interesting years for BestRideAuto and I. As we marched toward the intended merger of BestRideAuto and Greesson, our German parent changed from the Heidelstat Group to the German subsidiary of the Heidelstat Group, "BestRideAuto." While the Balkahi-Tar culture remained, the new parent culture was emerging as BestRideAuto Germany injected itself further into BestRideAuto North America. In addition, the German BestRideAuto was a much larger business, larger by four times, than the North American subsidiary, and by that, exercised greater control over the business, and they also took a strong lead in dealing with Greesson on the merger. Both 2010 and 2011 were full of due diligence and efforts at trying to get this merger executed. Challenging times.

As the merger neared, and knowing that in North America, Greesson was approximately four times BestRideAuto's size in the region, I sensed that I would need to find a new job. Often the larger company CFO will take full control of the business in the merger, necessitating that I would need to move on. I secured a position, that I considered to be an interim job, as director of financial planning and analysis and assistant treasurer for an aluminum die casting company in Sheboygan, Wisconsin. On the day I was to resign from BestRideAuto, in early December 2011, the German BestRideAuto senior management was in our North American offices and readying for a 10:00 a.m. business review meeting. At 8:00 a.m., I was called into Balkahi-Tar's office.

This was quite odd. As I entered his office, I observed our head of Human Resources, my German BestRideAuto indirect boss and the German BestRideAuto HR head. As Balkahi-Tar took his seat at the end of the table, he announced that, because of the merger, my services would no longer be required. I was provided a severance package that allowed me to cover most of what was remaining open for our son's college costs. Had I shared my news ahead of this, this severance package would never have been provided.

I hit the lottery! The following Monday, I was to

immediately start the new job that paid fairly well. I looked around the room and asked why everyone looked so somber. "Lighten up!" I suggested.

Approximately three months later, the merger happened. I was aware that Greesson was going to have to ante up approximately $45 million to adjoin these companies and create the largest global noise, vibration and harshness dampening company. I recalled that a "merger of equals" really doesn't work and often ends to divorce as in the case of Daimler-Chrysler. The Daimler side essentially controlled the combined company.

The fight for control at Greesson-BestRideAuto was ever ongoing. I recently received a call from an ex-colleague at BestRideAuto and was advised that the two companies could not agree on how to work together and that they could not agree on a payment value to divorce. The solution that they had arrived at was that Heidelstat would buy out the remaining 50% partner Greesson. After having charged Greesson a premium entrance fee into the merger, the 50% owner of the merged companies, Heidelstat, was now looking to pay a lesser amount than Greesson wanted to go away. Greesson believes that the merged companies are worth a much higher value than Heidelstat believes. But of course, Heidelstat was now on the buying side!

As for Balkahi-Tar, he was seeking to become the combined companies' CEO in North America. He lobbied hard and pressed his European colleagues on this for some time. Once the merger took shape, he was demoted to be a head of one of the product lines. His management methods did not improve over the course of his tenure.

In a recent call I received, I learned that the new

CEO of the North American Greesson-BestRideAuto business further demoted Balkahi-Tar to be a technical director for that same product line. This lasted for a few months until such time as he was fired.

After my "interim" position for Sheboygan, Wisconsin, aluminum die casting company, I was sought by a private equity firm to become the CFO of one of their portfolio companies, "PUFFiltration", Inc. of Faith, OH. You are about to read about this fine experience.

Consider a young Muslim Eastern Indian who lived with 10 families, one of which was his own, in an open floor plan on one entire floor of an apartment building, in India, with a communal bathroom. This person desires for a better life, so he becomes well educated in the hierarchy of the education in the schools of India with the expertise of electrical engineering. At a relatively early age, he then finds himself a way to get to the States. In the States, he continues his education as General Electric recruits him. At GE he is responsible for program management in the building and sale of large electrical generators, under contract with the US Government, Department of Defense. He is young, bright and successful in his job and is bred into the "GE Way." He takes very well to this environment. While he was successful in his job, he was not identified as a "key high-potential" employee. Continuing to be highly smart and self-motivated, he is interested in advancement and comes across a position with Motors Engine. He enters the Light Duty Filtration business segment (a noncore business of Motors Engine), as product quality manager, then moves into an overall plant management role and from there on and into general management within the Light Duty Filtration business segment. He is tapped to lead the sale process of the business segment to a private equity firm. This low-middle market business produces approximately 20% EBITDA returns on a pro forma basis, as was displayed in the winning PE firm's prospective financials for the business as a stand-alone entity.

He wants to be a star for this PE firm and amass a fortune. After the business that he has already sold once has several newly found bumps in the road, some of which were the result poor of diligence and deal making on his part and on the part of the PE firm, the business moves toward insolvency. His job is to show that the business is in line to be financially on track so that the company can live another day, achieve the business objectives that may make the company salable at a price the PE firm can mitigate the investment loss.

A tall order to fill, especially without knowledge of and cooperation from the company's lenders.

Consider the Eastern European, older, relatively used-up ex-consultant (AT Kearney and KPMG, big consulting houses). He, as the operating partner and lead-man/chairman of this new portfolio company, was joyously advertising to all with regularity, prematurely beating the drum with sounds of "what a successful investment this is." This was the largest investment of the PE firm to date! "This investment will be so successful and we all will win big on the ultimate sale of the business with cashing-in all of our options!" This, all the while with (the) more intelligent people being of the sound mind that the PE firm overpaid for such a business and knowing that the options may not be worth the paper that they were written on. First of all, options were only worth anything after the PE firm made a 25% internal rate of return on its investment, which the company was a far cry away from that milestone! I may have been born in the dark, but not yesterday.

Is this guy too far gone to even contemplate what his intentions are or the boisterous words that are coming out of his mouth?

Footnote Explanations

(12) Generally Accepted Accounting Principles call for the amount of bonuses, which pertain to a given year of results, to be reflected in the same year of those results (the year in which the actions leading to the bonus actually occurred). The payment of these bonuses does not actually occur until the year concludes and the audit of the financial information is complete (often March or April of the following year). So long as the bonus estimates, which are reflected in the financial results of the year in which the bonus is earned, are well supported with credible logic, if bonuses paid in the following year are different, in this case less than the estimate, this unpaid amount can be reclaimed as income in the following year (the year in which the payment is actually made).

The

PUFFiltration

An Accretive Industry Capital Partners Portfolio Company Experience

PUFFiltration is a portfolio company of a Chicago, Illinois, private equity firm called Accretive Industry Capital Partners ("AIC"). I was networked into an opportunity of the chief financial officer role by a mutual acquaintance, a Grosse Pointe, Michigan investment banker, Mr. Jim Rickman. Jim knew I was looking for active opportunities as I had met with him and described the merger of BestRideAuto with Greesson, an entity five times the size of BestRideAuto. I advised him that as a result of the merger, I would likely need to move on and into my next career opportunity. Mohammed Kahlmeny, the CEO of PUFFiltration who sold the business to AIC as he was an employee of Motors; Nick Ferdalez, the portfolio company operating partner and chairman on the PUFFiltration project; and I first met in the Detroit Metropolitan Airport Westin Hotel lounge in September of 2011 while we contemplated my fit to Puff as the company's chief financial officer. AIC was slated to complete the acquisition on Halloween of 2011 with the anticipation of carving out of the light duty filtration business of Motors Engine. The light duty filtration business of Motors services approximately 75% of all of the OEM light duty in-tank or in-line fuel filtration needs in North America. Said differently, Puff provides seven or eight out of every ten in-line / in-tank fuel filters for the North American automotive market. PUFFiltration also has a "dry" or air filtration business located in Bramalea, Wisconsin. The flagship for Puff's "wet"/fuel filter business was Faith, Ohio, as was its headquarters. Puff had unique fuel filter technology and was a leader in this industry segment.

The light duty filtration business of Motors had Asia operations located in Shanghai, European operations located in Quimper, France, and a very small operation serving the South American two-wheel (cycle) and automotive market in Sao Paolo, Brazil. The asset purchase agreement did not include the real estate or employees of the French operation due to the high social cost situation in France. The productive assets would later be moved to Faith to service the European market, warehousing the goods in Hamburg with a third-party logistics firm handling the inventory and making appropriate shipments to the European customers. It was intended that manufacturing would be the main activities of the above-named operations and regions, except for Europe.

Carving out the light duty filtration business out of the large Motors machine meant establishing buy / sell agreements for product between Motors and Puff (as Puff was both a supplier and a customer of Motors and vice-versa), divorcing all information technology systems from Motors, establishing legal entities and operations in Shanghai, China, Sao Paolo and an administrative operation in Basel, Switzerland, which consisted of accounting, legal and tax functions for the business. It also meant interim phases for both companies. You see, this was a complex situation.

Little did AIC know at the time of the transaction, but Motors was not empowered to speak for their landlord, nor would they allow a co-habitation of a manufacturing plant in Shanghai and Sao Paolo. This, as you will see, became a major blow to the anticipated return on investment ("ROI") that AIC would eventually realize; whether there would be any "R" in ROI is yet to be determined as the business is still held by AIC, far beyond the anticipated hold period (of two years) upon the acquisition.

Our September, 2011, discussions were quelled. I was told that they had decided to go in a different direction which was somewhat disappointing to me at the time. I later learned that meant that AIC desired to promote the Faith Plant controller to the position of chief financial officer. A thrifty move that some private equity firms attempt with many positions to internalize the cash and optimize the portfolio company profits. In other words, they look to get something for nothing by paying a plant controller's wage for the services of the chief financial officer position. Well, that didn't work. Neither did the trial hiring of a longtime friend of the operating partner as chief financial officer. This guy clearly never served a day as a bona fide custodian of assets, much less a CFO with the determination of maximizing value creation for owners and stakeholders.

AIC finally figured out that they would need to pay the going fare for a full-fledged chief financial officer. Having left BestRideAuto in December, 2011, I hooked up with Tom Nosgarter, the prior president of the Heidelstat Group's Automotive business, and he suggested that I come over to a firm that he was running as its chief executive officer. Tom was nearing the end of a long process of two bankruptcies at Moldmetal, a Sheboygan, Wisconsin, based aluminum die caster of automotive transmission cases and engine blocks. Tom and his chief financial officer, Pat Byrne, were readying the business for sale with advisors and investment bankers. While this was going on, their director of financial planning, analysis and treasury resigned which left a hole in the organization as they were busily working to sell the business. Tom knew that my mission was near completion at BestRideAuto, so he invited me to come work with him and Pat. While it was well known that my position would be interim, I took on a much broader role in the business. I led the initiative to synchronize manufacturing systems which were completely unsynchronized, in addition to spearheading the completion of the 2011 audit which was requisite to paying management bonuses and executing a deal. Any prospective buyer would want the most recent year's performance opined on by independent accountants. Also within my responsibility I worked with the operations controllers in the production of the month-end financial package that would be distributed to stakeholders. I also was responsible for treasury functions including daily / weekly cash management and interfacing with Moldmetal's commercial lenders.

Being that Moldmetal emerged a second time from bankruptcy, it had a long list of owners, including, but not limited to: trade creditors, hedge funds and private equity firms who bought up the debt at cents on the dollar to receive equity in return. These folks were anxious to get their money out of Moldmetal and it so happened that upon sale of the company, they would profit substantially in turning what could have potentially been a significant loss of money into gold. Tom was significantly responsible for the growth in both sales and profitability and an individual by the name of Jack Peregrine really was responsible for getting the company out of the doldrums of poor performance which led to the first bankruptcy.

My position was interim due to the fact that the company would likely be acquired by a larger enterprise that would take layers of management out and convert the operational structure of Moldmetal into purely manufacturing plants. I welcomed a March 2012 call from

AIC's Nick Ferdalez (Chairman of Puff and Operating Partner of AIC), to ask if I would still be interested in the opportunity. The answer was "yes," and I described my current situation to him. Soon after, I had dinner with Bob Tretis, Managing Partner and co-Founder of AIC.

AIC discussions continued beyond this time and things were seemingly on track. In mid-June, I had a final meeting with the boys from AIC, along with Mohammed Kahlmeny, the CEO of Puff, at Oakland Hills Country Club where a good friend, Phil Martini, was a member and—I soon learned—an outside director on the board of PUFFiltration. Phil and Ferdalez played golf at Oakland Hills from time to time and this was Phil's link to a position with AIC.

Things went well in the meetings. Kahlmeny was annoyingly persistent in hammering me on the deficiencies of the current CFO to be replaced, the friend of Ferdalez. This guy Kahlmeny, an Eastern Indian Muslim and ex-GE manager, was a freak of sorts and an elitist, believing:

1. He is above everyone and all else, and
2. He is the smartest guy in the room at all times.

These items should have been apparent to me through his actions in the Oakland Hills meeting, but it took some time for this realization to set in, about two days on the job.

I received a joint call from Ferdalez and Kahlmeny about the placement into the CFO role at Puff. We hadn't even talked numbers as of yet, and these guys were setting me up; hence, negotiating the way that they wished to proceed with me. I would offer to them, and in so many words, that their method and approach was unorthodox, given the certain set of circumstances, but they were insistent on their approach and were resistant to the change. Not hearing and considering my side was another strange sign in lack of professionalism.

I received a call from Ferdalez and we put the final touches on my offer / acceptance and settled on a start date: July 16, 2012. Onward and upward, as I was motivated to create value for the general and limited partners, as well as the remaining stakeholders, including myself.

The week of July 16 came quickly. Although I requested a great deal of information from Kahlmeny ahead of my start date, it was never provided. Things like credit agreements, recent financial statements, transition services agreement, the asset purchase agreement and supply contracts that would have made my integration seamless and allowed me to get the jump start that normally is afforded. Not wishing to become pesky, I relinquished from further requests and just assumed that I would be a fast study upon entry.

Allow me to present some hard facts related to the business and acquisition:

Normalized annual sales revenue of PUFFiltration:
$80,000,000

Trailing 12 months EBITDA,
as adjusted at the date of acquisition:
$16,000,000

Purchase price of business—to the nearest million:
$90,000,000

effectively paid for with:

Senior and Secured Debt:
$40,000,000 - $50,000,000

Subordinated Mezzanine Debt
$20,000,000

Contributed Equity Capital
$30,000,000

A note worthy of mention: Term debt with fixed payments was ~$40,000,000. A variable lending facility was in place, which, at low points in cash flow, was utilized to fund the value of working capital (accounts receivable, inventory) and the operations of the business.

One would think, upon entering a business as its CFO, that a company with one-third of the purchase value coming from ownership investment would be quite good, safe and conservative in contrast to a completely leveraged buyout where 10% or less is actually ownership capital put at risk. It seemed like a "decent" place to be, that is until you learned of what a shoddy job the private equity firm did at due diligence in learning about this business, the deal structure which clearly advantaged Motors Engine (the seller), the inexperience and youth (borderline negligence) of the chief executive officer and the resulting lack of negotiation strategy and intelligence that AIC put forth in executing this deal.

When I got there, everyone was deeply tasked with the "carve-out" (an in-vogue term that means full separation from the seller parent company), as if that was all that was required for this business to be a success and command a premium value from a buyer which is mostly the means in which private equity firms make money for their general and limited partners. Hardly was this the only issue and key success factor to be realized.

The other issue and weakness in the operation of the business was that Mohammed, the ex-Motors manager in place to sell Puff to a private equity firm, never left the "sell-the-company" mode. Instead of paying strict attention to the operation of the business and growing its top and bottom lines, a great deal of his attention was in portraying data in such a manner as if he was assembling an offering memorandum to market the business with. He required the accounting and finance function to deviate from the essence of the buy-sell contracts with Motors and reshape transactions as if the buy-sell transactions were conducted with other third parties, ignoring the economics of the transactions; hence, there was a requirement to keep more than one set of books. When I entered, there were only these bogus books and no fundamental GAAP books, no adherence to incorporating the essence of the business contracts into the financial statements that would be purveyed to third party lenders; hell, when I got there, they weren't even booking federal income tax liability as the company was profitable before tax and had no loss carry-forward.

Such fundamentals as bona fide purchase orders between a willing and able seller and a willing and able buyer were non-existent between Puff and Motors who were now separate companies buying from and selling to each other. I couldn't believe that after the two businesses legally separated, they continued to employ the prevailing practice when one division of a large corporation does business with another division. All they did was mark-up a cost sheet and part number log and input the price into the billing system. This was the practice. There was no diligent contract administration with an actual purchase order contract being tendered between the parties. "We couldn't enforce this approach with Motors," as I was told. "Motors will not cooperate with this," many said. I immediately stopped shipment until we were accorded valid enforceable purchase contracts for all of the products that we sold to Motors. Guess what? These contracts came within single days. Shipments began to flow, and the world became a lot clearer with much less bickering between the parties. Up until then, Motors would game the system and take advantage of Puff in each and every instance.

The international, non-domestic operations in Shanghai and Sao Paolo were not separated from Motors. While Puff owned the assets, and Motors utilized them, Motors continued to manufacture the products using Puff raw materials sold to Motors from the Puff Faith operation. Upon completion of product manufacture, Motors would then sell the goods back to AIC Filter (Puff) China where Puff would take title and then sell the products to Puff's customers. The full intention, at some point of maturity, was for Puff to manufacture the parts in these countries and sell to their Asian and South American customers. Cart ahead of the horse as an indication of oversold promises once again. For some reason, the transaction date whereby PuFFiltration was sold to AIC had to be adhered to and the full separation of the operations from Motors would have to come at a later date in these countries.

To add insult to injury, AIC really screwed up the China setup. First, they hired an inexperienced Chinese financial consultant, along with a US legal firm with a branch in China, to help them with the setup of the company. China is very strict about business operation, strictly requiring a business license that identifies the primary operations of the business; for instance, if your business is exclusively buying and selling merchandise, then the Chinese and regional government would grant you a "trading" license. If your desire is to establish a business that manufactures products and sells them, then the governments would grant a "manufacturing" license and allow the coincident selling activity, even so much as to allow the merchant trading activities as described in the prior scenario. Should you be a lender, or in the finance business, you would then be granted a "financing" license, and so on and so forth.

Well, you can guess what happened. Even though the ultimate business activities that would occur within several months after the acquisition would be manufacturing, a "trading" license was obtained by the private equity firm AIC. To add further injury, both Motors and Motors' landlord were resistant to Puff cohabitating with Motors on the existing factory site. When these two items collided, the Pudong district of Shanghai, the original grantor of the "trading" license, would not allow the existing trading license to be converted to a manufacturing license. Nor were they friendly to the situation in general. At that point, the person in charge of setting-up China and commencing with production decided and presented the concept of building a brand new factory in another district of Shanghai, a very large city, resulting in the need to <u>duplicate</u> the capital investment in China. Yes, DOUBLE the investment and do it with borrowed funds because AIC did not wish to alarm their silent partners of the mistakes they had mad by asking them to invest more to get them out of this debacle.

AIC's market intelligence in this product segment, in addition, was extremely poor. The air filtration business in Bramalea, Wisconsin, was dependent on the lawn and garden and agriculture segments. Customers like John Deere and Briggs and Stratton were extremely important to how well, or poor, the Puff air filtration segment would perform. With each successive month that passed, upon my analysis of sales volume, I would note significant reductions in the amounts of product sold to these customers when compared to the prior year, or compared to the acquisition model upon which the financing was hinged. AIC failed to identify that fully integrated products, manufactured in and shipped from China, were taking market share from the domestic producers who bought filters from Puff. In addition, AIC failed to understand the extreme cyclicality related to the air filtration business. Each late spring and summer of each year, sales would just plummet, and profitability of the company would follow suit. As time continued, the rebounds were less and less due to the off-shoring of ultimate end-product manufacture (lawn mower, etc.).

Fast forward a bit into my tenure and Motors was now enforcing a clause of the asset purchase agreement. This clause mandated that Puff assume all of the order to fulfillment activities of the aftermarket air filtration business. Operationally, that should not really be a problem. Put one or two order administrators in place and, so long as customer payments stayed current, this should not be a problem. After all, Puff-Bramalea was already manufacturing the parts. All that was needed was the order administration part of it…. OOPS!, except for an important piece affecting the economics of the aftermarket business.

Motors never revealed that there were customer volume rebates associated with this business that they internalized and never pushed down to the actual business unit; therefore, Puff had no knowledge of them. Worse yet, AIC never asked! This amounted to a $1 - $1.5 million per year reduction in sales and profits due to these rebates. Since there was no disclosure, AIC and Kahlmeny were making a case that Motors would have to bear this since there was no disclosure in the deal and Motors was protected by an indemnity clause that said damages had to top $3 million before Motors would be liable to make up the difference to AIC. Nowhere was this rebate of up to $1.5 million included in the acquisition and financing model. It was a huge gaff in the lacking diligence process that AIC performed in acquiring PuFFiltration.

Well, that's all good noise. Noise indeed. Incorporated into the deal was a topper of these items such that items that slipped through the cracks, such as these rebates, would have to top an economic value of $3 million before AIC could make a case of breach of contract. AIC and Puff had nowhere to go on this and no court of law would stand by them.

Young, inexperienced... chalk it up to that and the ivory tower 30-something PE know nothings.

There was a lot on my plate in leading the business out of the hole the private equity firm (AIC) placed it in. Incorporating cost reduction and continuous improvement initiatives into the broad business, implementing global cash management and forecasting for daily visibility, incenting strong working capital management, upgrading the staff in the finance and accounting areas, developing and implementing robust forecasts and budgets that began with the number of light vehicles that would be produced in the geographic operational regions of Puff. Add to that, implementing a strong internal control environment along with full analysis of what was going on with the business in terms of profitability and cash flow... and fixing the mess in China!

As if I didn't have enough to do, I had to babysit the chairman. When I say babysit the chairman, what I mean is field his juvenile attempts at convincing me to cook the books so that the bank would not really get any idea of just what was going on with the business and Puff's ability to abide by the bank agreement. To begin with, it was a real hoodwink of a job that AIC did on them to get them to pump $40 - $50 million into this business. This babysitting job lasted about five months and protected the truth that had become all-consuming.

As we closed the year 2012, and consequently my first six months with Puff and AIC, the numbers were not adding up to the expectations. As I had mentioned, the business was purchased on an average earnings stream of $16 million of adjusted EBITDA. The expectation was with such a great acquisition (as told to us by Chairman and Bullshitter-in-Chief B.S. Ferdalez), the first full year of earnings would indeed top that $16 million because of all of the "positive things that are happening in the business." What a line!

Early in January, the preliminary numbers were reported and consolidated. On increased sales, slightly above the $80 million, the company was barely reporting above $15 million of adjusted EBITDA. "What? Something must be wrong with the numbers," blurted Ferdalez.

At that point, Ferdalez was holed up in his office

adjacent to mine. He commanded the presence of Kahlmeny and I, and the three of us proceeded to go through twelve months of transactions, literally. These included those prior to my joining the company, first to understand the validity of the historical accounting treatment in the initial recording, and second, to conjure any possible way to reclassify some major ones that may have a dual character, but with the intention of relieving the expense line to bolster the 2012 profitability. Thirdly, to push the accounting rules hard, not within the realm and reason of GAAP, but to cross the line and build their own case that was justifiable in their own minds. It would be me who would be responsible to uphold positions taken and sell these (fraudulent) positions to our auditors, the bank and other financing sources. I was getting uncomfortable!

Not knowing how to convey to these guys—who were clearly up to no good—that these are things that we really ought not to be doing; certainly fixing errors is one thing and must be done, but to twist the truth, ignoring components of the acquisition that required expensing of such items and labeling the items a certain way in a manner to increase income? How do you persuade these guys who sign your paycheck not to be doing or suggesting these things?

After a few hours of these guys suggesting such things to obtain my approval to make such adjustments, and my declining the vast majority of their suggestions, I chose words that on appearance had a humorous tone to them, but got the message across. "Guys, I've gotta put my name on this stuff!" I exclaimed. I—as any CFO of a business that has third party debt where there is a credit agreement calling for the books and accounting records to be kept in "accordance with Generally Accepted Accounting Principles"—must sign a certificate at the end of each month and on a quarterly basis, where such credit is governed by the company's performance adhering to "covenants" and borrowings are outstanding, which states that to the best of his knowledge and ability, the financial statements are developed and produced in accordance with GAAP. Putting one's signature on that document and knowing otherwise constitutes a commission of fraud; therefore, I would be the one on the hook, so to speak. Ferdalez would regularly tell me that "this isn't a Collins & Aikman," having full knowledge of my history there and what had happened to the company. He would leverage these words as to imply that his suggestions weren't nearly as bad as what happened at Collins & Aikman. My position always was that a fraud is a fraud, no matter its size, and my body language would show that.

Well, the words "Guys, I gotta put my name on this stuff" would come to haunt me in my mid-year 2013 individual performance review. This was the only exception taken to extremely my exceptional performance that was proclaimed in my review by Kahlmeny. AIC and Kahlmeny jointly scolded me—through Kahlmeny's vocal chords—about using this phrase. I was told that using statements like that infer to the other side that what they are suggesting is to alter financials statements and effectively lie to the investors and lenders. Well, if it walks like a duck and quacks like a duck, it must be a duck!

I always knew what they were up to in trying to hide the real truth about this faltered acquisition from the real people that mattered: their investors, their lenders and the employees. It didn't matter much to the empty suits in the room. I was the gatekeeper. It mattered to me. It wasn't going to happen on my watch.

The debacle in Shanghai was unfolding. During the fourth quarter of 2012, we understood that we had to recapitalize the business—yes, double up on the capital invested in China; an erosion of value for the investors. With Ferdalez's drunken cheerleader approach to Puff, and all of the B.S. that he could spew about "what a great investment this is and will be in the future. In the grand scheme of things, this will work out to be fine in time. A few millions of incremental investment—here or there—isn't going to change much for "the Partners." Ferdalez was intimating that there was enough investor support for this investment that if we needed more money to come from the Partners to get over some hurdles toward eventually selling the company at a gain, this "would not be a problem."

"Not be a problem?" NOT! It *was* a problem!

What planet did this guy come from? I knew even before I was advised that I needed to incorporate the added $3 million of (China-doubled) capitalization into my cash requirements forecast and test if the credit line could absorb borrowing this money to send to China. My analysis said that this was viable as long as the company met its revenue growth projections while keeping costs in check. The company could live for a while until this money would be repatriated back to the US in some sort of engineered "round-tripping" of cash. Little did we know—and I claim ignorance on this until such time as I learned from the experience—that once you start the process of closing and liquidating a company in China, which was still at least 18 months away, the initial investment into the AIC Filter Trading Company would be withheld by the Chinese regulators who required a one-year close down period along with a statutory audit of affairs with the company to assure there was no wrong doing which opposed Chinese law. While I had some experience with business in China, I certainly articulated to AIC that I had no start-up or closure-of-operations experience in China. That was of no issue at the time because the young lads from Chicago assured me that things were well in hand with respect to the Puff business footprint. Unfortunately, AIC knew no better and had no grasp on these things. I learned to know better as the grasp on things and the responsibility to fix their major fuck-ups rested on my shoulders.

This news, supporting the commonly used phrase that it is easy to put money into China and extremely difficult to get that money out of China, meant that it would be at least two to three years that the trading company would have to be in existence and operating—while the (new) manufacturing company had launched and operated—before any invested capital could be returned to the US parent company. This was relatively a big deal because the hold period, as established with the AIC partners, for any portfolio company was approximately three years before the company would be sold and the capital return and gains would be paid to the partners. With the light duty filtration business of Motors being acquired on October 31, 2011, an anticipated sale would be planned for (at the latest) December 2014. With the delay in hitting several of the company milestones, in addition to the Chinese blow, the earliest the sale of the company could occur would be in the year 2016, unless the fund partners would be willing to accept a loss on the sale of the largest acquisition investment in AIC's history.

These milestones were missed, month upon month,

and the revenue targets were missed in the air filtration segment, in addition to forking an unplanned $1 to $1.5 million of rebates back to the aftermarket customers, in addition to cultural problems inside of the company that were holding us back from achieving improved profitability. My team and I identified and shared that results would fall short of expectations. Bear in mind that our credit agreement was tailored in such a manner to incorporate month after month of profit improvement as well as growth in the business which translated into higher earnings. The credit agreement, which was assembled and agreed upon the purchase of the business, contained aggressive terms. These aggressive terms called for profits to be increasing at a rapid pace after the acquisition.

As profits increase, more internal cash is generated. With more internal cash generated, the need for external financing of operations reduces; therefore, there were lending restrictions embodied in the form of covenants (agreements) that scaled back the available amount of lending as we were to generate the earnings which were put forth in the acquisition plan upon which the credit agreement was based. As we were not hitting the acquisition plan performance, internal financing wasn't sufficient to fund operations of the business over time. Due to the lending restriction (covenant) being set off of premium earnings in the plan, external financing was also not available.

With each month's financial results that were revealed, I was required to author a narrative explaining what was happening within the business, such that the business was yielding the results which were compiled and reflected in the company's financial statements. I developed methodology to determine exactly what was going on in the revenues and the profits, as compared to the business plan / bank plan, and articulate the deviations, both positive and negative, along with prospective corrections and what the future outlook was for the business. I would develop a matter of fact document that would identify strengths and weakness within the business and place a positive vibe on the proactive approach we were taking to remedy the weakness and exploit our strengths. This "management discussion and analysis" is customarily provided to significant stakeholders of a business (owners, members of the company's board of directors, commercial lenders and significant investors).

I submitted this to Kahlmeny and Ferdalez for their review, and then on to the big guy at AIC, Tretis, as Tretis had the relationship with our bank, ABC – Residents of Chicago. I would develop the most accurate explanations to deviations in sales revenue and profits and compare those to industry trends and feel quite confident of my presentation of events that occurred within the business. Upon submission to Tretis and his financial analyst, I received back an extremely altered document, diffusing the actual occurrences within the business, in an attempt to soften its reality so that the bank would not detect what was actually happening within the company, get nervous and either increase the financing cost, commensurate with the risk, or ask for an action plan for improvement within the company's operation. Mind you, the bank had $40 million at stake which was secured by assets in the company.

I received this altered document back from Tretis, was expected to sign it and forward it on to the bank and other lenders, with the certification that the books and records were in accordance with GAAP. Well, soften the truth as you may in the management discussion and analysis as to the goings on within the business, the books were going to reflect the actual events of the business, in accordance with GAAP, and I would sign the certificate on the financials, along with the letter and expect that if the bank had questions as to a mismatch between the dialogue and the numbers, they would come back and we could get to the bottom of it. That rarely happened. I was responsible for the financials. Tretis could twist the reality and spin it any which way he cared to cajole the bank into continuing to play the game with AIC and Puff. The financials would be right and that is what mattered.

Within the first two weeks of my hire, I was getting a sense of what these guys were up to. However, not really knowing the people, personalities and motivations, nor having a full set of circumstances related to some company issues, I could not prejudge and draw a conclusion that they were fraudsters at this point. Within these first two weeks (in late July 2012) I had learned that they reserved off a $1,100,000 gain in inventory valuation that was learned in January 2012. They had not recognized this gain in the financial statements of the company. Not to mention that after appreciating the complexities of this acquisition, AIC and their "professionals" really botched the acquisition accounting and purchase price allocation in the opening balance sheet. This lead to circumstances of "interpretative accounting" subsequently which were conveniently subjective with an ambiguous and misleading story line.

Upon learning of their holding back on recognizing the gain and not understanding how you could ignore such a significant item, I asked this exact question. The real answer came. "Well, we really didn't need any income in the first or second quarters of the year whereas the company will need this income in the third quarter, when the Bramalea lull in demand occurs and profits plummet. Since we're audited only on the year-end financial statements, we're just fine, and no one will have any issue," Kahlmeny, "the smartest guy in the room," advised me. (That is the mindset that comes from only big company employees who are trained that only year-end numbers matter because they are audited; actually, quarterly numbers matter just as much, but non-financial types are not knowledgeable about this.) I quickly responded that monthly and quarterly submissions are provided to the lenders, accompanied by a statement signed by the CFO being that the financial statements submitted thereon are expressed in accordance with Generally Accepted Accounting Principles. Within the current year and immediately prior to my entrance to the company, six of six such submissions were misrepresented and fraudulent. As a result, I mandated that this gain must be immediately recognized; however, so as not to badly distort the financials, we would spread the gain over three or four months.

Little did I know at the time, not having a full grounding of the business only two weeks into the job, I was unaware of the blatant earnings management that was taking place by Kahlmeny, Ferdalez and Accretive Industry Capital Partners. While I believed I was correcting an error in the financial statements, I was unaware that I was aiding their cause because the recognition would, by default, fall into the periods where the Bramalea volume problem would hit, therefore moving the income gain into the third quarter when it was most needed to meet the lender's required covenants. This, by definition, is earnings management and constitutes a fraud. With such short tenure with the company, I had no idea this played right into the hands of the fraudsters.

This adjustment received attention from the commercial lender upon my quarterly submission. The only explanation that I could derive—not being there seven months earlier at the time that this million dollar adjustment was developed—was that the company needed time to understand whether or not the adjustment was accurate and valid, and doing so would take three to six months to understand if the estimate of operating costs were accurate enough to include into the inventory valuation as a gain to the P&L. While I learned over time that this was not a pure answer, it did have a level of truth to it because the cost structure of the business, which was newly acquired, really wasn't well enough understood. For that understanding to occur, some time had to pass, and the operational costing experience of this newly independent business had to be gained. In addition, there was a level of sub-optimal competency in the financial ranks of the company. That being said, the level of understanding could all have been obtained in the first quarter and certainly have been booked correctly by March 31 of that year.

There are many methods, however, that the financial recognition could have (and should have) occurred, and the subsequent monitoring and adjustment would have followed in the future months. I was boxed in and gave the company and the individuals the benefit of any doubt at that time. Equally, a decision by me to re-open the month of January and book this adjustment in the proper period would have been unintelligent of me, given my short time with the company. Had I caused this—and although unlikely, the adjustment had been incorrect—I would not have exercised the required diligence to test the numbers adequately. That could only have been done with experience of running the company and monitoring the costs.

The adjustment also received attention from our auditors at the end of the year; however, at the end of the year, the numbers showed that a larger gain would be required to state the inventory accurately. Since the gain would be increased and the auditors identified other risks within our numbers, a favorable adjustment increasing the value of our inventory for cost incurred, with an increasing effect to the P&L bottom line, wasn't realistic.

Time marched forward. While the company was profitable, it was not going to meet the liquidity requirements of the lenders due to the increased investment required in China combined with the company not meeting its growth and earnings milestones. My back of the envelope math in December of 2012 also told me that. With this, I needed to instill a level of urgency within the senior management organization that didn't exist. I suggested to Kahlmeny that we hold a broad management meeting laying out the issues and inspire and motivate the group to deliver and pull ahead many of the cost improvements that were identified for 2013 in the 2013 budgeting process. Action plans and monitoring would be required.

The staff was, for the most part, ex-Motors people with significant tenure. Being that this business was a noncore business of Motors, the business, its employees and leadership were kind of forgotten as a stepchild of the greater enterprise. As such, a level of complacency existed. New suggestions for how to approach running the business and doing things differently were met with "We never have done it that way before" or "I don't think that's possible" when, in fact—having been there and done that before—I was more than confident that it could. The near dire financial circumstances were conveyed to AIC in a very informal format, with the promise that we would perform a diligent job of forecasting the remainder of the year, 2013, and would review this in the fourth quarter, 2012 board meeting that was scheduled for late February 2013.

Only slight improvements were made operationally and gains occurring in one month were reversed in the next month. This was quite concerning to me. At the same time, the "carve-out," or taking full control of the business of manufacturing and selling, was still quite incomplete. There were milestones in the asset purchase agreement that called for a timeline with firm dates on closure of these items as well as taking possession of the assets and remaining inventory to propel PUFFiltration into standalone operation, no longer to be dependent on a co-manufacturing agreement with Motors.

To pull together a comprehensive forecast for 2013, we needed to engage the general managers of Asia (Shanghai), Europe (France/Switzerland) and South America (Sao Paolo) to button down revenues and hammer out expense levels, along with their working capital needs as well as required investments in capital equipment. A similar, but more exhausting process took place for the wet filtration flagship in Faith, Ohio, as well as for the dry (air) filter business in Bramalea, Wisconsin. These two businesses' revenues comprised roughly 75%, or $60 million, of the $80 million company. Upon the full compilation and consolidation of the re-forecast, my first review told me that the results were not good. Once all of this was consolidated and pulled together, I then incorporated the required lending to continue the business and have it achieve the objectives which were set forth by AIC and Kahlmeny, in readying this business for sale in 2014 (the AIC investor mandated target date for sale). Based on the data, I was sure that we were to bust the covenants in the third quarter, certainly in the fourth quarter of 2013. That would mean higher financing costs, perhaps a whole re-write of the credit agreement, and perhaps changing commercial lenders. Nothing good was to come of the reality, but most certainly, addressing it head-on was the best approach and that was my recommendation to Kahlmeny.

Well, the smartest guy in the room always knew better, so he went to work calling upon various individuals in the organization to push them into better performance, higher sales and resultantly more profits and cash generation. His motivation was to change the numbers to move them into an acceptable range, even though it was not likely that there were actions to support these purported improvements. Being around the block more than once, I asked for a detailed action plan including timing, dollar values and who would be responsible. Sure enough, he would rally the troops and they would ultimately concede to him and he would produce such a schedule; whether or not it was attainable was a whole different issue.

After tempering these numbers with a "probability factor," I included them into our projections. Still the results were such that we would breach the bank agreement sometime in 2013. No way out.

The late February board meeting consisted of Kahlmeny and Ferdalez highlighting all of the accomplishments that had been made, on the sales and operational side, along with blaming "those bastards, Motors" for falling down on commitments that they had made which had cost us either money or time. I reviewed the prior quarter performance and provided my outlook for both profitability and liquidity throughout the rest of the current year, along with risks and opportunities. I hit the chart that said we would be in breach of our credit agreement sometime in the third or fourth quarter and suggested that forewarning to the bank, along with an action plan and proposal, would be highly recommended and warranted. For all intents and purposes, I was called an "alarmist" and that we shouldn't do anything rash with the bank to set them off. Obviously, these AIC guys and board members were greener than I had originally given them credit for, because anyone who knows their way around the banking situation knows that being proactive and working together with the bank is better than any late surprises.

As it was time now to begin to close off the transition services agreement and move from a co-manufacturing scenario with Motors being the other part of the "co," Kahlmeny nominated me to travel to Quimper, France, and Shanghai, China, to take the lead in this initiative. I had no problem with this as it involved a very significant and important piece of finalizing the deal. In addition, as things unfolded in China, we received notice that the taxing authority of the Pudong District of Shanghai had put the company on "red-flag alert" as the transactions that AIC / Kahlmeny had set-up were in violation of Chinese value added tax laws. On this trip, I would attempt to persuade the tax officials that we were victim of a component of the sales agreement with Motors and that we were not willfully violating their law. The company also had a loss in its 2013 Shanghai operations, and this would be another component of discussion with the tax officials.

The co-manufacturing transactions were set up as follows:

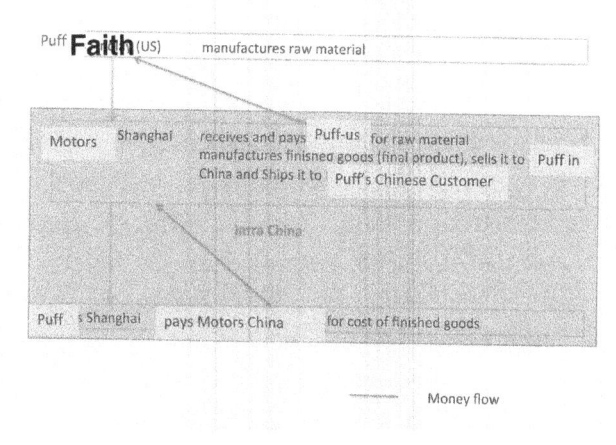

Puff **Faith** (US)	manufactures raw material
Motors Shanghai	receives and pays Puff-us for raw material manufactures finished goods (final product), sells it to Puff in China and Ships it to Puff's Chinese Customer
	Intra China
Puff's Shanghai	pays Motors China for cost of finished goods

----- Money flow

PUFFiltration China transaction flow chart - 1 page

To close off the co-manufacturing agreements in France and China, in addition to setting the values related to the purchase of inventories and assets, the hammering out of the cash exchanges on the inventory and fixed assets was fairly straightforward; however, the problems with the Chinese regulators mounted. The above set up is largely accurate. One deviation from the above chart was a premium market price adjustment that would be paid in a lump sum to Puff-US from Motors China for Puff's profit element in the price of the raw materials. AIC structured it this way within the co-manufacturing part of the overall deal. My wife and I enjoyed our finest bottle of wine that we possessed the night before I departed for China because I wasn't sure if I'd be wearing an orange jump suit and working hard labor on building a railroad somewhere in China after my first meeting with the tax officials.

Now in China and pleading the company's case, I was faced with convincing the tax authorities that the company was not colluding with Motors to take cash out of China while paying no income tax to China due to the recorded losses as the company was not making any money to pay tax from. After a span of three months, seven weeks of these three months spent there and three such meetings, I, along with some hired hands from AndersonMarwickCopland's Chinese affiliate, was successful in removing the red flags on the tax officials radar screen and, after co-manufacturing agreements expired (in effect at the time), the company would be in compliance with the Chinese law. This was some undertaking on my part, but I must say that my first experience with righting the errors of AIC in company and transactional set-up was personally rewarding and expanded my skill set and knowledge base significantly about conducting business in China.

While all of this China news bode well for the company, the company still was toiling with future liquidity that did not meet the requirements of the commercial lender. As such, my team and I were watching domestic and international cash daily. I implemented measures to push payment terms out to sixty days with our suppliers and this aided our cause significantly. In addition, the company's senior management were amateurs at managing inventory, so I brought in an old friend and the best materials and productivity expert in North America,

Mr. Slim Vickers, to help conserve cash. Tick-tock, tick-tock, the clock ran and we watched our cash. In my Chinese experience, I learned that it would take at least two years to receive the initial $3 million investment in the first Chinese company back from China, and that would happen only after a one year audit of the business ongoings of the company.

With all of this going on, as if it weren't enough, my babysitting job continued. Needless discussion, wasting time, Ferdalez tried to convince me to move money from the P&L to the balance sheet, thus shielding the income statement of operational costs and supplementing our liquidity by fabricating the financial statements to be the story that he wished to tell. The strong push of Ferdalez began in the May-June 2013 timeframe. It began with an extremely long discussion (three hours, minimum; about 50% in person in my office and the other half over the phone). Ferdalez enjoyed as many frequent flyer miles and Marriott Hotel points as he could possibly accumulate. There was absolutely no need for him to come to Faith every week. It appeared that all he did was sit in his office adjacent to mine and talk on the phone, schedule travel arrangements to go to and from his home in Tampa Bay, Florida, and work to convince me of his way of accounting. We spent one to two dinners together during the week and, early on, the discussion embodied a demonstration of his financial moxy as CFO of a division of a multinational conglomerate, then on to A. T. Kearney and KPMG as some sort of consultant with finance expertise. The conversation took me through some of the difficult times he experienced in his career, contrasting them to what we were experiencing at Puff and always—ALWAYS—advising me that Puff is not a

Collins and Aikman situation. These words were surely code for what was to come later from Nick Ferdalez.

Ferdalez advised me, David J. Burgundy, CPA, that all costs that had been incurred in Shanghai should be "startup-related" to getting things in place and ready to manufacture parts. No costs should be considered operational or related to sales and thus should not be matching against revenue and hitting the expense lines in the periods that the revenues are realized. Ferdalez' suggestion certainly applied to some costs, specific to readying the new facility for manufacturing, but not all the costs. There was a large proportion of costs that were caused by the operation of selling parts to customers and should be matched against sales revenues and expensed in the period, not hung up on the balance sheet to figure out their disposition at some later point.

I believed that my staff and I had been doing a diligent job determining what costs were (1) appropriate for balance sheet capitalization, (2) were "transition" related and those costs were given a pass by the bank as to excluding them from determining EBITDA for credit agreement benchmark purposes and (3) operational, which are the costs that generate and support sales revenue in the given period. Ferdalez was not satisfied after my demonstration. He asked that I contact our partner in charge of our audit, Michael Marcona, CPA, for the literature on start-up accounting. Sure enough, after reviewing what I had already known, I was spot on with respect to the proper accounting.

Ferdalez wasn't happy with this. He continued to "dog" me for the next several months about areas where we could push the accounting treatment and justify our treatment to the auditors with some such bullshit that he would fabricate.

Here's an interesting one: I came up with the position that the spare parts in our machine maintenance crib were actually inventory and if we could get an outside supplier to buy back these parts and resell them to Puff at such time as Puff used them in the production process, Puff would recognize the expense upon use of the items and not at the time that they were acquired and placed in stock inventory [13]. The prior practice was to expense these items upon their purchase. There was at least $1.5 million of these items in the spare parts crib inventory which would mean that if the Supply Chain Department could convince the suppliers to take these parts back and resell them to Puff upon their usage, there would be a $1.5 million pickup in profits because we would defer the expense recognition until the spare parts were used.

Well, Ferdalez, knowing that Puff Supply Chain would not do the hard work required, and with no true leadership from Kahlmeny, this was for sure, he literally directed me to put these items into production inventory (the inventory that we use to actually convert into saleable parts to our customers), and devise some scheme to say that it is product inventory and that 1/3000 of each of these bolts and screws that are installed on the machine are consumed with each product manufactured and for that reason, inventoriable (not to go to expense). This is so far from Generally Accepted Accounting that I was near to becoming ill. From this conversation, I determined that AIC knew that they were in deep with the acquisition of Puff, meaning it was a failed acquisition and that AIC would do almost anything to save face with its investors by lying to them and all concerned.

Watching and managing cash and liquidity on a minute-by-minute basis, we got by the second quarter 2013 with some room. The serious headwinds were to begin in August and continue for the remainder of the year. Projections that we all put together, actively, told the story that on a month out basis, we were to breach covenants with the bank, and I could not sign a management representation of covenants or certify the borrowing base as if it was within covenants.

As we got tighter to the covenants with time, I saw fitting that we do another full-blown forecast and compare that to our weekly liquidity forecast developed off of a different method, to see if in fact we were as close as we felt we were. Below you shall find the answer that we came up with.

For the remainder of 2013:

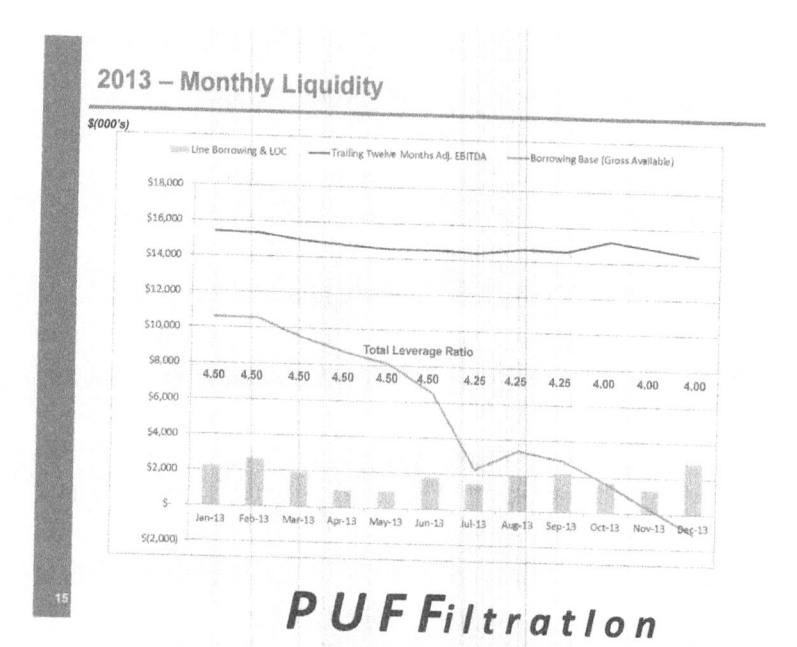

PUFFiltration 2013 Liquidity chart - 1 page

The orange line is equivalent to "bank allowed borrowing" and the green bars were the actual required amount of borrowing. As you can well see, for October, November and December—due to not achieving earnings and with the ratcheting down of the EBITDA multiples that indicated allowable borrowing per the bank agreement—we had less liquidity (cash-on-hand and available borrowing) than what actually was required to operate the business.

For the twelve months of 2014:

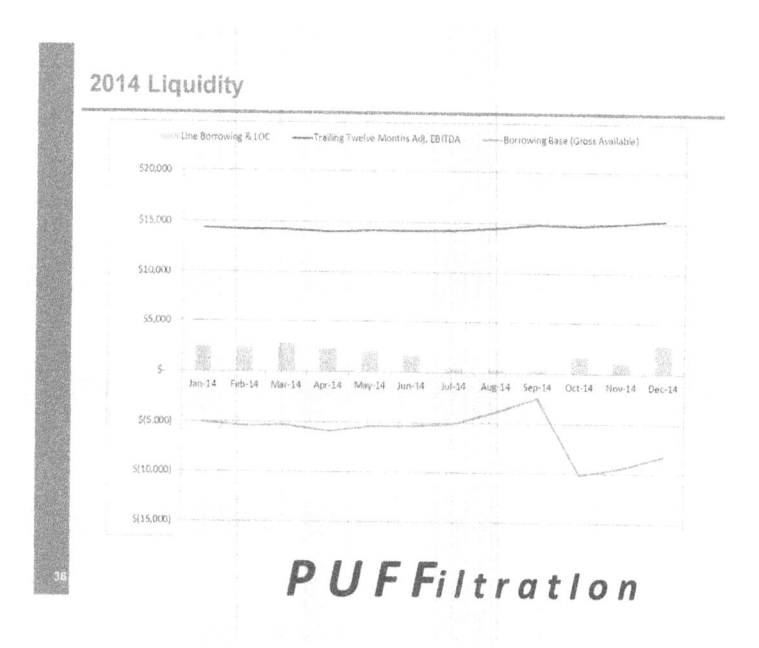

PUFFiltration 2014 Liquidity chart - 1 page

We were under water the whole year with respect to the same metric.

Covenants were worse:

2014 Covenant Performance

	Mar-14	Jun-14	Sep-14	Dec-14
Total Leverage Ratio - per Credit Agreement	3.75	3.75	3.75	3.25
Total Leverage Ratio - Forecast Outlook	4.30	4.22	3.92	3.95
	Fail	Fail	Fail	Fail
Senior Leverage Ratio - per Credit Agreement	2.25	2.25	2.25	2.00
Senior Leverage Ratio - Forecast Outlook	2.52	2.42	2.18	2.25
	Fail	Fail	Pass	Fail
Structural Financing:				
Senior Revolving Line — ABC	$ 2,531	$ 1,389	$ -	$ 2,506
Senior Term Debt -	33,409	32,935	32,461	31,987
Norwest Mezzanine	21,261	21,396	21,534	21,671
Seller Note Payable	4,088	4,190	4,295	4,403
-Total	$61,289	$59,910	$ 58,290	$ 60,567
Trailing Twelve Months Adj. EBITDA	$ 14,263	$ 14,186	$ 14,884	$ 15,339

PUFFiltration

PUFFiltration 2014 Covenant Failure - 1 page

PuFFiltration would fail seven of the eight covenant tests, prospectively. This was really bad, but not unexpected news. With the reneging of certain significant deal items with respect to revenues, with having to draw an unanticipated additional $3 million from a line of credit to recapitalize and fix the AIC screwups in China and a $1.5 million unanticipated rebate to be paid to the aftermarket customers of Bramalea, Wisconsin, it is no wonder that the company was in the shape it was. The creditors who were now into this deal for well over $60 million had limited information about the condition of the company. As it was, the creditors were aware that the company required more funding due to the AIC mistakes in company set-up in China, but were substantially unaware of the commercial issues that were adversely affecting the PuFFiltration's ability to service its debt across the time horizon.

And so it was that when my staff and I were confident and complete with the financial pro forma (primarily made up of a forecast along with attending assumptions) that we compiled over the prior three weeks, including the weekends staying down in Faith while my home and wife remained in Grosse Pointe Park, Michigan, I was supposed to be with Kahlmeny and Ferdalez on October 23, 2014 for a review of the information. Ferdalez was busy, so I went in to see Kahlmeny. I revealed the results and Kahlmeny was not in disbelief of the results, but, being "the smartest person in the room," he wasn't accepting them as being accurate and reliable.

I assured Kahlmeny that my team and I looked at each and every number that went into the projections and we were confident that unless something of a drastic change were to occur, these would be the results if certain "favorable" items that we included were to occur. Again, the numbers were developed with a realistically conservative view of "task" for the operational folks to perform to.

Kahlmeny rebuked the information and directed me to send all of the Excel worksheet files and PowerPoint presentation files directly to him and excused me out of his office. Apparently, this non-accountant, expert-of-everything was going to fix things his own way to pass the covenant tests that our expert work told us the company would fail. I knew his efforts would not be to paint reality but would be designed to tell a story that he would want told to the lenders: in a word, fraud. I instructed my staff that although we did a grand job, Kahlmeny felt he knew better and we were to comply with his direction on sending him all files per his request, but we were to change nothing, unless our changes were to be affected with reason and substantiation and met the GAAP criteria.

Kahlmeny was on his own.

I knew where this was going. The numbers would be changed so as to keep Kahlmeny and AIC out of hot water with investors and the lenders.

This would only work for so long.

Footnote Explanations

(13) Such pay upon usage contracts are commonly called "consignment agreements."

Ferdalez Wisdom

Being as my staff and I had nothing of a productive nature to do for the later part of the afternoon, we camped in my office: Gerry Hoover, corporate controller and Justin Sutton, director of financial planning and analysis. We were in disbelief of earlier events of the day and pondered what Kahlmeny and Ferdalez could be doing with our numbers after the level of diligence that we all put forth over the prior solid three weeks.

At approximately 3:45 p.m., my mobile phone rang. It was Ferdalez. You see, against my, Hoover's and Sutton's advice, Kahlmeny pumped our Shanghai and Brazil operations full of raw material from Faith, expecting to realize the profit from the intercompany shipments. Our advice was not to do this because it would cost the company cash AND there was no profit increase on these shipments because we performed an intercompany profit elimination (profit does not exist unless the sale is to an outside party, not a sister manufacturing plant of the same company who manufactured the goods).

Ferdalez was HOT. He was suggesting all day long that he could argue that there is no profit on the raw material sales to our affiliate and that he could convince our auditors of this. "This is worth $250,000 in a month that we're tight on our covenants!" he exclaimed. I contested this, knowing financial statements quite well and the inner workings of them. I advised that if profit is declared by the seller of a related party recipient, then the profit which was declared must be "eliminated" by the corporate entity because profit is only earned on sales to outside customers, not related party customers. Shanghai and Brazil were owned 100% by Puff. Ferdalez instructed me to put back in the profit that we had eliminated, and he would argue and justify the numbers to the auditors and I advised that I could not do that. He then suggested that we get a subject matter expert on the topic and pay him or her some money to tell us the rules. I raised the possibility that because my good friend, Mike Marcona, was named AMC Partner on the Puff account, that if I called Mike, he would be in Faith at 8:00 a.m. to discuss inventory valuation and intercompany profit elimination and provide his insights and opinions. "Oh, I didn't want to get the auditors involved," said a timid Ferdalez. "I thought that if we could get a real expert, he could give us an opinion." I suggested that there were no more experts than the folks who would opine on our financial statements and that was Mike Marcona. Ferdalez punted.

I suggested, "Nick, why don't you Google 'intercompany profit elimination and inventory valuation' and see what you come up with. Call me when you do."

My colleagues (after hearing every word) and I looked at each other in amazement. How in the world can someone rise to a level of influence, such as Ferdalez, and drive others to perform acts of illicit commission such as the one that he directed?

… as the world turns …

I called my wonderful wife, relatively soon that evening, after that awful exchange. I advised her that the Puff experience was no longer going to work and that it was in our best interests for me to tender my resignation as soon as possible, if not earlier. Understanding as she is, but thorough, she asked me to make sure and if I was sure, then she was on board with the decision. After all of the illicit attempts and near misses with these amateurs and crooks, I knew the one and only answer: "I'm out."

I had dinner that night with my dear friend and the best materials management and productivity expert in North America, Slim Vickers. I apprised Slim of the situation. I told him as of noon tomorrow, I'm gone. I also said that he is making a great difference there and so long as the company wants him to return and keep on doing the good things he does, to absolutely do so without hesitation.

We left the dinner table. I walked to my apartment. I changed into my jeans, a sweatshirt and ball cap. At 10:30 p.m., I returned to the company and cleared any personal belongings from my office. I returned to my apartment, authored my resignation letter to be submitted at noon the following day, October 24, 2013.

With no stimulation from Kahlmeny the morning of October 24, 2013 on getting together, I held my final cash meeting with my crew, scheduled a noon meeting with Kahlmeny and waited for that time to arrive. At noon, I entered Kahlmeny's office, "always the smartest guy in the room" and he proceeded as if everything was totally in his control. I expressed my disdain for positions that he has taken relative to the financial management of the company, along with his lack of support because he had paid my employees under market levels of compensation and that he effectively blew me off. I suggested then that it was high time that I provide him the writing that I developed the night before. This Muslim Asian Indian turned white after he comprehended what was happening.

"You know better. It's all yours now. I'm done here."

About a year after this all had occurred, I had been getting calls from some of my finance staff at Puff asking for my help out of the company (for them to leave Puff and find new employment). They told me that the financial performance is bad, the bank is mad at them and if I was there, it would be a different situation and they would not think of leaving or breaking any loyalty.

In November 2014, they fired Gerry Hoover, the corporate controller, for "non-performance," they claimed. Gerry was awarded 2014 "Salary Employee of the Year" at Puff and received accolades in front of the whole salary workforce. This was not a performance issue with Gerry, I can assure you of that. The fact of the matter is I advised Gerry to renegotiate his under-market salary when I left because he was the only one capable of holding the accounting and finance stuff together with me gone. He did so and received a raise. I am sure that Kahlmeny despised that action and got his retribution by firing Gerry.

Gerry called me to share his news that he was "in the job market again." What he told me was not surprising, but still interesting to me because after spending almost two years there, I wanted to fix Puff the right way. Gerry told me that the company was struggling to hit $7 million of EBITDA (remember, AIC's acquisition case was based on $16-$22 million), and that they had $3 million of defrauded income/expense hidden into their balance sheet which should have hit the P&L and subtracted from profits. I suspect this $3 million was the Shanghai operating costs that Ferdalez was persuading me to capitalize, plus the ignoring of the right-pocket, left-pocket intercompany profit transactions that he did not want to eliminate.

He also advised that Greyrock Group, a Chicago based insolvency workout firm, was into the company to perform turnaround services at the bank's request. Further, he said that most of the management staff left after I did, and that the customers now hated the company as delivery and quality performance were "red" with all customers.

Diagnosing the ills of companies that have turned insolvent always results in the disease of "mismanagement" being the cause. This mismanagement stemmed from AIC's lack of due diligence and ranges from overpaying for the beleaguered asset to the drunken rah-rahs put forth by the "Chairman and Cheerleader-in-Chief" Ferdalez through the inexperience and "green/wet behind the ears" management style and lack of execution by Kahlmeny, always the smartest guy in the room.

From the Author

Truth. Honesty. Intelligence. Trust. Freedom. Ingenuity. Hard work. Integrity. Creativity. Fairness. Liberty. Respect. Teamwork.

Simple words, but it is the concept embodied in these collective words that spawned the greatness of our country and the basis of our free enterprise society. This framework is one of greatness and must be preserved. It is why we fight for what we know as our beloved United States. Fighting for the meaning and spirit of each one of these is what is tucked deep inside each of us Americans. The system just plainly doesn't work if you cherry pick and live by only the ones you like. They are entirely interrelated because it is the concept of exchange.

I expect truth, so I must give truth in exchange. I expect respect, so I must give respect in exchange. I expect fairness, so I must give fairness in exchange. You can go right on down the line with each one of these concepts and it is the same. It cannot and must not be "I expect fairness, so I must cheat" or "I expect honesty, so I must lie." If this was the case, then what could we rely on in society?

I have experienced a great deal in my career. Among all of the vast experiences, I was integral to a team who employed the above concepts and in 1995 and won the Shingo Prize for Manufacturing Excellence. This was one of the pinnacles of my career. I know the power of what happens when all of these elements are combined and create a force of excellence. Unfortunately, I also know and have experienced individuals who want such results of esteem, accolades and premium compensation without the willingness to contribute the requisites that I have referred to in my opening line.

I have struggled over the necessity of writing this book and vacillated from one extreme to another, from not writing the book to a full disclosure expose, telling it all in each of my three (now four) "sideways" experiences, including the names of the companies and individuals who were involved. I was half-pregnant with the thought of this endeavor until I treated myself to an extended weekend by myself in the great town of Toronto. I decided that progress on this book would be my mission and a side-benefit to the treat of hanging out and treating myself well during the weekend. My wife was hosting some relatives on their annual business trip to the greater Detroit, Michigan, area and I had decided another venue would be best given my state of mind. So I chose one of my favorite North American cities.

Even though this book was intended to be a major part of the extended weekend, at this point I could not claim that the book would ever be finished, much less published for distribution; that is, until I met an attractive young lady at dinner the first evening of my trip. Being a loner on this trip, I pulled up a seat at the bar of "Colette," a new, upscale and trendy French restaurant in the downtown area. As I enjoyed a glass of nice French white **"Burgundy"** wine—the Burgundian that I am—and took in the ambiance of this great place, along with the young lady who sat nibbling at her dinner and pounding her laptop on the bar. Type, type, typing away, I had decided to ask what the heck she was working on. Being that we were near the financial district of the thriving city of Toronto, I was betting that she was carrying on with unfinished business of her day job.

Surprising to me, I was wrong. "Writing my book,"

she responded.

I said, "How very interesting." I asked her what the subject was and she told me it was a blend of fiction and some of her real life experiences and that the book had a spiritual overtone. She went on that she had been following a prominent book writer of similar context as her book and shared with me that people who write books have a purpose to write their book and a message to deliver in it. I pondered for a moment and thanked her for the information as I had finally decided that for many reasons, I needed to write this book. Let me touch on the purpose and message, once again.

First, I imagine that there are many men and women choosing a career who will opt to move into the financial management side of business. I also believe that their perspectives on the field are very similar to what mine were upon making the decision to pursue such a career: there are standards to be upheld, your performance will be judged on how well the company performs, holding you as a contributor to that performance while making sure that the company is playing the game "inside of the white lines" and that everyone involved in the business, including your superiors, "get it." In other words, the goal is to make money and grow value, legally and ethically, with the interests of investors, lenders, employees, customers, suppliers, the community and the environment at heart. In my experience, the vast majority of CEOs, chairmen, presidents, COOs, boards of directors, investors, private owners and private equity firms are interested in furthering their own financial interests and aligned with the interests of doing that fairly, truthfully and legally. Initially, my perspective was that "everyone" is aligned with these interests (I guess that is why you see my phrase "a career first for me" repeated a few times in this book). Admittedly, although I know all of the rules like the back of my hand, I was naïve to the greed element in business, how pervasive it can be and how it can be perpetrated. Shameful, but true.

The fact of the matter is that everyone is not aligned with these interests. There are folks out there who will place their own interests and financial gain ahead of fairness, integrity and abiding by the rules. I believe this book serves a purpose to those individuals making a decision to move into this career direction as well as to investors and lenders in businesses. Don't be shocked about running into such circumstances. If you are "out there" in the field of business, rest assured that you will. Someone, even those you would least suspect, will try to pull one over on you. You will need to decide a number of things when this happens. One of the things that you must not decide, or pass judgment on, is objectivity. Preserve this and you will preserve all, including your integrity.

The next comment may be a shock to at least one person: the guy I did not vote for in either 2008 or 2012, Mr. Regulator in Chief, Barack Obama. Barry, "YOU CAN'T REGULATE THIS." Substantially, the rules in place prior to your becoming Emperor were adequate. What was needed was effective enforcement. More regulation and stricter rules punish 100% of the participants, thwarting the creativity, objectivity and competitiveness of businesses in the United States, when maybe around one-third of the business leaders might present an ethical problem.

Also, Barry, these types of frauds are not caught on the level where you seek to implement more regulation.

As I have demonstrated in this book, often these violations go unsuspected. People who are willing to put their name on fraudulent financials will do so even with stronger regulation that yields more punitive consequences. They're going to perpetrate regardless. It's like drug addiction, which you may or may not know about, having done heroin. It's the fix that is important and unless they get their fix, they're not going to be happy.

You see, in the case of Collins & Aikman, the company's executives involved third party suppliers to fabricate bogus agreements that would be shown to the auditors so C&A could pass the annual audit and not recognize the true liabilities that really existed and ultimately would be paid back to the suppliers if in fact C&A survived into the future. This involved alignment of chairmen, directors, executives, management, purchasing agents, suppliers, accounting departments, lawyers, on and on, to perpetrate the fraud and lie to creditors and investors. Auditors cannot, nor do they have the ability to, detect such fraud. The hush-hush, wink-wink, behind the scenes secretive activity goes undetected. The auditors rely on signed statements by the people in charge of the company to attest to not being aware of any misstatements in the financial statements in addition to being unaware of any fraud occurring within the company for the subject period. You cannot get at this to fix it with more regulation. It settles with the integrity of the people involved and that's it!

The one area of Sarbanes-Oxley that I believe is beneficial is the separation of auditing firms from any of the other consulting services that can be provided by the same firm. Prior to this law, an audit firm could perform I/T consulting, operation improvement consulting, financial services consulting and the list could go on... The separation of the audit function is fundamental. Not to be accusatory, but you can readily appreciate that if a CEO needs a clean opinion of his financial statements, perhaps to get a deal done, and the auditor detects a material misstatement of the financial results of operations, the CEO may very well tempt the auditor firm with award of non-audit type work should the auditor sign off on the statements as they were. I sense of late that this aspect of the law is administered somewhat loosely as I learn more and more audit firms are again providing services other than audit and tax. They probably say that they can maintain their independence, but that will always be questionable in my mind. Most business people have an allegiance to "more money."

While I hope that this book helps to apprise and to educate people considering a career in financial management and the broader public of investors, lenders and other interested individuals, I wish to advise the reader that experiences in this book are becoming more commonplace. As I become more acquainted with many individuals through meeting people in business or otherwise, I have become comfortable enough to share snippets of what had happened to me in these notable career circumstances and the response I receive is, "Oh, I was just talking to someone who went through something similar." I am not alone from the standpoint of having experienced the potential influence to commit fraud. I may be alone from the standpoint of handling it as I did.

While I did not take you through the notable accomplishments of my career, I had become expert at leading manufacturing companies to successive value creation through enterprise growth and efficiency on my watch, while improving business processes and systems, satisfying customers, upgrading employees, adhering to standards, observing and improving the environment, coaching colleagues, creating and abiding by value-oriented agreements and had gained significant recognition throughout my career for doing so. I am happy that I can say that these accomplishments were the result of hard work on the part of all, fairness, integrity, some intelligence, playing the game within the white lines and abiding by the concept of mutual respect among colleagues. I am happier, though, to sit across the dinner table from my loved ones and say, with the right amount of emphasis and meaning, "Do the right thing."

During the C&A debacle, Bill Waldon sent me this note of encouragement relating to all of the "Enronian" articles that he would read.

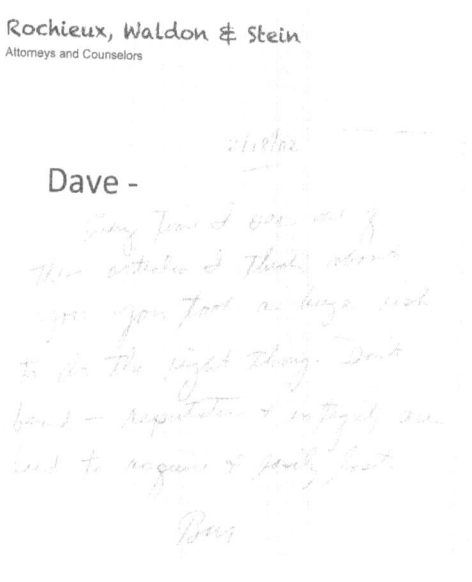

Rochieux, Waldon & Stein
Attorneys and Counselors

Dave -

Note of encouragement from Bill Waldon - 1 page

Epilogue:
Meet Mr. Patrick Sulyeam

What is the deal here? I am quite sure that by now and after all of my experiences, I do not have a label on my forehead that says, "Cheap date for hire! I will do anything for money, including lie and commit fraud for you—that is, if you pay me well."

As you know, one of the facilitating factors allowing me to write this book is the fact that I have been "in transition" for some time now and exploring future employment possibilities. In case you haven't done the math on me, given my lengthy career experiences, I am in my mid-fifties. After my wife and I have collectively put four children through a Big-Ten college, in addition to living a slightly above-average lifestyle, I need to work. I need to work and earn so that my wife and I will be able to afford a cat food-free diet in our retirement.

I have had the luxury of meeting a number of great professionals during my lengthy career. Lawyers, actuaries, insurance and risk management specialists, management consultants, business owners, board members, independent accountants, private equity professionals and investment bankers. There are many types of investment bankers. An individual, like yourself or I, may consult an investment banker to buy and sell securities (stocks and bonds) of publicly traded companies listed on the New York Stock Exchange or the NASDAQ. Goldman Sachs, JP Morgan, Morgan Stanley and Merrill Lynch are among some of the most commonly known investment bankers who have significant segments of their business devoted to the buying and selling of securities on behalf of investors, in addition to advising investors in accordance with the investors' best interests.

Another type of investment banker, who holds similar credentials, may broker entire businesses between buyers and sellers; often a buyer of a business will engage an investment banker for advisory services related to the specific purchase of a business and, similarly, a seller of a business will engage an investment banker for advisory services related to the sale of a specific business. The aforementioned investment bankers also buy and sell entire businesses on behalf of investors; however, some smaller firms specialize in this type of activity. Relationships with investment bankers may prove key to revealing certain other broad opportunities which are not specifically tied to the buying and selling of business, more so than any other business professionals, because, as you can imagine, their span of relationships can be great as well as their span of "inside" knowledge of changes to an industry, a business and the buyers and sellers thereof.

Through my transition period, I have stayed close to one particular firm, due to the fact that one of my close friends and (next door) neighbor had been working for one of these firms for a number of years. Craig Campenelli had been quite instrumental in making introductions internal to his firm, including to the principal in the firm, Cliff Paslin. As my transition continued, in addition to my making reciprocal introductions, we had contemplated my going to work for the firm in an advisory / transactional role; however, compensation is not too different than that of a fisherman–hence, "You eat what you catch." That is, any compensation is purely on a contingency basis: my bringing the firm a business to package-up and sell would yield me a small percentage of the enterprise value for which the company ultimately is sold. Also, bringing the firm a business which meets their clients' criteria on a buy-side transaction would also yield similar compensation. While this can be quite lucrative, the odds can be quite low for an individual like myself to land such a deal in their hands; therefore, my quest for other productive employment continued.

Just as the referral side of our relationship was bilaterally active (I had made such referrals to the firm which resulted in only near successes), I received a call from Cliff advising me that he had provided my CV, name and contact information to a Mr. Patrick Sulyeam, the owner of a growing business, who was in need of a chief financial officer. After now knowing each other for quite some time, Cliff understood that I was "above board" on all things and "played inside of the white lines." For this, I had reason to believe that Cliff would have made only referrals which were complimentary to my mode of operation and code of ethics. Cliff, from all indications, was an above-board kind of guy, worked hard at satisfying his clients through providing them value in his field, and would do so with a manner full of honorable integrity and ethics. Knowing this, I had thanked Cliff, advised him that I would be interested and approved of his sending my CV to Mr. Sulyeam. Within ten minutes after that discussion, my mobile phone rang, and it was indeed Patrick Sulyeam on the other end.

Mr. Sulyeam's tenor and aggression, off the cuff, seemed to be hard driving and entrepreneurial, but the man's delivery should have been a huge warning sign. Instead, I welcomed the exchange as someone who can help him add value to his portfolio.

His disgust with customers and his perspective on

how customers should pay prices far above fair value (in my interpretation of the dialogue) caused me wonder because in those introductory moments, he demonstrated his deep belief that he deserved their money and they did not, no matter the consequences. This clearly should have been a real red flag and telling of what was about to unfold in the coming weeks and months. This did cause me to pause due to the fact that his belief of entitlement could not only be applied to customers, but suppliers and probably employees. Thinking back, hate and greed clearly came through the cell phone microwaves.

Another (huge) red flag was he was not interested in talking through / learning about my career experiences and marrying them up to the task at hand. He merely advised that he reviewed my resume and that I clearly had the credentials he was interested in and could do the job. I laid this off to the quality of the referral and that perhaps Sulyeam had a fully trusting relationship with Cliff. This was not the case. I learned that such level of intimacy between Cliff and Sulyeam did not exist.

After this exchange (far less than a discussion), Sulyeam advised me that he would turn my contact information over to his (holding company) chief financial officer, Steve McCracken, and that McCracken would be contacting me shortly. The call came within two days of the conversation with Sulyeam.

McCracken was interesting. The promotional aspect of the Sulyeam-McCracken show was in full force. "Growth through acquisition" was the big theme. "We're currently profitable and sitting with a virtually unused line of credit of $75 million with an accordion [expansion] feature of an incremental $25 million, should we execute an acquisition and we are pursuing three at the moment." "The business is split into two parts: aftermarket, which includes Clean Swipe Window Wiper Blades, and your business, should we elect to move forward, the Automotive Original Equipment Group. The aftermarket business is approximately $400 million in revenue and the original equipment business is running between $300 and $350 million."

Like Sulyeam, McCracken was passive in delving deeply into my professional past. Although I am proud of my accomplishments, I left that piece as is; if he was good, I was good. You're taught that when "they" do most of the talking, that you are in a power and control position in the world of job hunting.

"Patrick and I fly each week to Detroit and spend the first part of the week in Rochester Hills, Michigan, at the Clean Swipe facility. Can you meet us there Tuesday morning at 8:30? Can you be prepared to talk 'key performance indicators' and 'controls' when we get together?"

"Sure to both," I said willingly.

Over the next few days, I developed a PowerPoint presentation that demonstrated I had both the knowledge and the know-how as to bringing proper business measures and operational and internal control to a manufacturing business from concept to implementation. To 'professionalize it' for presentation purposes, I then sent it via email to my own email address and planned to show it on my iPad in the breakfast meeting the following Tuesday.

I had received an email from McCracken asking to move the meeting to Wednesday, instead of Tuesday, and the venue to the Townsend Hotel restaurant, mentioning that they would treat me to breakfast. The Townsend

Hotel is a status driven, high-end, full-service hotel, restaurant and bar in Birmingham, Michigan, an upscale metropolitan Detroit town about 20 miles northwest of downtown. This agreed with my schedule and I accepted the change.

As I approached the hotel restaurant on time, a shabbily dressed guy with straw-like, ungroomed hair and a roller suitcase brushed past me and through the door of the restaurant. Nearly avoiding a collision, I approached the hostess and mentioned that I was to meet someone there. She looked at me and it was obvious that no one had left a name to match with mine. At that point, I decided to approach the "near-miss" guy as he was just getting seated at a booth in the restaurant. "Steve?" I queried.

"David?" he queried back. "Patrick will be down shortly. He's just pulling a few things together and had to take a call," McCracken mentioned.

"Fine, fine, no problem," I replied.

Patrick Sulyeam entered the restaurant and booth with such energy that I nearly had to question its source as being a synthetic stimulant. This guy got right into the customer bashing all over again (as if this was his theme), advising me that "the customer has to pay more than their fair share." I wasn't sure what industry this guy was talking about, but it surely wasn't the automotive supply industry that I operated in since 1978. It's all about price/cost, technology and customer service that translates into a value proposition where a supplier can receive a fair price when all of these criteria align in such a manner that the said supplier provides a "premium" value package to the car-maker, when compared to other suppliers providing similar products.

In the case where new/better/best technology enters

the situation, customers (Original Equipment Manufacturers such as GM, BMW, Ford, Daimler) will allow a premium price when compared to the less technology-rich competitors' products. This technology often replaces additional value-add processes that the customers would have to pay separately for or adds features or functionality to the prior generation products.

It is often that when product technology matures and competitors acquire similar rich technology, the carmakers will seek to commoditize the particular product by bidding the incumbent supplier's prices against their competitors'.

I didn't know then that Sulyeam's companies produce (shit) lower food chain products that have been long-ago commoditized by the carmakers and the angst he demonstrated was one of undeserving entitlement. The technology was low, (I later learned that) customer service was suffering and the only thing that would get such a supplier through such conditions would be an excellent relationship and reputation. Early on in my relationship with Sulyeam, I could easily tell that he wasn't winning any popularity contests. I later learned that Sulyeam's companies were "RED" in all of the important categorical measures of technology and customer service, including quality. Pricing was appropriate because of the overall value proposition; customers were getting what they were paying for and, consequently, not paying for what they were not getting in terms of technology and customer service. Hence: ANGST! RESENTMENT! HOSTILITY! (from Sulyeam). That is just how the guy is built.

As the meeting progressed, mention from Sulyeam about business measures came. I had offered that I developed a bit of a presentation about the subject matter to share with them and asked if it was all right to show it to them. They agreed. I walked through the iPad presentation and they were awestruck in that I had the elements that they were indeed looking for. I knocked the ball out of the park. Sulyeam and McCracken finished their breakfasts. I did not order any food as I knew I would be talking most of the time. We parted and they both advised that we would be talking soon. It was the next day that I received a joint introduction email from McCracken addressed to Mr. Bob Belenhoff and me. Bob was the president of the GoldHat Automotive Original Equipment Group. The email was a request for Bob and me to get together to conduct further diligence on my prospective hire.

Bob and I exchanged contact information. Bob asked if Sunday morning at 11:00 a.m. would be good to meet at the restaurant he owned in Plymouth, Michigan. I agreed. This seemingly was going at a relative fast pace (to my liking as I had to get to again making a living after approximately 16 months of no income having worn our after-tax savings relatively thin). These guys were collectively motivated to fill the spot of CFO for the Automotive Original Equipment Group and I was their guy.

An ex-Navy Seal, Bob was a very cool guy in every sense of the word: temperament, history, comfortable with his position in life, etc. It was evident that there was one thing in his life that he was not "cool" about and that was GoldHat and Patrick Sulyeam. Bob had mentioned that he reviewed my CV ahead of our breakfast meeting and wasn't interested in reviewing my qualifications nor my professional history. He had made a simple statement that he was "confident that I could do the job." Bob advised of his ex-Navy Seal status and his "doing things right for all stakeholders is totally what I am about, but something just wasn't right at GoldHat". "I am a lean manufacturing guy, and a big proponent thereof. That's how my team and I have been trained. I have brought in most of my management team in the Original Equipment Group. Now, Patrick has us building inventory, as much inventory as we can make. I do not know why this is, other than the fact that we generate income through fixed cost absorption when we build inventory. He is in need of showing the banks that his operations are profitable while he is attempting new company acquisitions with the borrowed funds. Steve shared with you how they are doing these deals, right?"

I acknowledged that he did via a large credit line that they are able to utilize to buy companies, "something like $75 million that can expand to $100 million should viable acquisitions occur", I responded. Bob was extremely uncomfortable with this. Having led XYZ, a successful Heinz Loften owned automotive supplier, he was quite aware that this was nothing but temporary window dressing and one day would need to be properly dealt with.

"Now, you're going to have to have my back on this one," Bob injected, as if to say that I would be responsible to raise the valuation issues about the excess inventory. Excess and obsolete inventory requires a negative valuation adjustment or P&L loss, because often, at the ultimate time of sale, an enterprise is paid a value that is less than its cost of its excess or obsolete goods. I offered that this valuation adjustment would need to be made at quarter-end, consistent with the bank reporting date. Usual bank reporting protocol requires an officer of the company, most usually the chief financial officer, to sign a borrowing base certificate and covenant compliance certification. I assumed that this would be me, but even if it was not me, being attached and responsible for financial statements that are not representative with proper GAAP valuation methods and resulting income statement recognition is something that I will have no part of. Bob made reference to the incumbent currently holding the position that I was interviewing for, that he had a long history with Patrick Sulyeam and wasn't the type of individual to stand up to Sulyeam in order to do the right thing. Bob, having a history with McCracken, also had mentioned that McCracken ought not be a party to this stuff, as he knew Steve from jointly serving on a company's board of directors at some prior time.

From this day forward, I became aware that I would have a fight on my hands and that Patrick was "gaming" the system for his greedy, self-serving result. Having sited my history of doing the right thing at the (temporary) cost of my career and income at C&A and some of the other experiences noted in this book, I assured Bob that I had an extremely thick skin when it came to things like this and that on my watch, the right thing would be done. I was confident that the meeting went well and that I would wind-up being Bob's savior as he really didn't know how he was going to overcome the wrath of Patrick.

From the close of that meeting onward, I was Bob's guy. Upon parting, he mentioned that he would get back to McCracken and that McCracken would come back to me, probably in fairly short order. The next day, I emailed McCracken and advised that "Bob and I had [what I thought to be] a good Sunday morning breakfast meeting and would be awaiting next steps." Within a couple of days, McCracken responded and said he would be in touch with me shortly. A little concerned that this had not occurred by Monday of the following week, I sent a follow-up email to McCracken. He replied by saying that he would be calling me the next day. He did so and beyond the cordiality, he extended an acceptable monetary offer of salary and bonus.

McCracken asked, "When are you available to start?"

Anxious to be positively productive again, I asked, "Being as we are coming upon the end of the month, would Monday work for the company?"

McCracken responded positively, although he mentioned that "if this is the case, he would have to terminate the incumbent this week." He assured me that he would do so, and that March 2 would be my starting date. I agreed and thanked him.

Monday, March 2, rolled around quickly. The morning had started off with me meeting Bob Belenhoff at the door as we both entered the Original Equipment Headquarters office at 7:25 a.m. This was slightly odd in that there was no one else in the 10,000 square foot Livonia, Michigan, office. I asked, "Why so much space?" Bob responded by saying this is left over from one of the companies that Patrick acquired in the aftermarket and they consolidated operations in Rochester Hills. It seemed to me to be quite expensive for two or three people to occupy and only periodically as a fair amount of our time would be spent at the operations.

The place was dark and resembled the ghost town of Detroit's vacant offices in the 90s. Bob suggested that I take any office that I care to, but I opted for the one next to his as a CFO's close proximity to the president can be both collaborative and, in some respects, foster the confidential relationship required between the two senior leaders of a manufacturing organization. Bob referred to "Diane" as our part-time secretary who worked two or three days a week and that she would be in tomorrow and would help me get situated with phones, computers, etc.

"I've got a nine o'clock call with the attorneys who are helping us with these lawsuits that customers have brought against us due to Patrick's unilateral thousand percent price increases, and I would like you to sit in on the call as this is something that you will have to be dealing with," Bob advised. I agreed on all counts. As it goes, disputes between suppliers and customers on pricing can be commonplace in this industry; however, for it to be reduced to an actual customer lawsuit is a whole level of scrutiny that is unusual and has the propensity of customer success. This was another "red flag." The industry is protected from unilateral price increases, in that the proverbial "gun to the head" approach (give me my price otherwise I will not ship you the parts) is generally reversed by the district's judiciary as no vehicle assembly lines will be shut down due to lack of parts supply under these circumstances. The governance of the system calls for mutually agreed prices for most anything bought and sold in a supply contract scenario. The automotive industry is no exception.

I religiously took notes through the meeting after cordial introductions. As I know it now, someone along the way—perhaps Bob himself—must have known the attorney involved and been friends, as I later had found out that the attorney's specialty was marital divorce. The attorney spoke sense; in any case, all the while expressing these two cases were problematic for GoldHat. We were in the discovery mode, and it was all about digging out as much evidence that would justify the increases. As I learned, the gun was held to the head of the customer by Sulyeam (pay or no parts), and as soon as possible, the customers re-sourced their business to alternative suppliers. The amount of the "damages" in both suits was the excess value above the original contract price which was paid while the customers were busily attempting to re-source the product. As long as this went on, these amounts approximated $2.0 - $2.5 million among two customers (States Rubber and Phister). Follow-ups were decided upon and were to be executed. These lawsuits were aligned with the Windsor plastics business unit of GoldHat known as Noir Plastics.

The plastics business was a significantly profitable business for GoldHat. Seaway Plastics and Noir manufactured mold-in-color plastic, structural (non-decorative) components for the autos. One major reason for this profitability came from the fact that one of the automakers, GoldHat's customer, specified the use of Dow plastic resin which is a more expensive brand of plastic resin; therefore, the company priced into its sales value the value of Dow plastic resin. The actual resin purchased and used in the product was not that from Dow, but from a supplier providing a significantly lesser priced plastic resin; hence, they were selling a product which did not meet the full customer specification, at an agreed price that was based upon providing Dow resin. This was another financial fraud awaiting recognition. Should the customer learn of this, they could immediately come back on GoldHat, claiming fraud and, at a minimum, sue for every dime above the actual purchase price of the actual materials used (which amounts to most or all of the profitability that GoldHat realized through the sale of these parts).

Bob and I met early in the office the next morning on a day that was even more enlightening about Sulyeam business dealings than the first day. Bob appeared nervous about the situation. Bob had been with GoldHat about five months prior to my joining. Bob explained to me that for the first few months, Sulyeam consulted Bob on most any Original Equipment Group business decision. It was now March 3, and Bob had expressed that Sulyeam did not consult him on any of the matters related to the business since December and that Sulyeam—essentially—was the senior manager of this business and making all of the decisions. Because the metallics side of the business, comprised essentially of tube manufacturing from steel coils, was losing money, Sulyeam would chair daily meetings focusing on sales units and dollars, manufactured units and dollars, various cost categories and compare the prior day results with some arbitrary targets that Sulyeam had made up. This was supplemented by a weekly P&L review, chaired by Sulyeam himself, that would be comprised of reviewing the line items in the P&L and once again compare them to arbitrary targets that he made up. Please understand that these were targets that just simply could not be achieved. These meetings were a self-fulfilling prophecy as Sulyeam enjoyed belittling most people and making sure that everyone involved knew that he was the boss, had the power to fire anyone and was the smartest person in every room.

Clearly there were incompetents involved in the management ranks at GoldHat. I later learned that Bob used his retirement hobby—his restaurant / bar—as his recruiting ground. I first learned of such nepotism when someone helped me understand that Bob hired his nephew to be the general manager of the Detroit tube mill business, Tubeworks International. This guy had no knowledge or experience at running a middle market, $50 million per year revenue business. I also learned that he hired the financial controller of this facility because he learned that she was a financial-type looking for a job. She was an accountant who had no manufacturing experience, per se. She doubled as a singer/guitarist performer and Bob had featured her and her band in his bar. A major account executive that frequented Bob's bar was also hired and had little to no automotive experience. Bob also hired someone near to him as a brother-in-law to run the Madison, Indiana, tubing facility. This guy had absolutely no clue how to manage a business and run a company. So Sulyeam's criticisms may well have been warranted; however, his manner of execution was certainly not fair nor humane. There were a few others, as well, but it doesn't warrant my calling them out in this writing for any purpose other than to demonstrate the incestuous methods in which Bob would operate.

Just before lunch, Bob had what I would consider to be his first meltdown. Prior to our getting together for a discussion, I had heard him through the wall on the phone with an individual. When we got together, it became revealing, not only what Sulyeam was potentially up to, but also Bob's ability to gather intelligence through his (Navy Seal) connections, his ability to assimilate, interpret, hypothesize and conclude on such information. We first chatted about Sulyeam's direction to withhold payments to our suppliers for goods and services way beyond the "agreed-to" commercial terms. It was coincidental that just the day before, I learned from the singing controller that direction was given through my predecessor to withhold payments on certain employee withholdings, to bolster the company's cash flow, and window dress the financials of the company. In some cases, these withheld payments would be 45 – 60 days late. This didn't make any sense to me. In the automotive supply world, you try to strike your best deal with your suppliers and hold to that deal, including payment terms, except for certain circumstances which would be communicated to the suppliers. Then Bob, placed this bombshell in front of me (unsure of its source):

7/26/2009 2:34:00 PM

Millions sought from Santa Maria Component Group owner

A Pennsylvania bank has sued Santa Maria Components Group's owner to recoup millions of dollars in defaulted loans, and a Delaware company filed suit seeking hundreds of thousands of dollars from SCG for non-payments of goods.

SCG, whose longtime community presence started decades ago with Azo Industries, is closing the plant at 15th Street and Central Avenue on Friday.

SCG owner Patrick Sulyeam and former owners Jay Gaven and Mike Hammersmith have closed at least 10 manufacturing plants in North America in the last 10 years, eliminating at least 1,500 jobs and leaving suppliers and employees owed money.

Pittsburgh-based Penguin Capital Bank filed suit June 26 in Ohio against Patrick Sulyeam, four companies he owns or has owned Santa Maria Components Group, Brock k Stamping, Belair Manufacturing and Magpie Manufacturing - Elizabeth Sulyeam and Columbus resident Charles Domingo, SCG s former chief financial officer.

Penguin claim Sulyeam efaulted on more than $6 million in loans, and accuses the defendants of fraud, conversion and conspiracy in obtaining the loans, lying about their ability to repay them and taking money from one company that should have been paid to the bank.

Molvmer Sciences Corp., which coats and laminates steel coils, alleges in a suit filed June 29 in Illinois that SCG as not paid for $272,220.80 in goods delivered to SCG between Jan. 28 and March 3. MSC also alleges that SCG n February made an unauthorized $32,107.99 deduction of goods. MSC seeks $304,328.80, plus attorney and court costs. Five other lawsuits and two liens against SCG seek a combined $413,130.81. Four default judgments have been awarded against SCG totaling $75,511.84.

Bank sues

Penguin alleges that the $6.25 million in loans given to Arizona-based Brock and Ohio-based Belair t on April 30, 2008 was based on false and inflated accounts receivable and inventory figures for the companies, and did not reflect money they owed to other companies, which misrepresented the companies' financial strengths.

Brock and Belair also fraudulently overstated their ability to borrow by hundreds of thousands of dollars, the suit alleges.

Patri Sulyeam informed Penguin Dec. 16, 2008 that Brock operations had shut down, and on Feb. 12 told the bank that Belair operations had been terminated, the suit alleges, and subsequently both companies defaulted on their loans.

The defendants also collected more than $1.5 million in management and consulting fees from Brock and Belair, even when the companies could not have "satisfied the criteria" for such payments, and in violation of loan terms by Penguin he suit alleges.

The bank claims that the defendants were not forthcoming in turning over collateral, particularly business records for R Brock and Belair t, after the companies defaulted on the loans.

After obtaining the records, the bank learned of the financial discrepancies hidden from Penguin and of $575,000 in inventory that was allegedly sold from Brock to Belair, and then billed to SCG r the same amount, the suit claims.

This caused the value of inventory to be misleading, and the transfer of inventory was unlawful because Penguin had a secured interest in it as collateral for the loans.

Penguin alleges that Patric Sulyeam lizabet Sulyeam d Domingo were the principal decision makers for the companies and controlled the companies' funds.

The bank seeks compensatory and punitive damages, possession of collateral and the management fees paid to the defendants.

Elizabeth Sulyeam's lationship to Patrick Sulyeam not stated in the lawsuit, but an address for her is the same as the one listed for Patr Sulyeam in the suit.

Domingo claims in his response to the complaint that his employment at SCG nded Jan. 21, 2009, and that many of the allegations occurred after his departure.

He also claims that he was a "plantlevel" employee and not an elected officer, and that he did not create and direct account entries.

July 26, 2009 article - "Millions sought from Santa Maria Components Group owner - 2 pages

Bob revealed that he, I and anyone else caring to perform diligence on Sulyeam and his company, were unable to perform any level of due diligence (background check) because he had it on good advice from one of his contacts that Sulyeam had his name wiped clean from the internet after this 2009 episode of fraud. It is obvious that revealing such information could impact Sulyeam in attracting good and credible senior management, professionals, financial sources, etc.

It now was becoming clear to me the reasons why Steve McCracken told me that Patrick likes to fly beneath the radar and that the website is spartan and not up to date with a full set of company information. This was not a matter of spending the resources to keep things up to date or being late / lackadaisical in getting things done. This was purposeful.

Bob's (unrefined and unproven) theory was as follows:

3. Sulyeam hired Bob and I to hide behind our credentials and reputations,

4. Sulyeam was directing the withholding of payments to suppliers to amass a sum of money (just as in the case of Santa Maria Components),

5. Sulyeam was running up inventory balances (manufacturing inventory far in excess of customer orders) to increase the collateral and therefore amass further monies through borrowing on this inventory collateral from banks, and

6. Sulyeam's business model was established in the Santa Maria Components Group manifest. Sulyeam was soon to bankrupt GoldHat Group and abscond with these amassed funds for personal gain.

I can understand Bob's thoughts on Sulyeam's motivation. Sulyeam did not consider himself a colleague of anyone. Sulyeam was a pre-Madonna of sorts, barking his orders in a deeply condescending and intimidating manner to most anyone within earshot. As I had mentioned, he thought himself to be the smartest one in the room and wasn't about to let anyone in his thoughts, plans or process of pushing toward his end goal—an end goal which at this point was a highly guarded secret, leading anyone of sound mind at the top of the GoldHat Group to become highly suspicious of where he intended on taking this broken company with broken and intimidated people.

I personally witnessed many times when Sulyeam showed disgust, disrespect, abruptness, disdain for the people that he hired, whom he would shut down in the midst of their sentence by stating "We're done" and either changing the topic or closing the meeting. In March, Bob mentioned to me that Sulyeam quit talking to him sometime in January; Bob surmised that this was due to Bob's promises for improvements which most were not delivered upon.

Sulyeam did have some legitimate issues with the competency of certain individuals that worked for him, but his weak management style held him back from replacing people in a fair and equitable manner only to prolong the suffering on both sides with his simpleminded belittling of those who were incompetent. The sad thing was that this self-fulfilling prophecy was holding the business hostage by delaying the much-needed improvements, the reason that I was there was to drive the organization toward making the right data-driven decisions. This initiative was essentially usurped by Sulyeam because—as I would roll out a rather excellent work product that would allow the management to set goals by area, key success factor and areas requiring improvement, develop roadmaps, monitor their progress in comparison to those goals—Sulyeam would tell / direct me not to roll those items out because it would be like trying to teach calculus to a kindergartener, that is, our staff is not sophisticated enough to use, manage and interpret the information that this tool would be bringing forth.

Fielding what Bob was surmising about Sulyeam, I suggested to Bob that I make a couple of calls and inquire if friends, colleagues and business associates had heard anything negative in relationship to Sulyeam, GoldHat Group or potential upcoming events that GoldHat Group may be taking part in. The first and only call I placed was to Cliff Paslin, the investment banker who made Sulyeam's referral. I described the conditions to Cliff and he was immediately apologetic for having gotten me involved in such a situation. Further into the conversation, Cliff knowing, as I knew, that Sulyeam was embarking on acquisitions, suggested that all of this window dressing may be designed for the purposes of looking good in front of Sulyeam's banks as he was to utilize bank-borrowed funds to acquire the target businesses. I tended to agree with Cliff, but just wanted another professional's perspective on this after having to deal with my boss who was clearly "over the edge" by now.

Bob's frustrations with Sulyeam built to an unhealthy obsession. Bob now related every unfavorable element that was going on inside of the business back to Sulyeam's control of the business and his perceived motivations. Through Bob's coaching and leadership, the staff was now mimicking this behavior. This developed into a severely unhealthy condition for the business, Bob's followers, the employees and ultimately for Bob. On several occasions, Bob expressed feelings of "betrayal and lies told" because McCracken was his prior acquaintance and business associate, having served together on other companies' boards of directors.

Weeks passed with nothing but more of the same:

the same daily and weekly degrading Patrick Sulyeam meetings, the continued long hours for me—including working 10-12 hours on the weekend as the weeks were consumed with answering Sulyeam's idiotic questions—and embarking on paths that produced no real value, I had no time during the week to make the real progress that I was hired to make. This would fall to at least one and one-half long days of work on the weekend.

This situation continued to wear on Bob to the point of becoming a huge distraction from what we had to get done. Be as it was, I still had objectives to accomplish, those under which I was hired, and I continued with that. One of those objectives was to pull together a monthly reporting package that included those business metrics that I referred to earlier. This consumed a great portion of my weekends and three weeks prior to the first planned monthly reporting meeting, I completed the package and sent it to those responsible for their individual business segments of the Original Equipment Group. I strongly suggested that those responsible must spend time with the package, understand how it worked and what it was actually measuring, and how best to portray the corrective actions that were being managed to right the business and begin to produce a cash-profit which was non-existent on the metallic side of the business.

This change in practice met with resistance in the field. The responsible heads claimed to be too busy to give attention to this. In some cases, they pleaded that the information was just not available and that it would have to be developed. This was unnerving. If we were not able to take command of the data necessary to manage the business, perilous doom would be the result. What you cannot measure, you cannot improve! I constructively expressed my concerns to Bob about this regularly. One week before the show and tell, Bob asked that I call a meeting with him in attendance, for once the boss is involved, somehow the troops find the time and begin to pay closer attention.

The meeting started out by the responsible heads echoing what I mentioned earlier about the information not being available and that it would take an army to construct all of it. Bob caved and suddenly, the meeting turned into a negotiation between me and the responsible business heads such that they wanted to carry forward the legacy reporting system, which I believed to be useless for what we needed to accomplish. I knew the right road to improvement, which was my proposed package. Bob pushed for meeting me halfway, with the promise that we eventually would get to producing my full reporting package each month, but that would be a ways off. I agreed and provided my full support to the team to develop the information and get it right.

The next week was pretty tough, trying to meld five different business units and pretty much five different approaches to preparation of the package into one consistent package and way of doing things for the entire Original Equipment Group for which Bob and I were responsible. Right up until the last minute, we were pushing to get it right. Bob and I travelled to Madison, Indiana (Milestone Tube), to follow-up on progress and to prepare for the meeting, the week before the meeting. We headed down early on Monday morning. We drove separately as Bob wanted to bring his wife and dog, a massive Bernese Mountain Dog, down to Madison with him. Due to the hotel being oversold, Bob and family stayed part of the week with Keith Carlton, the general manager of the Madison operation. Bob and his wife were close friends with Keith and his wife so the occupancy condition at the hotel was supplemented by Keith.

As it pertained to the package, we still were negotiating the content on Wednesday of that week; this was among a myriad of other priorities, including these lovely Patrick Sulyeam meetings. Steve McCracken was useless as the holding company CFO. My sense is that he gave in to Patrick whenever there were any points of discussion / decision. I advised that the quality of the operations and the content of the monthly review meeting was subordinated to the need to prepare for these daily and weekly meetings, a true fact. This didn't seem to matter much as McCracken spouted, "The meetings will continue until we see that the business turns the corner and there is reliability in the information." Well, McCracken was neither smart enough nor in tune with the situation to understand what was really going on.

The march toward the Monday meeting continued. On Thursday morning, McCracken decided to lob an email to me stating that he had certain additions and modifications to the presentation package that I put together. He had had the package for three weeks, but then three business days before the meeting he decides to make changes? This was an arrogant move and one unlike any business leader with whom I've engaged. I marched into Bob's office and shared this with him. This was probably a mistake, in hindsight, but because he was so vested in the process, I had to make him aware of this. This situation fueled his second meltdown and one that he could not recover from. He literally went off the deep end. Now, Bob's mind was set on Sulyeam and McCracken setting him / us up for failure and that these mandated changes coming from McCracken were not navigable in the short time that we had before the meeting. My thoughts were that McCracken was clearly unreasonable and arrogant to throw this upon us in the closing hours before the meeting, especially with the internal difficulty that we had with getting the package to the stage we had.

Bob's position was that we were going to stay with the package we originally developed. I interjected that since we now knew McCracken's and Sulyeam's requirements, we had to meld them into the presentation in some way. Clearly, there was some middle-ground that would accomplish their perceived needs and what we had addressed; there was certainly redundancy in what they asked for and what we already had prepared. Bob wouldn't let go of it. He repeatedly tried to reach Sulyeam on his mobile with no success.

It was around noon, or shortly thereafter, when Bob asked everyone to join in on a conference call. His senior managers who were on site had come into the plant general manager's office. As we gathered around the conference table, Bob was clamoring to the last bit of sanity that he possessed. Struggling, he showed his disbelief of what he perceived "Patrick" was now up to. "Setting us up for failure," was Bob's clear mind made-up position on Sulyeam.

Being a leader of a large organization, no matter whether it is a platoon of U.S. Marines, Navy Seals or a major sector of a large company, one must place the mission first, the team a close second and all else behind that, including oneself. Bob had this exactly backwards as whatever thoughts were popping into his head, his mouth blurted them out to the team. What was happening to Bob came first; then, he projected what was happening to him onto the team, with no thoughtful consideration that he was hired to accomplish a job. His mantra always was "his team came first," but it really didn't manifest itself in that way.

Bob proceeded to continue to try to diagnose what was ailing Sulyeam (I knew Sulyeam was diseased, but he was the owner who deserved a certain level of respect—that is, until he crossed a line where ethics, people and intelligence may be compromised). Although Sulyeam advertised he was from a south Pacific country, Bob had pegged that Sulyeam was Eastern Indian and part of the "caste" system. Bob's diagnosis for what was ailing Sulyeam was that Sulyeam's father got a lower caste female pregnant with Patrick and Patrick was forever trying to get even with whomever was inside of his world by projecting his father's disapproval of him onto them, in a derogatory and defamatory way. I must say that I believe that truly could be a possibility as I have seen how Patrick Sulyeam operates, up close and personal. The other element, of course, is unfettered greed that I believe is at the core of Sulyeam's being.

Bob proceeded to tell the entire senior management team of the Original Equipment Group, "I am outta' here! I wish you all well. I have tried to protect you and you know that I am all about the team coming first. I have shared with you all of my concerns about how Patrick operates and it's not good. You're a good team, but now you must decide for yourselves what is right for you. I'm done. I cannot predict the future of this company, but Patrick knows best and he's running it. I'm outta' here. On Monday, when Patrick arrives for the meeting, I will get some time with him ahead of the meeting and explain this to him, and that McCracken has betrayed my trust, but for all intents and purposes, I'm outta' here!"

A couple hours earlier, I learned that Bob had a similar meltdown in the front of a low-level engineer and a materials manager where he had proclaimed that he was "outta' here." Bob's announcement meeting along with this hallway outbreak of mutiny clearly told me that there was no way that Bob could (or should) manage this business as its most senior leader. His emotional stability was gone, and this was in the way of him being effective as a senior manager. I immediately lost all respect for him as our president.

Approximately two weeks prior to this event, Sulyeam had engaged two consultants who made their mark for themselves as senior management operators of HI-LO Industries, an automotive metal working concern that was bankrupt and these guys turned it around and won the lottery as they were paid in stock that appreciated to nineteen dollars from two dollars at the low. Theodos Tratoperis was the CEO of the business and Nikidemos, his son, was a vice president and meneral manager. Since then, with a $40 million payout, they had been lying low—that is until Sulyeam, who shirked them out of millions of dollars in a prior life (Santa Maria Components Group), called them. The lure was $7,000 per day of consulting fees—yes, $1.4 million annualized. These guys were at the Madison facility and gathering the necessary data, information and conducting interviews to conscionably develop an improvement plan for the business as Sulyeam had lost all confidence in Bob and his team (this became evident).

Theodos (Ted) and Nikidemos, who had a prior life with Steve McCracken, were pros by any measure. They knew (and had implemented) the concepts of lean manufacturing and were engaged by Sulyeam (McCracken) to either educate the managers of this self-induced dysfunctional and defunct Sulyeam business and facilitate the implementation of the concepts in an effort to move the businesses toward profitability, or decide on the level of management competency. They assured both Bob and me that it was not an assignment of the latter; however, we all knew that when asked by the person paying them, they would certainly opine.

It was midday on Thursday and Bob, along with his family, was slated to leave for home, which they did. The people (management) in the company were an absolute emotional mess and, as of Bob's "coming-out" meeting, absent of leadership. The troops were disheartened and didn't know which way to turn, or if their job would be safe given the circumstances. I was equally concerned for the folks as I was for the destiny of Patrick's business. As I have described earlier, the CFO holds a duty to the owner, which is the highest duty known to law, the fiduciary duty, to protect his investment and act at all times in his best interest. It was clear to me that not only had Bob put the business and the owner's capital funding at risk, he also had compromised the effectiveness of the $7,000 per day consulting activities of Ted and Nikidemos Tratoperis.

Because of the level of jeopardy here, I was compelled to let the owner and his loyal few know of what had happened here. Sulyeam, however, as I perceived, was impenetrable and not easy to communicate with. It seemed to me that as I knew he was communicating with Ted daily, that if I shared this information about Bob's pending mutiny, he would likely convey this to Sulyeam and the fireworks would begin. I knew Ted Tratoperis for the better part of two weeks and felt that was long enough to judge that he was trustworthy; he had demonstrated numerous times that he was only interested in creating value and had the leadership required in doing so. I was confident that if I shared Bob's incidents of the day with Ted that he would have used the information only in the right way; after all, the word would soon get out and the happenings of that afternoon were destined to become public information inside of the company in rather short order. My motivation for sharing this was first and jointly to protect the owner's investment and the employees' jobs. I did so later that late afternoon / evening while Bob's friend, Keith Carlton, general manager of the Madison operation, was present. Ted assured me that he would share the information that evening with Sulyeam, as he told me that they talked every evening. I had no issues with making this known to the people who deserved to know for the aforementioned reasons. Effectively, I had done my job of providing the right information to Sulyeam, even if it did not come directly from me. No matter how it was conveyed, that was my job: to make sure that the proper and necessary remedial action took place. Bob essentially declared himself to be ineffective as the leader of this business. Leadership, at every moment inside of a large manufacturing concern, is primary. Strategic vision, mission and leadership are what all employees are looking for, and, absent of one of these elements, chaos will dominate and ultimate demise will occur.

With the major diversion that Bob caused during the day, it was clear and evident that my work would and should take me entirely through the weekend and that the time taken to travel back to Grosse Pointe Park, Michigan, would encumber my ability to complete my required task. As such, I called my wife, explained the situation and told her that I'd likely see her in the middle of the following week at the latest. Having made that declaration, I was dedicated for the duration. I closed out the evening with dinner and headed to my room, anxiously awaiting the next day.

With an attempted normal start to Friday, I walked into the Madison facility just like any other day. It was approximately 7:30 a.m. I stopped in the operation controller's office for a brief greeting and chat of what had occurred the day prior. Deb White was a solid woman and controller. Although she had advertised regularly that she was tough and had a thick skin, once I shared this information with her about Bob, it was clear to me that she hadn't experienced anything of this nature. To her credit, not many people have. Deb sat there in mere shock. I emphasized that we needed to conduct business just as if this was any other day and we must not advertise of the happenings of yesterday so as to not upset the employees and further disrupt the company's operation. She agreed that would be how she would operate.

It was about 11:30 a.m. when the call from Steve McCracken came. "Whoa!" he exclaimed. "I wouldn't have expected this from Bob," but we both knew that at the end of the day, his issues had to be resolved and Bob had put himself in a spot where that could not be diverted. Bob's public disdain for what was going on and—more personally—for Patrick Sulyeam could no longer be hidden. This was clear and there was only one way that this was going to end.

Well, it was evident that McCracken did not know

my caliber as the phone conversation continued. Perhaps as a retention effort, he was talking as if he was consoling me and advising me to "hunker down" and stay the course. I advised him that there was no other way. This clearly told me that he, himself, did not have a grip, not on what was going on inside of the business nor as to the thick skin that I had developed after my thirty-plus years in the automotive industry.

We concluded the discussion with their flight arrangements on Patrick Sulyeam's private jet, their arrival time and where they were flying into so I could pick them up on Monday morning. I said, "I have no problem with that, and we shall see you at 9:30 a.m. on Monday."

I worked the solid weekend, late into the night, fixing, correcting, developing the subject matter charts that were to be reviewed and discussed in Monday's business meeting. My staff was less than credible when it came to the understanding and compilation of most of the data into an intelligible form; so it was left up to me. I had no problem performing these tasks for the first meeting as I would expect the team to catch on to the concepts, methods and objectives; however, with some tender loving care and coaching from me. Seriously, having spent it in this way, the weekend was a literal blur.

Monday morning rolled around quickly. As you may imagine, I didn't predict that I would be staying over the weekend to work, so I ran out of clean clothes and spent time nearing the dinner hour on Sunday in the local public laundry, cleaning "the necessities." I also located the only dry cleaning operation in the greater part of Madison, IN, and dropped those items off which would not be ready in time for the meeting, but I had enough slacks to get by.

Bob showed up on Monday around 8:00 a.m. He offered that he and Sulyeam had made contact on the weekend and that they would hold a meeting on Monday to discuss the issues. I advised Bob that it would be in the best interest of the company and managers if he should have this discussion with Sulyeam prior to our business review meeting so that the air would be cleared, once and for all; after all, this game of tit-for-tat between Bob and Sulyeam had become highly distracting and non-productive for Bob's direct reports, including myself. Bob agreed that this was appropriate and said he would do so.

McCracken was in communication with me such that their plane was about 30 minutes behind. As Sulyeam's and McCracken's pick-up time neared, Bob was insistent on me taking his BMW SUV to pick them up, but I insisted that my car, a two-door Cadillac CTS (Sport) Coupe would be just fine. I had predicted the result that Bob would be excused from his duties after his juvenile mutiny of the prior week and didn't want any confusion over what is in whose car, etc., etc., when Bob would be required to vamoose!

Just before I was to leave for my retrieval of these two, I stuck my head into Keith Carlton's office, where both he and Bob were, just to see if Bob needed anything. Instead I got a question from Bob: "Did you tell Ted and Nikidemos about the meeting that we had on Thursday?" Keith obviously shared this information with Bob and Keith was holding his head quite low when this question came.

I was caught slightly off-guard by the question, but maintained my composure by responding, "Yes, I did."

Bob queried further, "Why did you do this and how would this be an advantage for you?"

I thought that this was a very strange question for him to be asking, but given his level of derangement, I gave him a pass and responded, "Bob, we've got a hell of a mess on our hands now." My implied message to Bob was, "You not only sold the team out, you sold yourself out with your undying rampage."

I fetched Sulyeam and McCracken and delivered them to the facility at 10:00 a.m. Immediately, Sulyeam, McCracken and Bob locked themselves into the conference room where the business review meetings were scheduled to occur. The management team was holding tight until Sulyeam, McCracken and Bob were done with their important business. I went back to my office and was productive on the long list of items that needed to be accomplished.

It was after 1:00 p.m. when the doors opened. Just prior to this occurring, out of my temporary visitor office window, I watched Bob drive off without any words spoken to anyone. Apparently, the employment separation occurred. At the point of the doors opening, the management team, minus Bob, was summoned to the conference room. After getting the entire team present, for those on location and on a conference call, for those managers who were remote, Sulyeam announced that Bob was no longer with the company and revised all reporting relationships to which Bob was a party. At this point, I was the only and the most senior manager of the GoldHat Original Equipment Group. In this revised scenario, I was to report to Steve McCracken. As a point of time reference, it was Monday, March 30. Quite a turbulent first 28 days on the job, and a sign of more "fun" things to come.

The meeting went painfully long, well beyond 7:00

p.m. As I had mentioned earlier, the meeting materials were a parsing of my new tools and the old, which were far inferior, but Bob blessed keeping some of the old as a comfort item he gave to his buddies. This made the meeting difficult at best, with Sulyeam blowing through otherwise important materials. I finally dropped Sulyeam and McCracken off at their plane nearing 8:30 p.m. and headed to dinner. It was an uncomfortable ride back to the air field. Sulyeam sat in the front seat and McCracken in the passenger rear. For the third time that day, Sulyeam slammed the car door, in the middle of McCracken attempting to pull himself up from the coupe's back seat and exit out of the same door. "Damn it," exclaimed McCracken as I laughed under my breath. Gotta love that CTS Coupe!

As this book displays, one of my credos is good and appropriate accounting. I reflect on my early years of accounting education and the "old adage: accounting is an art and not a science." I prefer to think of it more along the lines that accounting becomes an art once you master the science of accounting; then and only then, in its pristine form, is it an art form. Good accounting is not easy. Maybe that's why I am such a stickler for it. I went through great pains to learn how to get the accounting right and violating those rules would be in and of itself a violation of me as I dedicated more than 50% of my entire life to learning how to get it right.

Part of getting it right is identifying liabilities. The rules state that a liability (an amount owed to another business or person) must be recognized if it meets the test of being "probable" for payment and "estimable." Therefore, by the nature and definition of what a liability is, you can't recognize 50 percent of a liability because the business can afford only 50 cents on the dollar of the liability. Hence, if it is a valid liability, its value is 100 percent of the value. Conversely, allow me to help you understand the topic of asset valuation. The rule is simple. It states that assets (something such as machinery and equipment, inventory or buildings which are owned by a business) must be valued at the "lower of cost or market value," or "net realizable value" (these terms mean the same thing). Just as with liabilities, if an asset's value is X, it is recorded on the books at X, which is its cost, and if it is determined that the "net realizable value" of that asset is $-0-, the asset must be written off. This is synonymous with a loss being taken for the full value of the asset that was reflected on the books prior to any adjustment. Along the same lines, the full loss must be recognized, not 50 percent of it because the company cannot afford such losses while it attempts to meet the profit targets as set in company's banking and financing agreements.

After having been in both Patrick Sulyeam's and Steve McCracken's presence in meetings, both in person and remotely, I was confirming that the smell in the air—from early on in my tenure at GoldHat through today—was the smell of a rat. In taking my first tour of the Detroit tube manufacturing facility, I observed the infrastructure: the machinery and equipment, both in operation and just sitting idle and in ill-repair, employees with the appearance of being productive, the building full of roof leaks. I also observed a massive amount of product inventory: work in process and finished goods (much more than the quantity required to fulfill any order backlog on record). Intertwined was a mess of disorganized and defunct machine tooling and manufacturing supplies sitting all over the place in open shelving. The production and quality support offices were old and run down. The "cold storage room" contained another mess of excess and obsolete inventory. This stuff was so old and dilapidated, it may as well as had mold, moss and rust on it; and there was A LOT of it! (Sudden flashback to the Sunday morning breakfast discussion and concerns of Bob about running machines to make products for which there were no orders, Sulyeam's means to pump up the earnings to impress third party lenders).

As I well understood the need to apply the valuation rules of accounting for inventory, I asked Jeff Sarkin, the general manager of the Detroit facility, if Steve McCracken was aware of this. Jeff advised me that upon his walkthrough with McCracken and Sulyeam and coming across the cold storage room, they both turned their backs on it, asked that they not see it, but advised Jeff that he must not dispose of it. I knew that *there was only one reason that they wished not to see all of that junk that was declared as having value in the financial statements. If they had seen it, they could not deny its existence and the need to devalue it (write it off) against their financial performance.*

I asked Jeff what the approximate value was. Jeff advised, "Between $800,000 and $1,000,000."

I asked, "Is this at all reserved for in the financial statements?" meaning, has the loss been recognized?

"No," he replied.

If I recall correctly, my next statement was, "Ouch!" I had begun to think that this was only one of the five facilities within GoldHat under my management. *Could it be an equivalent amount at each? My God*, I thought.

I immediately asked Kathy Norman, the current Detroit company controller, whom I had a dotted-line relationship with, to quantify this problem for me. I was expecting that with some immediacy, I would need to compile the whole of the inventory valuation problems across the Original Equipment Group. By evidence of the age of the inventory and it not being properly dealt with for so long, this neglect was purposeful and habitual. This problem was not a one-off coincidence (déjà vu, Santa Maria Components Group). I was going to have a tough row to hoe.

As I had mentioned, the metallic side of the business was losing money. Operating income was significantly negative and after the add-back of expenses not requiring cash, such as depreciation and amortization, before paying interest and taxes, it was slightly positive on a good day. There were few good days. In addition to the effect of poor earnings on the cash balance, Sulyeam had an affinity toward building inventory without any orders to support it. As he liked to say, "We must get ready for the Tsunami of new business that is headed our way." This was more of a myth than anything else; what he should have said instead was, "Just in case that new business actually comes to the company." Good companies do not build inventory with no sales orders.

Unfortunately for Sulyeam and GoldHat, there was a long list of unhappy customers with the company's performance across the metallic side of the business. In reality, Sulyeam knew what to say to the folks to get them to do what he wanted, and it seemed that all of this big hoopla would occur around the end of each quarter, another clear sign of upward earnings management. This allowed Sulyeam to pump-up the borrowing base (creating an ability to borrow more money), an end with means supported by unethically fabricating income through reclassifying costs and expenses that would normally hit the profit and loss statement to an inventory asset classification, declaring the inventory has such value. The problem is, however, without customer orders, the proper financial statement value is the scrap metal value that this excess inventory could be sold for. Generally speaking, this is the net realizable value.

While the plastics business was doing quite well (to a large degree, due to the defrauding of the customer over using cheap customer **un**specified plastic resin), the metals business was failing on all counts. It was clearly not evident, with Patrick Sulyeam's leadership, how Gold-Hat could ever become a competitive and value oriented supplier of metallic tubing components to the automotive industry, especially with no knowledgeable leadership in the form of a president of the original equipment group in-place, nor any in the foreseeable future. It was obvious through the shell game that McCracken played with both Bob Belenhoff and myself about Patrick Sulyeam's past that they hoodwinked the both of us into joining this fraud machine. This was not going to be the job for me to retire from, as I had planned.

As April marched forward, after so much talk about surplus and obsolete inventory and evidence that Patrick had a tendency to build inventory to pump profits whenever he needed them, I put soft "feelers" out to my direct reports such that we needed to begin the process of quantifying how much over-valuation was contained in the balance sheet for inventory and related items. In addition to the over-valuation of inventory, there was large reclassification at the end of the prior year to take income and capitalize "spare machinery parts," most of which were junk and worthless. The way this worked was in the prior periods in which these spare parts were purchased, the cost of the spare parts was expensed against the profit and loss of the business. Being as they were expenses, they were a subtraction from profit. Now that the company decided to classify them as "valuable" assets, these prior period expenses were now added back to income, all in December of the prior year. This was a large number. Typically, auditors will disallow this due to two reasons:

1. To declare the items have value, evidence of the value must be demonstrated; e.g.: a business or individual must contract to purchase the item(s) at a stated value (it is not enough to say that these items will be ultimately used in the manufacturing process, and because of this, they have current value to the company and upon usage, the company will then expense them against their profit and loss statement), and

2. If the change is implemented for a mere change in accounting method, such change in accounting method presents a discontinuity in the financial statements and renders them non-comparable.

I shared with the group what the thought process should be regarding the proper valuation of this stuff. For the obsolete inventory, the appropriate value would be the estimated proceeds from scrap dealers or other distribution outlets (customers willing to take it off our hands) who would purchase this stuff from us. Scrap values are in the neighborhood of 10 percent of the value for which the goods were originally purchased.

It's not such an easy estimation for the old stuff, dubbed "surplus" or extra on-hand inventory. First, the items in the inventory must be "aged" according to the date it was acquired, in the case of raw materials, or manufactured, in the case of items made by the company. At this point, based on historical recovery, percentage of original cost is applied to each bucket of time-phased inventory; for example, the automotive industry is a make to order business. Therefore, anything sitting around for a long time is perceived to be "de-valued" and ultimately, when it actually sells, this reduced value would be realized upon the sale. In this case, it can be conceived that inventory sitting around for six months, but less than one year would recover approximately 75% of its originally acquired or manufactured value; items older than one year but less than two years would receive a discount of 50% and anything older than two years, scrap value would be appropriate. All companies are not consistent in their methods of valuing excess and obsolete inventory, but this is a fair representation of what most companies do pertaining to this topic.

While managing the (onerous, impractical and repeating) requests, and running the business as best could be done, my group was formulating their numbers on what we knew to be significant impending loss on the company, once we performed our due diligence in the inventory valuation area. As all of this was going on, and without any knowledge sharing from McCracken and/or Sulyeam, Caesar Napoleon was announced to assume the vice president role within the metallic group of the GoldHat Original Equipment Group. The announcement came on the Friday ahead of the Monday that Caesar was to start with GoldHat. Some time ago, Caesar tagged along on the original walk through that Ted and Nikidemos (consultants) performed at the Detroit operation (Tubeworks International).

Caesar is about five foot five inches tall, is Italian and is a spitting image of Caesar from the Roman Empire. As most of us are familiar, a stereotype has been formed for those who are "vertically challenged" in that they must make their presence felt, known, and acknowledged, and they have the need to believe that they are "influential," thus the pseudonym "Napoleon Complex." This was now an added ingredient to the clusterfuck dysfunction known as the GoldHat Group.

Caesar is a fast study, to his credit. He did receive (strong, influential and accurate) tutelage from Theodos (Ted) Tratoperis in his prior life of working for Ted, as Caesar often gives credit to Ted for bringing him along the curve of becoming a manufacturing professional. Nothing here, mind you, is rocket science as we all have been trained in and ascribe to "lean manufacturing." The Japanese taught us to get our manufacturing act in shape in the eighties by eating our lunches on the competitive automotive landscape. Most all automotive suppliers use lean techniques in the contemporary automotive supplier space. Much of what you see today regarding the level of quality in the US automotive manufacturers' products is the result of this.

I was a level above Caesar in the management structure of the GoldHat Group, but I had a sense that while this was the case, it was incumbent on me to demonstrate both my proficiency and my knowledge base of manufacturing to Caesar. Due to Ted's and Nikidemos' high praise, Caesar would have a direct line to Patrick Sulyeam and Steve McCracken, as McCracken, Caesar and the Tratoperis boys all worked together in that prior life. Caesar would often come into my office and we together would roll our eyes in bewilderment on some of the items that we both were revealing about the management and the condition of the GoldHat Group metallic business. This would occur more than three times a day and would be rather comical. While it was comical, it was a serious issue that was costing the company and Sulyeam's banks' money. Notice I did not say "Sulyeam's money."

In case I haven't yet mentioned, there were approximately $550 million of assets in the GoldHat Group and $539 million in liabilities. That's 98 percent leveraged (WOW!). A business is considered heavily leveraged if it has more than 67% (or, two thirds) of its asset base financed by debt. Virtually all of the financing at GoldHat is debt financing with a pittance of equity, only two percent. That is what Patrick Sulyeam can rightfully claim.

I have absolutely no idea how in the world a guy who has Patrick Sulyeam's history of defrauding individuals has been able to persuade and cajole banks into providing a line of credit of up to $100 million. My theory is that someone else is financially backing Patrick Sulyeam and the relationship must be unknown to the public at large. Clearly, if they knew of the operating conditions and results of the metallic side of the business, as well as the continued fraud of not having disclosed the value of the excess and obsolete inventories (which is pledged as good collateral and borrowed upon) while pumping the income line, as well as the lawsuits opined by our own counsel to be GoldHat losers, the conditions in financing would change dramatically. This I know.

Just as I had made it clear to both McCracken and Sulyeam that all of these improper reporting elements must be cleared at the end of the second quarter in order to produce credible financial statements and provide them to our banks, I also made that clear to Napoleon.

Napoleon and I would go back and forth at times on Sulyeam's motivations and how he has amassed such levels of bank credit, given his history. When Napoleon was considering joining GoldHat, he was curious about two items that needed Sulyeam's answer, prior to Napoleon agreeing to join the company. Napoleon told me that Sulyeam attested to no one else, that it is only he who has been able to secure this much bank credit. In addition, to spite the theory that Sulyeam's interest is a short-term spin, flip, sale or bankruptcy, Sulyeam told Napoleon that he plans to "own GoldHat for a very long time and as soon as it is righted, I shall approach his banks and make the request of regular distributions to take care of his family and provide for his retirement income."

While he had Napoleon convinced, I was not. The reason I was not convinced is because you cannot run a business like Sulyeam runs his and expect any longevity of ownership nor improvement enough to warrant this expectation. Sulyeam may buy companies well (for low/reasonable/fair-value prices), but he runs them terribly, and instead of the steady pursuance of lean manufacturing concepts, he changes up the game plans in accordance to meet his current financing needs (more inventory build, more profit, more ability to borrow). Stability is a strong requirement for businesses to flourish well into the future. Sulyeam's manic-depressive approach to running the business in accordance with his personal needs presents only a perpetually chaotic situation.

The unreasonable, illogical and repeating requests continued as did the grilling and embarrassing weekly calls (the daily calls were continuing; however, they were with Sulyeam's permission and under Napoleon's scrutiny.) As many of the folks who worked for me did not have a strong grasp of the connection between cash flow and income generation, it was nearly impossible to ascertain what was going on in the cash side of the business. This was not only causing credibility issues, but it was creating large variances from cash projections that were developed and assembled so that the company could predict where it was going to be with cash and how much borrowing was required to fund operations. As such, I personally took on the challenge of diagnosing what was going on with cash, particularly in the Madison, IN, operation known as Milestone Tube. As it was, I diagnosed that the majority of the cash "burn" (the negative cash flow in the periods successive to the large inventory build) was due to the need to pay our raw material suppliers for the materials that went into the building of these massive amounts of inventory. The remainder of it was due to the mucked up and poor separation of "company headquarters" cash activity, like making payments on loans which were used to acquire the individual businesses. These were reflected in the cash flow of the plant operations, thus confusing the whole cash flow situation at the operations level.

I spent a couple of weeks at the Madison facility trying to make all sense of this business' cash flow. I reviewed historical disbursements, time-phased all prospective disbursements, with the help of Controller Deb White, and signed all checks for those two weeks after cancelling them off of the cash disbursement projections. This was long, laborious and painful as it took me away from the other job requirements that I had as vice president and chief financial officer. While this was absolutely necessary, I had no one in the field nor any staff helping to diagnose the issue.

I also had learned that the company had just "accepted" that customers were paying the company late for goods it had provided, outside of the normal payment terms. I directed immediately that this condition be fixed with proper communication to our customer base: "No timely payments, no future goods" would become the message in time. That being said, my overall diagnosis was credible.

Napoleon and I had a discussion, shortly thereafter, that since all of my time spent had been to get the metallic side of the business in order, for an undisclosed and indeterminate period, I would report to him. While I had some heartburn with this, at face value it made sense and I agreed. The "Napoleon concept" reappeared in this instance as it did in most of Napoleon's management activities. In his mind, he was an all-knowing, better-knowing individual on all issues about manufacturing and it was a challenge for him to not be trite and disrespectful to the average colleague. I dubbed "young strappin' buck" to Napoleon, as this was most usually his modus operandi.

In the meantime, the compilation of exposure related to the inventory valuation issue and the unrecognized liability were coming in. The number approximated $6 million (see below exhibit). There was $2-3 million in bad inventory values and $2-$2.5 million liabilities from impending litigation. It was May 6, after I wrapped all of this together and compiled this into a report. McCracken had advised that upon the next acquisition (pending to be executed within the second quarter), we would recognize all of this bad news because of an accounting rule that would allow a gain on a transaction that would be deemed a "bargain purchase." In other words, if you purchase a business for less than its "fair" value, then upon the transaction, the acquirer is allowed to write-up the value and recognize a gain. Bear in mind that these bargain purchase conditions are not common and occurs once in a blue moon.

McCracken was planning to blame all of this bad news on "transaction costs" and effectively bury them under the rug from true explanation. While I do not ascribe to McCracken's approach, I didn't much care at that time about McCracken's method. These were to be his doings, but at the end of the second quarter, I could opine and sign off on the financial statements of the operation for which I was responsible. I hoped and prayed for this deal to be complete in the second quarter, allowing for the proper accounting treatment for the items in my control; however, a second quarter closing for the transaction was becoming more unlikely as time marched forward.

All aside, I was anxious to get the news of loss to be booked in the second quarter out and in the hands of McCracken, Sulyeam and Napoleon. Also, because of my mantra to do the right thing, I copied the plastics vice president and general manager. I included verbiage and the PowerPoint summary that laid it out quite well.

Can't Regulate This   D. J. Burgundy

OEG – Impairment Summary for 2Q 2015

GoldHat Auto — **ORIGINAL EQUIPMENT AUTOMOTIVE GROUP**

	Obsolete Inventory				Excess / Surplus Inventory			Product Inventory	Stores / Spare Parts			
	Gross Value (before recovery)	Estimated Proceeds	Value Impairment		Gross Value	Reserve Required (25-50. Less: Reserve 75-100)	Current Reserve	P&L Impact (Value Impairment)	P&L Impact (Value Impairment)	Gross Inventory	Aging Reserve Required	Fair Valuation	Total Impairment (P&L Impact) Required
TWI	119.1	11.9	107.2		750.9	515.0	123.6	391.4	498.6	559.8	545.2	14.6	1,043.8
Tube Finishing	40.5	6.1	34.4		130.0	51.5		51.5	85.9	700.0	624.2	75.8	161.7
Milestone	840.2	246.9	593.3		673.0	201.6		201.6	794.9	655.5	255.5	400.0	1,050.4
Totals - Metals	995.8	264.9	734.9		1,553.9	768.1	123.6	644.5	1,379.4	1,915.3	876.5	1,088.8	2,255.9

Plastics $
Balance Sheet
EBITDA Potential
Adjustments –
Description of item:

Adjustments – Description of Item:	Amount	Booked	Appl. Year		Plastics $				Total OEG				
Inventory Excess/Obsolete	89.2	TBD	2013		Potential Reduced Tooling Sales	69.5							
Legal Bills for Arbitration	100.0	TBD	2013/2014		MRO Inventory Adjustment	86.3							
Claim Arbitrator	750.0	TBD	2014		Severance Pay	10.7							
Claim	1,643.5	TBD	2013/2014		Slow Moving Inventory	28.0							

Total Pending 2,622.7   194.5 $ 5,465.6

    2,628.4
    372.5

*Total is to be revised for Fixed Asset Impairments .... d
                                                                 r
Note: no significant IQ adjustments for out of period or abnormal items were recorded.

Goldhat Impairment Summary - 1 page

These numbers are expressed in thousands of dollars. For your ease of interpretation, inventory was

-331-

over-valued by $2.7 million and the effect of the Plastics business segment lawsuits pending result was an additional $2.7 million. This is $5.4 million dollars of fraud (each reporting date), as this was not disclosed to the bank; surely, if it was, the bank would have had a different perspective on GoldHat and their willingness to support future acquisition via bank lending.

I fully expected that I would have received accolades for pulling this together as it truly was nearly impossible with the level of sophistication and systems contained within the company, not to mention that this was planned on and requested. Then came the red flag that was not only a red flag, but also a smoking gun email from McCracken, which is below:

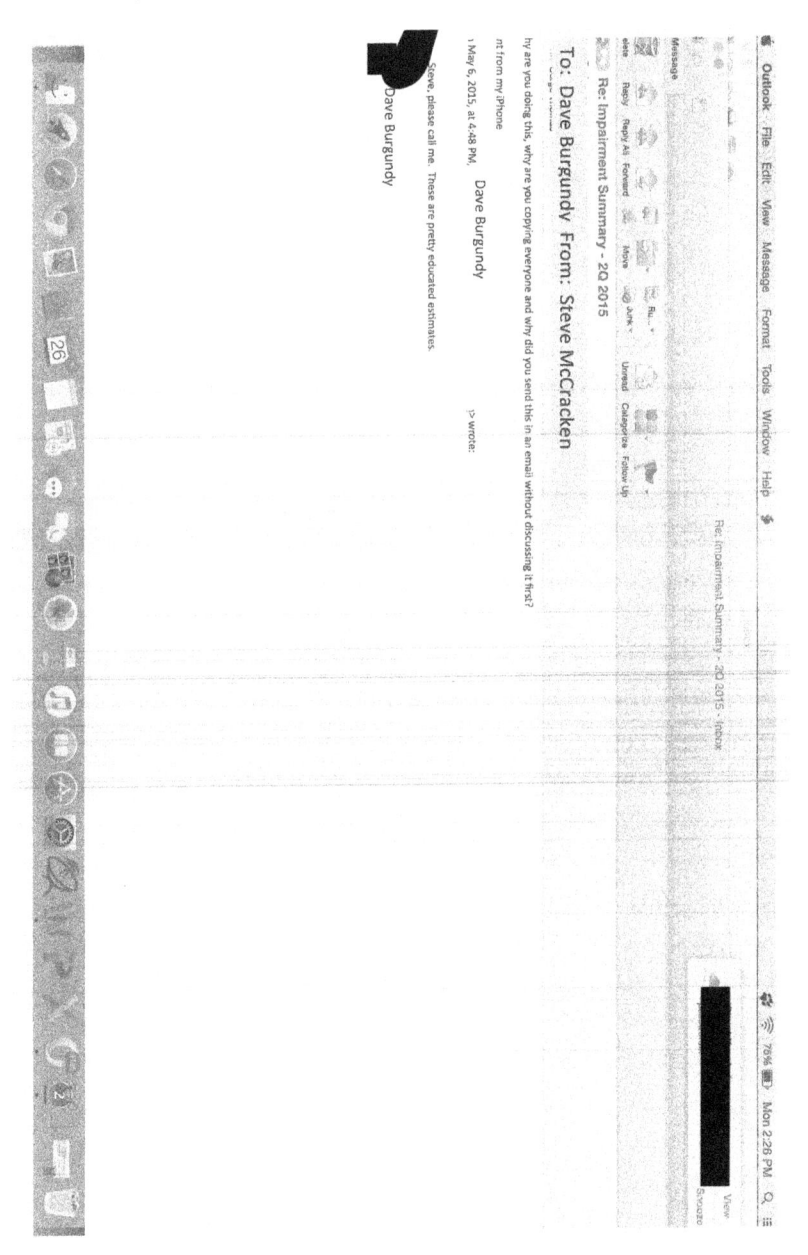

May 6, 2015 McCracken smoking gun e-Mail - 1 page

Can't Regulate This   D. J. Burgundy

It was well understood that I was undertaking this study and that I would make its results known to the concerned parties when the results were available; after all, we were to record this in the second quarter, right? Apparently, I was the other side of the (supposed) wink and I didn't wink back. It was with forwarding this email as my first communication to my attorney, Bill Waldon, to begin the process of protecting me and my income stream, as I remained steadfast in the company doing the right thing on my watch.

The cash flow was an issue at all of the metals businesses as the businesses were in bad shape. The company also suffered the turmoil of poor competency levels in the financial controllers' chairs. This also led to poor reporting, financially, of the reasons why the cash flow was not as predicted, and miscommunication of what the actual cash flow was, in the case of one of the more stable businesses. The financial statements themselves were a mess and, in the case of this aforementioned business, which had a positive cash flow of approximately $100,000, the financial statements reported a negative $950,000. Since the financial controller had just resigned due to the poor circumstances and perceived fraud of Patrick Sulyeam by this individual—and a new guy was in place only for a short time—I decided to go with the financial statement number, - $950,000, thinking that since this would go into the company's consolidated financial statements; this must be the right number and the controller would have made sure of that number. Well, myself being in place for six weeks at the most, I didn't have a real good grasp on every number within the business and felt it safe to report the most conservative one, given that everything was going to hell in a handbasket.

Instead of understanding how poor the condition of the business was and giving me a one-time pass on using a wrong number which showed up in the financial statements as prepared by another party, I was absolutely grilled by Sulyeam. McCracken did not come to my defense. This was more McCracken's problem than mine as he was there far in excess of my tenure. These were more his financial statements—as holding company CFO and controlling the global financial statements and condition—than they were mine. It all seemed to make sense that these guys were going to seize upon any and all opportunity to paint me in such a way that unless I played ball with them, they were going to try to make me go away before the second quarter reporting period. Recall, I advised that we must clear all known financial reporting inconsistencies with generally accepted accounting principles before we report to the bank for the second quarter.

Caesar Napoleon now appeared in an attack on me that occurred in a late afternoon phone discussion. He dared to claim that "Never, ever, never, never had I experienced such a bad meeting where one of his direct reports had been cited / called out for poor performance by his owner and by that, this was a direct reflection on me. I was completely blind-sighted by this. "Why didn't you share this with me ahead of the meeting? I am disappointed?" he exclaimed.

"Well, I must say that I am equally disappointed, Caesar," I volleyed back. "I tried to call you no less than five times before having to submit our results, with my goal to review these financial results with you, the head of the metallic business, before I submitted them. Never, never in my career have I released financial results without reviewing the results completely with the head of the business unit to whom responsibility is beholden. I never got a return call and therefore, against a time deadline, I was compelled to submit the results. I know just how busy you are and that you were travelling for an important and confidential reason, but one thinks that when your CFO is calling you with such frequency, that there is a reason he is doing so. Yes, I am disappointed in you," I finished.

Napoleon continued, "Well, David, I am sorry that you are disappointed with our business and the GoldHat Group."

"STOP right there, Caesar," I rushed in. "Apparently, you didn't hear me. I'll say it again: I am disappointed in you and with you, Caesar, for not returning my important calls to the point of coming to have this conversation with you."

"Oh, well, no one has ever told me that," he explained.

"Well then, let this be the first time, Caesar," I shot back.

This was the first strong indication of the Patrick Sulyeam – Steve McCracken "setup" job to purge me out of the GoldHat system before the required bank reporting date. They were going to use Napoleon to execute me during their charade of financial gamesmanship. The young strappin' buck was too young and intent on showing the world how magically impressive he was in management and manufacturing and how he could quickly turn this defunct metallic GoldHat business around. He was lost as to what was really going on with the business and how exactly Sulyeam and McCracken were using him to help perpetrate their mission. Napoleon's ego got in his way from seeing what they were up to.

The metallic business continued to struggle, though perhaps "limp along" would be a better description. The condition of the company was a self-infliction of Sulyeam who had absolutely no clue how to satisfy customers, manufacture product, meet delivery schedules, price the company's products, recruit people, compensate people or, for that matter, even treat and motivate people. In a word, he couldn't manage his own navel. I recall one of the first meetings that I attended with Sulyeam (and McCracken). Sulyeam had put upon me that I must make an evaluation of the Detroit company controller as to whether she (Kathy Norman) was a keeper and if not, fire her immediately. I explained to Mr. Sulyeam, in no uncertain terms, that I refused to do that. I said that approach was unfair to me as the new group chief financial officer, but more importantly, unfair to Kathy. I said I needed a minimum of two weeks with Kathy, under my management, and if she needs to be replaced, she would be within an additional two weeks after my determination. I knew from that moment on, that this job and my relationship with Sulyeam would not be characterized as a love affair.

Every interaction with Sulyeam resulted in his mandating and engineering the end result of the most money for him, whatever the case, with the absence of any experience or reason as to how to intrinsically get there. Forget about methods, systems, approaches, strategies and (least of all) ethics—he wanted what he wanted and that was all that mattered. I should liken Sulyeam to the seven-year-old in the toy isle at the department store who is throwing a tantrum, crying and screaming at his mother to buy him that toy he wants. Sulyeam's vindictiveness comes out and manifests itself in the treatment of his employees, his buying and selling of people, a character feature that he has honed well over his years. I'm sure it comes out in other even less pleasant ways, also.

Since the business was not improving, even with the "young strappin' buck's" perceived magic, Sulyeam's rage was multiplying. As we marched toward a potential date for a new business acquisition with such poor results, Sulyeam was getting rancid. The whole of his efforts was dressing the windows in such a manner to keep the bank as far away from the truth as possible. As an example, a raw material steel supplier granted only 30-day payment terms, from the time of receipt of the steel. Sulyeam wanted to hold the supplier's money longer, vis-à-vis' pay for the materials in greater than 30 days; therefore, he instructed someone at GoldHat to renegotiate pricing of the steel in such a way to allow GoldHat to pay in 60 days, in lieu of 30. This added 2.5 cents per pound to the original purchase price of the steel (noteworthy point: the contract and inherent price is for the purchasing "steel" and is not for acquiring money as in a financing contract). Sulyeam had given me the directive that we must quantify the aggregate value of this 2.5 cents that we paid in steel purchase price (number of steel pounds purchased annually times 2.5 cents), and reclassify this as interest expense, not the cost of production materials. His reasoning for this was that this 2.5 cents per pound was financing cost (or interest) and that we should show it as interest expense instead of cost of goods sold expense.

As the bank measured our performance on "earnings before interest, taxes, depreciation and amortization," this erroneous fabrication would serve as an add-back to net income, of an amount that was otherwise deducted from income, as cost of product material, that is reported to the bank. Hence, this was another book cooking exercise to increase the income of Goldhat that would be reported to the bank. Quarterly reporting to your lenders, and maintaining a certain level of income is required to keep your credit line in tact. The bank regularly assesses a borrowing company's financial viability and this is a lender's mechanism to ensure they have made a good loan. Should they detect something is awry, they would "call the loan" (request immediate payment) or seize the assets pledged as collateral. Because Goldhat was tight (close to not meeting that criteria), Sulyeam and company were attempting to fraudulently increase the earnings by counting things that do not belong in the earnings formula.

I advised Sulyeam that I would take that under consideration and think about it; however, I knew that there would be no way in hell that I would reclassify the cost of materials, or a portion thereof, to interest expense. Consistently applied, if this was correct, why wouldn't every company peel off a portion of the prices that it pays for everything from its raw materials to office supplies and coffee and call it "interest expense" because, surely, the price contains some element of financing cost?

A couple of weeks later, I received a call from one of Sulyeam's henchmen, Andrew Grommers, GoldHat's director of financial planning and analysis. The purpose of the call was one of persuasion. Grommers' mission was to convince me that this was interest expense and not material cost of goods (classifying this cost as material cost of goods is the right approach and a deduction from bank reported earnings). We spent the better part of two hours on the phone, mostly me hearing his debate and my standing firm on what was right. As my patience waned and wore thin, I concluded the discussion by advising Andrew that, "The purchase order states that we are buying steel for the given price and that price does not cite any specific financing cost as a component of that stated price. Also, to the best of my knowledge, Allegheny Steel is in the business of making and selling steel. We buy steel and therefore if we are buying steel, it must be classified as material cost of goods. Now if we were buying money, or borrowing money, we would have a contract that stated we were buying or borrowing money, but that we do not have." I then hung up the phone.

See, the "disciple concept" is interesting. Just because the guy who signs the paychecks turns to this spineless paycheck-loving idiot to sell me on the concept, all due to the owner wanting the result that he wants, doesn't cause it to be right. ...but he is the owner, so therefore, we must do what he wants. NOT! That is all the more reason to push back and drive the right, fair and ethical position on the matter. You must know that this issue did not die with this last conversation. Sulyeam continued to bring it up regularly, as if to say that I am disobeying his order. At a later point, Grommers asked for all of the raw data, just before bank reporting day, and I'm sure they massaged the numbers to achieve Sulyeam's desired result. I would have absolutely no part of it. Sulyeam didn't like it, nor did he like me. It is typical for me to point to a situation for blame. Not in this case: Sulyeam = liar = fraudster = scum = low-life = vermin = maggot.

The young strappin' buck took operations as his. He

thought much better of himself than he actually was, so this dynamic was interesting to watch. He didn't want me to participate in his daily operations' reviews that were regularly and consistently unsatisfactory, not only to him, but to the promised improved results that never showed up. I wasn't going to get in this kid's way as I had enough enemies in Sulyeam and McCracken, so I just let him go on with his charade and didn't try to manage upward.

Since operations largely dictate the level of cash earnings, and our operating performance was notably poor, cash generation therefore continued to be negative on a normal day to marginally positive on a good day. Again, I credit this to Sulyeam's ineptness and inability to drive an organization to his desired result through proper motivation. People want to do well under the right conditions; however, the culture that Sulyeam would bring to any situation was only one of fear, no matter what level of the organization you talk to. Week after week, the focus on cash was obsessive. Sulyeam was hoping for a diagnosis other than reality. The reality was he had shitty pricing, shit operations generating shit margins and when combined with his personally directed explosion of working capital (inventory) to aid his borrowing capacity, there was significant negative cash flow to explain in the second quarter. He didn't want to hear this, though. As we continued the cash study across the business, these indeed were the only definitively acceptable reasons for the net outflow of cash from this dysfunctional business.

Week after week, the focus and efforts at putting together a 13-week rolling detailed forecast of sales, expenses, earnings and cash flow was all consuming.

This item would be reviewed every Wednesday morning with Sulyeam and the Cleveland headquarters financial crew. The young strappin' buck wanted so badly to stick his chest out with victory, but he may well have been the weakling on the beach where the beach-punk kicks the sand in the weakling's face and takes his girlfriend. Being humbled by his own performance and that of the business under his control, he was looking for a proverbial whipping post, and you could see it in his eyes daily. Hormones without a head. He would be quite humbled during the operations portion of the weekly reviews. As for me, I had to talk to the cash side of the business and when Sulyeam's had had enough of my matter of fact responses, he would go off the deep-end and assert to the team, in a discrediting and disparaging way, that I wasn't doing my job and he would get Caesar Napoleon the help he needed and so desperately deserved. What bullshit. The fact of the matter was the business didn't meet with Sulyeam's storyline to the bank and he hid behind his scolding that also would ostensibly help facilitate my termination. This was fine; I was fully prepared for what would ensue. I was going to stand strong and they would have to pay me to get rid of me.

I sensed as we were approaching the end of the second quarter and the need for another report to the bank on the financial status of GoldHat that my time was coming near. As such, I consulted my attorney, Bill Waldon.

Recall the role that Bill played in the Collins and Aikman saga? He was clearly invaluable throughout that process and I never would have achieved the same result without him. Well, Bill gave me some advice, again invaluable, and proved to me just how smart he is. He suggested that if and when the call came that has some indication that they are going to can me, whether in person or over the phone line, he advised that I was to respond as follows: "So you guys are going to fire me because you think I am going to blow the whistle on you."

On Wednesday, July 1, 2015, I received a call from Rick Sayer, a colleague from the CFO in transition group to which I belonged prior to joining GoldHat. Rick said he was solicited by a recruiter seeking to fill a position of vice president of finance for the Metals Group of the GoldHat Group. Rick was sincere in asking if he would be working with me or for me since the Metals Group was a component of the Original Equipment Group. We had a somewhat high regard for each other, and his assumptions were conveyed warmly.

I advised that Rick was probably interviewing for my job and the situation was deteriorating; I was sure I was to be leaving the company. I asked Rick for the position spec for which he obliged and provided. He was sorry to hear of my situation, but very thankful that we talked, and I could apprise him of the internal workings of Mr. Patrick Sulyeam and Mr. Steven McCracken of the GoldHat Group.

As I was at the Detroit company, I pulled aside the new controller, whom I had carefully chosen for the job and trusted. I advised him of what I knew to be happening. He couldn't believe it and responded, "Well, if not for you, how do we do the right thing?"

I had to respond with some appropriate advice which was: "Keep your nose clean, don't find yourself complicit with their fraud and keep a personal file full of their directions to you and how you resolved with dispensing with them." He then told me that it was all becoming clear to him.

He explained that in the last few month's borrowing base submission to the bank, he was instructed by Paul Glen—the very green assistant treasurer of GoldHat—to leave off the foreign (non-US domestic) accounts receivable from the ineligible collateral report. The ineligible collateral report is a report of items that the bank sees too much risk in to make borrowings on. Good collateral is something that the bank sees as having value, enough to lend an equivalent amount of money (or a factor of). If the borrower should not pay the loan back, the bank would then take the collateral and sell or monetize it, thereby becoming whole again. The bank will not lend on these particular receivables because they could be subject to another country's confiscation for one reason or another. By leaving these ineligible receivables off of the report, this "kited" or over-stated the amounts eligible to borrow upon. At the Detroit company, this was an amount of over $900,000. You see, this was Sulyeam's and GoldHat's goal as they were in need of funding their next acquisition. See the confirmation by Glen on the requested practice. I asked the new Controller, Mike Teloni, for this email chain of evidence that he provided:

From: Paul Glen
[mailto:pglen@GoldHatGroupLLC.com]
Sent: Thursday, July 02, 2015 6:25 PM
To: Mike Teloni
Subject: RE: BBR *("BBR" – acronym for borrowing base report)*

Hey Mike:

Sorry, you don't have to include AZI as ineligible

this month.

> Paul Glen
> Assistant Treasurer
> *GoldHat Group, LLC*
> *100 Town Square Suite 21*
> *Cleveland, Ohio 44114*
> Direct Dial: (216) 413-0009
> Cell: (440) 869-4768

From: Mike Teloni [mailto:mTeloni@istube.com]
Sent: Thursday, July 2, 2015 2:00 PM
To: Paul Glen
Subject: RE: BBR

Paul,

Any update on the Foreign Ineligibles for June and also, when will it be due?

Mike Teloni
Controller
O: (313) 937-2110 ext.960
C: (248) 876-4400
From: Mike Teloni
Sent: Wednesday, July 01, 2015 3:09 PM
To: Paul Glen
Subject: BBR

Paul,

As you requested last month TWI didn't include the Foreign Ineligibles (Canada AR) on the BBR, how do you want us to handle those for June month end?

Thank you,

Mike Teloni
Controller
O: (313) 937-2110 ext. 960
C: (248) 876-4400

It was Thursday, July 2, 2015. I sensed this day was going to be the day. I was scheduled to go to the Original Equipment Group Livonia headquarters. I expected that Napoleon would be there. I wanted to make Napoleon work hard at his assignment to discharge me. I decided that I would first go late to work, then a more brilliant thought came to mind. I would text him and leave him a voice mail (thank God he didn't answer—I didn't expect him to as he had been ignoring my calls) that I would be going into the Detroit company to finish up on some important work with a deadline. The Detroit company was literally 10-15 minutes from the front door of my home.

As I pulled into the parking space at the Detroit company, Napoleon's call came. Napoleon asked if I had arrived at TWI yet. "I'm just about to get out of the car and walk in," I responded.

He said, "Don't do that as I would like you to come to the Livonia office. We need to have a difficult conversation, David."

The Waldon words rolled right off of my tongue, "You mean to say that you guys are going to fire me because you're afraid I am going to blow the whistle on you, right?"

This wet-behind-the-ears intimidator, at best, responded "Well, uh, what do you mean? I haven't done anything wrong."

I said, "Well, you may have not 'done' anything, but you are complicit in the actions."

"What actions?" he queried.

I suggested, "There are things that are actually going on that you have no idea of, and they involve certain degrees of fraud. Patrick Sulyeam and Steve McCracken want me gone, and they have elected you to do the dirty work. I know exactly what is going on, and I have all of the evidence. They set you up perfectly, Caesar."

Napoleon responded, "You mean they are using me as their pawn?"

I said, "Those are your words, but effectively you are beginning to get it. They put you at your weakest point. They moved you and your family to Detroit from South Carolina; you don't have a home, no foundation, but you're here doing Sulyeam's work and you're all in, bud! Right where they want you."

He insisted, "Well what is the fraud and what evidence do you have?"

"I have all the information and it will not become available to you, whatsoever. It is for me to know and possess. That is how it will be."

"You mean to tell me that you and I have worked closely together, the closest of any of my other direct reports, and you have kept this from me for all of this time?" he exclaimed. "Why didn't you share this with me?"

"Because, Caesar, I predicted that we would be having this kind of a conversation, the one which you are calling me into the office for. Caesar, another thing you should know, Detroit is my town and I'm really fucking well connected! This is not Cleveland, and this is not South Carolina; this is Detroit, where I have been working in this industry for over 30 years. I received a call advising me that you folks are looking for a vice president of finance for the GoldHat Metals Group. As a matter of fact, I even have the position spec. Would you like me to share it with you?"

I sensed this kid began to shit his pants. With this, he tried to pressure me for more information, but I resisted. "Caesar, I'll be across town in 35 minutes and we can take the rest of this up then. Goodbye."

When I arrived, Caesar Napoleon was on the phone. I waved at him and told him I would be in my office. I proceeded to begin to gather my belongings and separate with all company property which was to stay with GoldHat. Caesar eventually came into my office and suggested that we go to the conference room for our discussion. I agreed.

Bear in mind that here were two guys in approximately 5,000 square feet of uninhabited office space. "Ghost-town." I was glad that I would not be returning.

Caesar was in awe and beside himself. I had never seen him like this. He's usually "macho-like" and letting everyone know he's the boss. Twitching with discomfort, he let me know that "he expected to have a completely different conversation than we actually had and that he was totally taken away and now 'just off.'"

"Understandable," I replied.

He asked me what evidence I had. Again, I advised that, "This is not for you, Caesar, not at this time." He asked for my help, given the situation, and I advised him that he should consult an attorney given the situation and that he should inquire what level of directors' and officers' insurance there exists inside of GoldHat and if it covers his level of management. "That is the best advice that I can give you, Caesar."

He then explained that he worked it out to provide me a little severance to tie me over (little is not an exaggeration). I looked at it and advised him, for obvious reasons, that this would not be enough to allow me to find a comparable position. We left the conference room and I suggested that I needed to finish gathering my things. He offered his help and I refused. He said he'd walk me out upon my exit and to call him when I was done with the gathering. I obliged.

We shook hands like adults and both mentioned that we wished for a different outcome. I said it's fine as I would be much more comfortable being away from Patrick Sulyeam and his culture. "You know, I am friends with people who have worked for me in the past and even the ones that I let go." I said well, let that be the case here, then (without my care to keep in touch, actually). He advised he would provide me his personal cell phone number.

July 15 (third quarter of operations), the acquisition of H2O-Form was consummated and executed.

The personal cell phone number never appeared.

I still keep in touch with my direct reports from GoldHat.

September 30 (the end of the third quarter) came and left. Bank reports were provided.

The recognition of the losses from the lawsuits and from the improperly valued inventories still haven't been recognized.

The fraud and saga of Patrick Sulyeam continues.

Zebras do not change their stripes.

Can't Regulate This!

Fast forward to December 2018:

I decided to call on an old friend, George Panaplos who was tapped by a New York private equity firm to shepherd a roll up strategy in the automotive steel components space to see if I could help with identifying acquisition targets. In meeting with him I learned that he and Sulyeam met in April where Patrick touted he had a business producing many millions of EBITDA and that George should buy it Of course, being the good businessman that Panaplos is, he had engaged some professionals to conduct some due diligence.

Upon conclusion of the due diligence, it was learned that in fact the company was producing zero – to – negative EBITDA which caused Panaplos concern enough to study it further before considering it a viable investment.

In January 2019, I learned that creditors took control of the company; there was "debtor in possession" financing in place and major customers were providing accommodation payments to Sulyeam's company in addition to the invoice cost of the components, just to keep the company supplying its component parts and cars could be made. If not for that, the doors would shut automatically due to insolvency. In addition, all of the Goldhat Auto Original Equipment group was being liquidated for literally pennies on the dollar.

I also learned that Sulyeam was buying more companies, potentially with funds from the accommodation payments made by the customers of the failed business. These funds were intended to keep the parts flowing and cars being built.

CAN'T REGULATE THIS!

Steel Company Drowns in the Downstream

In May 2016, a friend and business colleague referred me into a private equity deal to join, potentially, as the company's CFO. The name of the company was Exacto Products Holding Company. I met Exacto's CEO one day in mid-May and we seemed to hit it off well enough to schedule a meeting with the private equity partner overseeing the company. Exacto had four operations and was about to acquire a competing company with the same product lines and expertise that would double its size and footprint.

After meeting the private equity firm partner overseeing Exacto, I was nominated for the job. First order of business, in addition to co-running the business as its CFO, was to integrate the newly acquired (to be) company. Later in the month of my hire, the company was acquired on August 30.

Being as both of these companies were run like "mom & pop" enterprises, they were in need of professionalizing and that meant operating structure to me. One operating structure based on all of the functional areas of the business, where one person, along with their teams, would be responsible for the total function across the entire company; old-co and new-co, the combined businesses.

When I presented this concept to the CEO, it was denied, and in his words, "It is just going to be me and you running these companies as if we are the private equity holding company and the operating companies are our portfolio." I didn't like it, tried several times to integrate these companies, tried to convince him that this will not be successful, but I was denied on those successive occasions, as well.

I began the pseudo integration of the two companies whereby I was to instill the same policies and procedures across the full enterprise, old-co and new-co, but have only myself be accountable for the functional integrations and the post-integration operational results. Well, working diligently at it, it was on its way in October 2016, when the private equity firm (owner) announced it wished to commence with the sale of the entire business of Exacto. *Ugh*...I thought.

Well, we put our heads down. I continued with the integration piece because we would sell the business as if it was "one" business and then proceed along the path of working with advisors and investment banks in readying the business for ultimate sale.

There was high interest, without solicitation, for the business. In the end, it whittled down to seven finalists who submitted bids in an acceptable range. It just so happened that a company named "Group-Think Steel" wanted to go exclusive and they submitted a premium bid. The company, based on the CEO's mandated assumptions, was not taking constructive criticism from someone who had been doing this for about forty years (me). These mandated assumptions were among achieving the best performance without putting in place the proper company infrastructure to do so. With EBITDA of $56 million in the projections, Group-Think Steel put in an offer of greater of $400 million because they recently were granted a free spending spree by their board to acquire companies downstream of the value chain, so that they could test and integrate their steel in actual steel applications. The money was burning a hole in their pockets!

After further review, they retuned their offer to $360 million.

The first four months, the company was tracking to the time adjusted performance of $56 million, but May was a whole different story. One of the plants was undergoing a major launch for Honda; 62 parts and terminating like 25, based on Honda design changes and new models. Well, my CEO did not grant me or the company structure enough to digest this kind of activity (keeping profits only in mind from his perspective because this would ultimately drive the selling price of the business, upon which he would make boodles and oodles of cash!). Further, he was directing the newly acquired company to expend resources in areas that were not stabilizing of the business, creating further disruption to the overall company.

Well, that being said, the acquisition was completed on August 3, 2017 and with deteriorating operating results (do remember that the senior executives of GroupThink Steel were so far down the line and committed, that not a one of them had the male gone's enough to cause a pause in the deal for fear of falling out of favor with their board of directors. They had an earnings release in the third quarter, for the second quarter, that they wanted to stoke their stock price with the news of an acquisition, and timing was of the essence. To be fair, though, the Exacto business was a good strategic fit, but not at the price that the business would be transacted at! They did the deal at $360 million, sorry for them.

It is interesting that their due diligence advisor advised them that they should value the company at a $30 million earnings level, after their diligence. GroupThink Steel could not go back to their board, jeopardize the deal, and say we need to revise our offer to like only $200 million at the stated earnings multiple of near 7. Therefore, the deal was done, and everyone was paid. The problem is that Group-Think Steel did not do a level of operational diligence to really understand the business. Sure, we held out projections, but it was their job to validate those projections through relentless questions and investigation of the facts. They did not do that, so only they are liable in such a situation.

The end of August caused me to re-forecast the remainder of 2016, after the ownership change and the private equity firm was paid-off, as well as senior management of Exacto, of which I was one. After I circled the wagons with all of my financial controllers and management, the best we could come up with was $20 million of EBITDA. Okay, now get this: the company was purchased on an earnings stream of near $50 million, the buyer paid $360 million, or a multiple of 7.2. Now, due to the significant launch difficulties in a plant somewhere in Alabama, this sucked more than $30 million out of earnings. There were really expensive planes flying parts, delays in sales of components, quality issues, overtime to an excess, premium costs that you would not believe… on and on. Given that Group-Think Steel paid $360 million for the company, and the company's 2017 earnings were but a meager $20 million, this yielded an earnings multiple of 18 (UNHEARD OF EVER!... for such a business) Group-Think Steel EXCEEDINGLY overpaid for the company.

I subsequently left the company because I did not want to be the "answer-guy" for the CEO's erroneous and unrealistic assumptions which were incorporated into the financial projections that the company was purchased on. That would not go well for my future.

When asked on the third quarter earnings conference call, by Jose Bounesteine, an analyst for German Bank, if Exacto Products earnings are on track with expectations, the chief operating officer, whose father was a mukety-muk at "Group-Think Steel," responded, "Oh yeah, everything is 100% all that we expected."

Let me just say that lying to that magnitude on an earnings call is akin to written fraud and is subject to wire/mail fraud laws, because the fraudulent statements are transmitted over wires and air waves that cross state lines. If there were ten people on the phone line, that's ten counts of wire fraud. Assuming that these people tie other people into their lines, it becomes exponential: if each line has ten people tied in, then it becomes an offense with one-hundred counts, and so on.

I bought Exacto's stock at something near $5.00 per share, just to show that I was a (short-lived) team player, as the CFO of one of their major subsidiaries. The stock is somewhere in the $2.00 range today. Do you think that if people/investors really knew the truth about this situation and Group-Think Steel's management team that they would have bought or stayed in the stock (and suffered the losses) after the promises of accretive growth through the acquisition?

Author Bio

David J. Burgundy has been focused on increasing enterprise value in public and private equity companies since 1989. David is a registered Certified Public Accountant in the state of Illinois and knows the rules of financial statements and disclosures required by regulators and, potentially, when they are intended to be knowingly or unknowingly violated. He has performed in various leadership roles, exercising his entrepreneurial spirit and financial acumen with the utmost integrity and ethics throughout his dedicated career. With strong intrinsic value creation emphasis, David has led organizations to significant turn-around in profitability and top line growth and was responsible for the revitalization of a (then) large corporate, publicly-traded losing subsidiary, turning it into a key strategic core growth platform producing premium returns. As a result of this increased productivity and customer service, this key business became the recipient of the Shingo Prize for Manufacturing Excellence under David's tenure.

David has performed most all financial and operational functions in manufacturing for both SEC companies and private equity portfolio enterprises. While exercising the utmost integrity and ethics in the most senior financial leadership role, he has performed these functions in domestic and international, small, medium and large companies.

CPSIA information can be obtained
at www.ICGtesting.com
Printed in the USA
FSHW020200090620
70866FS